AN IMPACT OF CROSS LISTINGS ON THE VALUATION OF INDIAN STOCKS

AN IMPACT OF CROSS LISTINGS ON THE VALUATION OF
INDIAN STOCKS

Dr. ARIFA BEGUM

WhiteFalcon
Publishing
www.whitefalconpublishing.com

An impact of cross listings on the valuation of Indian stocks
Arifa Begum

www.whitefalconpublishing.com

ISBN - 978-1-63640-560-5

INTRODUCTION

Indian economy has seen an incredible success over the most recent couple of decades. The economic reforms in India since LPG took place in 1991 have accelerated growth, enhanced stability & strengthened the economy. There has been a great transformation in money markets, government securities market & foreign exchange market over the period. Indian capital market plays an important role in financing the growing needs of various sectors of the economy. In an era of rapid globalization, investors are looking beyond the boundaries of their countries for investment opportunities. This has given opportunities for companies looking to expand into new markets, tap new customers, get new investment base and raise more capital in international markets through listing and trading. In the 1980's and in the first half of the 1990's, the fragmentation of the capital markets was the main objective for the corporate managers to consider an international cross listing as a means of getting control over investment barriers and making a company's stocks accessible to foreign investors. There was a great demand for foreign capital in some of the lesser developed countries, at the same time supply of capital was in excess in the countries like U.S.A & England.

There was a need to bridge this gap and make a channel to enable the flow of funds from these countries to the countries that require the funds. Investing without such a channel was a challenge not just financially but also administratively. The transactions were complicated and the settlement of the transactions was very difficult owing to currency values. In an effort to bridge this gap, JP Morgan introduced a system of depository receipts in 1927. JP Morgan intended to provide a channel that allows for easier flow of funds from developing countries like U.S.A to other countries by offering them investment option overseas. Globally markets for DRs are 90 yrs old. DRs are traded on major global securities exchanges with large investment banks running this program. The depositary receipts were intended as both an investment vehicle as well as an investment option. Today, DRs are not only used for capital raising purpose but also used for number of benefits like strategic, reputational & risk mitigation.

Cross listings have been extensively covered in the literature (karolyi,1998). Cross listings gained popularity in early 1980's facilitated by liberalization of cross border capital flows & by internationalization of companies (Dodd, Olga 2011). Cross listing of shares is when a firm lists its equity shares on one or more foreign stock exchange in addition to its domestic exchange (Baker, Nofsinger & Weaver, 2002). Cross-listing refers to the situation whereby a firm lists its stock on an overseas exchange (Karolyi,2006; Bris, Cantale, Nishiotis(2012) ; Magnan, M. & Kim, (2012). Generally such a company's primary listing is on a stock exchange in its country of incorporation, and its secondary listing (s) is on an exchange in another country. Cross-listing is especially common for companies that started out in a small market but grew into a larger market (Wikipedia). Cross border listing has become one of the avenues for the integration of global securities markets (Dodd, Olga 2011). From the view of various investors, cross listing eliminates some of the uncertainties and costs involved in making direct listing in foreign markets (Abee, Zimmerman, 2006). Cross listings is a vital for international financial markets. Foreign companies majorly are interested to invest in American & US stock exchanges, and follows by British & European countries. European markets are improving its quality & are becoming favorite destinations for Cross listing. After US has introduced Sarbanes-Oxley Act 2002 (Marosi & massoud (2008), stringent & costly norms, issuers are seems to be switching to other destinations for listing (Doidge, Karyoli, Stulz (2010).

Over 3,000 foreign firms have secondarily listed on over 40 major stock exchanges (Karolyi, 2010). New York Stock Exchange (NYSE), NASDAQ, London Stock Exchange, and London's Alternative Investment Market (AIM) have attracted significant cross-listings. In addition, NYSE Euronext (Europe), Deutsche, Hong Kong, and Singapore have all become popular destinations for cross-listed firms.

Cross listing through DRs provide more benefits than direct listings as it offers a friendly mechanism for individual companies who want to enter foreign markets according to their needs. Depository receipts an equity instrument representing shares listed on foreign exchanges are still very little known among Indian people although their history reaches back to 1927(Kumar, 2003).

Cross-listing of stocks on international exchanges makes sense for many reasons. The first is that stocks tend to demand better valuations even in the domestic markets once a stock is listed on, say, the NYSE or NASDAQ (Alexander & Janakiramanan, 1988). Secondly, such listing also enhances the status of the organization in the eyes of investors.

Thirdly, it provides arbitrage opportunities as trading spans across time-zones will be different and will increase with the advent of capital account convertibility (Karoyli, G. A. (1998)). A good company can use this channel to raise capital especially in foreign currency as these funds can be used to finance projects involving foreign exchange outflows. Through cross listing customer base will increase, visibility of the company in the market will develop, it will also help to improve stock liquidity through its liquid secondary market (Nasser, 2005). According to US Federal Reserve data, US investment in non US equities in 2016 was $ 7.6 trillion, which is 9% more than 2015 with $ 6.6 trillion[1].

Companies normally weigh the costs of doing such listings as the regulatory pressures in the west often involve higher level of disclosures and better accounting standards which lowers the levels of information asymmetry. All this means higher costs to be incurred by these corporates.

From the perspective of investors, cross listing mitigates some of the uncertainties and costs involved in making direct purchases in foreign markets (Ayyagari & Doidge, 2010). Cross listing through DRs has more advantages compared to direct listings as it offers an easier and flexible mechanism with less stringent regulations for individual companies to enter foreign markets according to their needs (Olga, Dodd, 2011). The listing of a company on a foreign exchange through a DR framework exempts the firm from many stringent regulatory requirements compared to those required for direct listings on foreign exchanges, thereby enabling the investors to realize dividends and capital gains in another market. Previously, companies from emerging economies listed either on the US exchanges or on the European exchanges through ADRs or GDRs, respectively. However, the phenomenal success of DRs in the US and in European countries combined with the evolving liberal conditions that are conducive for capital market development in Latin American and Asian countries prompted the securities market regulators to allow DR programs in these countries. Another factor that contributed to the popularity of DRs is that investors are looking beyond their national borders to take advantage of new opportunities for diversifying their portfolio (Kumar, 2003). Even

---

1   Citi group, depository receipts.

many multinational firms are interested in the local DR program to take advantage of the growth prospects of Latin American and Asian countries.

Given that Indian companies are now in the frontline of M & A activity overseas, it is tempting to evaluate the option of cross listing of Indian companies on other bourses, starting with say the South Asian markets. Indian companies are performing well on international front. ICICI bank is considered as the third top most liquid DR program with 2771.9 DR million listed on NYSE[2].

This chapter includes Introduction of cross listings, Forms of cross listings, DR structure, issuance & trade mechanism, issuance process & participants of DR market, Types of DRs, corporate governance rules for ADR issuers, evolution and performance of DRs, performance of DRs, evolution of the DR scheme in India, Indian depository receipts, regulatory frame work of IDRs, Statement of research problem, objectives of the study, hypothesis of the study, need of the study, structure of the study.

1.1   FORMS OF CROSS LISTINGS:

There are two forms of cross border listing, namely, direct listing and indirect listing.

Direct listing implies that the firm directly lists its shares on a foreign stock exchange. Direct listings can be of three types are:

- **Primary listing:** A firm not listed on any domestic exchange lists its shares on a foreign stock exchange. It has to follow only the foreign jurisdiction listing rules.
- **Secondary listings:** A firm listed on a domestic exchange subsequently lists its shares on a foreign stock exchange. It is basically regulated by the rules of its domestic jurisdiction.
- **Dual primary listing:** A firm listed on a domestic exchange subsequently lists its shares on a foreign stock exchange. It has to follow the listing rules of both jurisdictions.

When the firm has already listed the securities on a domestic exchange & simultaneously lists its DRs on a foreign exchange is referred to as "cross listing". Indirect listing on exchanges is done through depository receipts.

When considering which of these options to pursue, a firm will consider:

- The legal restrictions the firm faces in the home jurisdiction including exchange controls, capital controls and corporate laws.
- The legal restrictions to be followed in the international capital market.
- The economic costs involved in each mode of access.

Securities of a firm are deposited with a domestic custodian in the firm's domestic jurisdiction and a corresponding DR is issued abroad which can be purchased by foreign investors. A Depositary Receipt is a negotiable instrument denominated in US dollars or Euro, which is issued to the investors in one or more foreign countries. DRs are issued by the overseas depositary bank to the international investors against the delivery of local currency shares of the issuer company to the domestic custodian bank (Kumar, 2003). A Depository Receipt contains features of equity shares and carries rights, which are similar to rights attached to equity shares. The Depository Receipt holder, thus, enjoys the right to appropriate disclosures by the foreign company issuing Depository Receipts; The right to corporate benefits/ dividends attached to the Depository Receipts; and the right to vote under certain

---

2 Bloomberg

circumstances. "Depository" means a company formed and registered under the Companies Act, 1956 (1 of 1956) and which has been granted a certificate of registration under subsection (1A) of section 12 of the Securities and Exchange Board of India Act, 1992 (15 of 1992). (Sharma, 2012). Depository Receipt'(DR) means a negotiable security issued outside India by a Depository bank. A Depository Receipt (DR) is a negotiable instrument in the form of securities that is issued by a foreign public listed company and is generally traded on a domestic stock exchange. For this, the issuing company has to fulfill the listing criteria for DRs in the other country. Before creating DRs, the shares of the foreign company—which the DRs Represent—are delivered and deposited with the custodian bank of the depository creating the DRs. Once the custodian bank receives the shares, the depository creates and issues the DRs to the investors in the country where the DRs are listed. These DRs are then listed and traded in the local stock exchanges of the other country.(Padhi, Pallavi, NSE, 2012).

DEFINITION OF DEPOSITORY RECEIPTS:

As per the new scheme notified by Ministry of Finance, 'Depository Receipt' is defined as:

Depository receipt means a foreign currency denominated instrument, whether listed on an International Exchange or not, issued by a foreign depository in a permissible jurisdiction on the back of permissible securities issued or transferred to that foreign depository and deposited with a domestic custodian and includes 'global depository receipt' as defined in section 2(44) of the Companies Act, 2013. (Ministry of finance)

1.2   DR structure, issuance & trade mechanism

DR Program structure

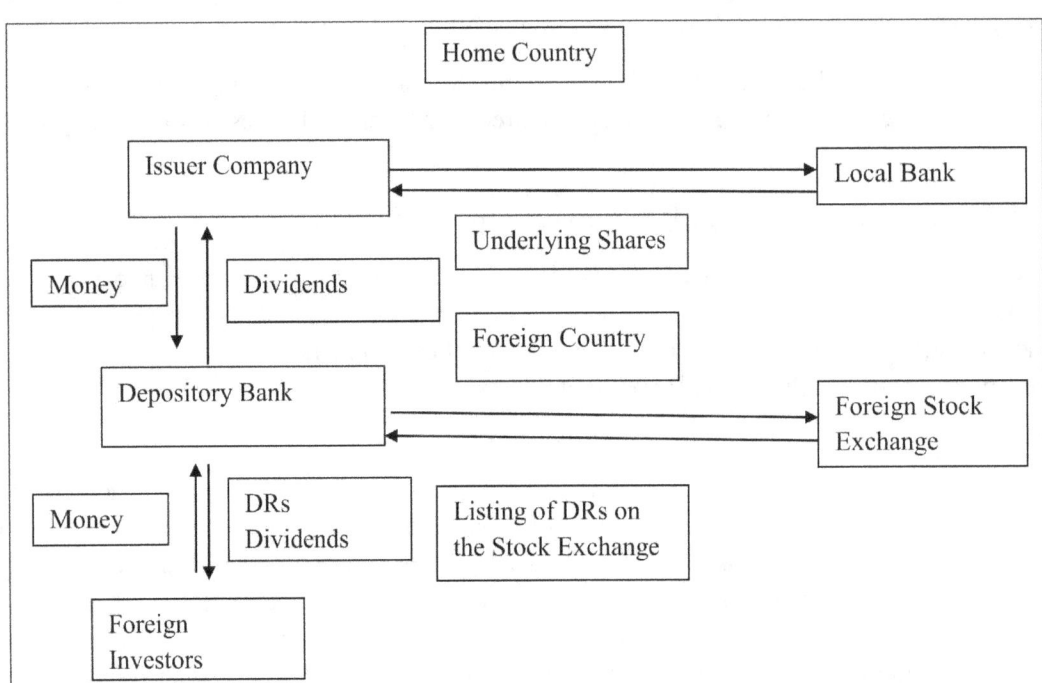

Source: - Desai & D'Souza (1998)

Figure 1.1 DR Structure

DR programs are classified as American Depositary Receipts (ADRs), Global Depositary Receipts (GDRs), Indian depository receipts (IDRs) & global registered shares on the basis of the countries where they are issued and/or listed. While ADRs are issued and/or listed only in the US markets, GDRs are simultaneously issued and/or listed in more than one market, typically in the European and US markets.

1.2.1   ISSUANCE PROCESS & PARTICIPANTS OF DR MARKET:

Setting up of depositary receipt program will require close coordination between company, depositary bank, and each firm's legal counsel. Depositary bank will need to closely coordinate with the custodian bank selected in the home market. If a company is raising capital or listing its depositary shares, it needs to rely upon other experts such as accountants, investment bankers, and Investor Relations firms. The depositary bank acts as the intermediary between your depositary receipt holders in other markets and activities in your local market. The roles and responsibilities of each program participants are summarized below.

Depositary Bank

- Provide assistance on type of program, exchange or market on which to list or quote
- Advice on ratio of depositary shares to ordinary shares
- Appoint custodian
- File Form F-6 if Level One, 2 or 3 program
- Review draft registration statement or offering memorandum, depending upon type of program to be established
- Coordinate with all partners to complete program implementation steps on schedule
- Coordinate with legal counsel on Deposit Agreement and securities law matters
- Prepare and issue certificates and/or direct registration statements
- Solicit market makers (Level I ADR only)
- Announce DR program to market (brokers, traders, media, retail/ institutional investors via news releases and internet).

Issuer

- Provides depositary with notices of stockholder meetings and corporate distributions.
- Provides custodian and depositary with notices of annual and special/extraordinary stockholder meetings and corporate distributions including dividends and rights offerings.
- On-going compliance with any applicable stock exchange and SEC regulations, including disclosure and reporting, and corporate governance requirements (in coordination with legal counsel and accountants).
- Executes US-focused investor relations (non-US-focused in the case of Regulation S GDRs) plan that may include management visits to targeted US investors, the development of sell-side research, and on-going shareholder communications.

Custodian

- Advises the depositary of deposits of shares, including complete delivery instructions.
- Registers the shares in the depositary's account as necessary with the issuer's transfer agent/ registrar.
- Confirms release of local shares upon cancellation of depositary receipts.
- Notifies the depositary of corporate actions announced in the issuer's home market.

- Provides the depositary with copies of notices of shareholders' meetings, annual reports and other shareholder communications.
- Remits dividend payments to depositary.
- Maintains and communicates up-to date local market information on tax withholding, reclaim, regulatory and settlement issues.
- Provides statements of share balances for reconciliation by depositary.
- Receive local shares in issuer's home country
- Confirm deposit of underlying shares
- Hold shares in custody for the account of depositary in the home market

Legal Counsel (depositary's and issuer's)

- Prepare draft deposit agreement (depositary bank's counsel) and file required registration statements with the SEC
- Manage compliance with US securities laws, rules and regulations and perfect any securities law exemptions (if Rule 144A/Reg S program)(issuer counsel)

Accountants (Level II/III ADRs only)

- Prepare issuer's financial statements in accordance with, or reconcile to, US GAAP
- Review registration statement or offering circular

Investor Relations advisor/ firm

- Develop long-term plan to raise awareness of issuer's program in the US
- Develop communications plan and information materials for launch activities (road show and presentations to investors, launch day promotion, meetings with financial media)
- Coordinate with issuer's advertising and public relations teams on specific program plans to support and develop company image in the US

Investment banks/Underwriters (Level II/III/Rule 144A/Regulation S ADRs)

- Advise on type of program to launch and exchange or market on which to list or quote
- Advise on ratio of depositary shares to ordinary shares
- Cover issuer through research reports/promote DRs to investors
- Advise on road shows, investor meetings, investors to target
- Advise on capital market issues
- Where applicable, advise on potential merger/acquisition candidates, and other matters such as rights offerings, stock distributions, spin-offs, proxy contests, etc.
- If concurrent public offering:
- Advise on size, pricing and marketing of offering
- Act as placement agent or underwriter in offering
- Conduct road shows with management/ introduce issuer to institutional and other investors
- Line up selected dealers and co-underwriters for offering

DRs can be created or cancelled to satisfy investor demand in either the market where the DR trades or in the local trading market where the ordinary shares trade.

A primary step in establishing a DR program is to determine the ratio of underlying shares to depository shares. The share to DR ratio is established as a multiple or fraction of underlying shares & this ratio can influence the price trading range. In setting the ratio, the issuer should consider:

- **The industry peers:** - Securities of companies in the issuers industry generally trade in a certain price range and the issuer may want to confirm to industry norms in the market where the DR will be listed.
- **Exchange options:** - Each exchange has different average price ranges for the shares listed & issuer wants to confirm to that range.
- **Investor's point:** - Institutional investors and retail investors will be interested to buy securities that they perceive to be well priced and valued fairly.

While many DR programs are established with a 1:1 ratio (one underlying share equals to one DR) DR programs have been known to have ratios ranging from 100000:1 to 1:100. In a sponsored issue, this ratio may be determined by the depositary agreement between the issuer and the foreign depository. In an unsponsored issue, this ratio may be determined by the foreign depository. The Committee is of the view that this ratio, being guided by commercial realities prevailing in the domestic and international markets, is best left to the prudence of the parties involved. The Committee could not envisage a market failure arising out of a freely determined conversion ratio. Therefore, the Committee recommends that the parties should be free to choose any ratio of DRs to the underlying permissible securities.

The depository will work with issuers to determine the most appropriate ratio at the inception of the DR program. Ratios can be adjusted to future date for example whenever there are changes in market conditions. The issuer may also undertake a stock split of the domestic shares so as to keep the market price of a single DR within a comfortable price range for the foreign investors. At the time of setting the ratio, three factors have to be considered. First, the issuer decides the ratio in a manner so that DR prices conform to the price range at which most securities of issuers companies generally trade. Secondly, issuer wants to conform to the average price range at which most shares listed on the stock exchange trade. Last, DR ratio is decided to give a sense of just pricing to the prospective investors.

The DR is created when an investor contacts a broker to make an investment in a company with a DR program in that market. The broker can either purchase DRs in the secondary market or create DRs by purchasing the company's shares in the local stock market and then delivering them to the depositary's local custody bank. The broker converts the local currency received from the investor into the corresponding foreign currency and pays the local broker for the shares purchased.

The custodian bank instructs the depositary bank to issue the DRs and deliver them to the initiating broker, who then delivers the DRs to the investor. Conversely, when DRs are sold, the sale can take place in the secondary market, or the ordinary shares held outside the market can be released into the home trading market through a cross-border transaction. In this case, the DRs are cancelled and the shares held with the local custodian bank are delivered to the broker within the home market.

1.3   TYPES OF DRs

Basically, they are two types of depository receipts. ADRs and GDRs represent a simplified and cost-effective way for investors to gain international exposure and portfolio diversification. The ADR trading process is efficient, by passing many of the hurdles and costs associated with direct investing in ordinary shares of foreign companies. ADRs are U.S. dollar-denominated negotiable U.S. securities that represent the publicly traded equity or debt of foreign companies. Since their introduction, they have become the premier vehicle for U.S. investors who want to access foreign markets. ADRs offer issuing company access to the world's largest and most active capital market. GDRs, meanwhile, are typically used by foreign investors seeking global portfolio diversification, as well as by U.S. companies as a way of accessing foreign markets. GDRs are similar to ADRs in many aspects, including pricing in U.S. dollars (although this is not a requirement of a GDR, which can also be denominated in pounds, euros, and yen, for example). Unlike ADRs, GDRs can trade in two or more markets. When traded in the United States, the U.S. component of the GDR, or the U.S. "tranche," can be in the form of an exchange-listed ADR that must comply with SEC regulations. The GDR can also be privately placed in the United States, available only to institutional investors. First created in 1927, ADRs were little used as recently as three decades ago, when global portfolio diversification did not carry the weight it does today and many foreign public companies stayed within the boundaries of their local exchanges. However, a lot has changed over more than 30 years. Foreign companies have found the United States to be an ideal place for raising capital. American investors, meanwhile, have become familiar with the idea of international diversification and aware that some of the largest and most profitable companies in the world are based outside of the United States. ADRs have neatly served the needs of both parties, and in the process have come into their own. As stated previously, there are more than 3,000 DR programs available to investors today, representing companies in 76 countries. From mid-2008 to mid-2009, almost 1,000 new DR programs were established (an approximate 50% increase), mainly due to the new rules adopted by the SEC in October 2008, which made it easier to establish over-the-counter DR programs, greatly expanding the potential of the DR market. The major U.S. stock exchanges, the New York Stock Exchange (NYSE), the NYSE American Stock Exchange (AMEX), NASDAQ & US OTC are the largest markets for DR trading, executing 90% of all DR trading value worldwide.

1.3.1   AMERICAN DEPOSITORY RECEIPTS

In the US, you can select from programs that are listed on a national stock exchange or traded over-the-counter, tap retail or institutional investors, and are designed to expand your shareholder base or raise capital. To trade in ADRs, different registrations, regulatory reporting & financial disclosure requirement are needed. Detail explanations of these programs are given below.

a)   Depository receipts issued in United states---- ADRs

Program type	Listed on NYSE or AMEX or NASDAQ	Unlisted	Retail investors	Institutional investors (QIBS)	Develop shareholder base	Raise capital
Level I Unlisted (OTC)		*	*	*	*	
Level II Listed	*		*	*	*	
Level III (Listed/public offering)	*		*	*		*
Rule 144A (unlisted/private placement with QUIBS)		*		*		*

Source: - JP Morgan

Table 1.1: American Depository Receipts Options

UNLISTED PROGRAMS (LEVEL I AND RULE 144A DRS)

LEVEL - I ADRs: - A Level I ADR program is not listed on a stock exchange, but is available for retail investors to purchase and trade in the over-the-counter market via NASDAQ's Pink Sheets. A Level I program does not create new capital in the US; rather, it gives company the opportunity to develop or expand its shareholder base by establishing a foothold in the US market. Level I ADRs

- Maintain home market accounting and disclosure standards.
- Use existing shares to satisfy investor demand and liquidity. New DRs are created by issuing and cancelling ordinary shares in the issuer's home market.
- Are exempt from US reporting requirements under Rule 12g3-2(b) compliance.
- Are registered with the US Securities and Exchange Commission using Form F-6.

Bid and ask prices are electronically updated at the end of the trading day by the Pink Sheets LLC information service. Real-time and intra-day quotes posted by market makers are available to investors, by subscription, from vendors such as OTCquote.com.

Rule 144A:- A Rule 144a DR is the quickest, easiest, and most cost-effective way to raise capital in the United States. New, restricted shares are created and then privately placed with institutional investors. Rule 144A facilitates the resale of privately placed securities to Qualified Institutional Buyers in the US. These institutions manage at least $100 million in securities, or are registered broker-dealers that own or invest, on a discretionary basis, $10 million in securities of non-affiliates. Rule 144a DRs

- Are not subject to US reporting requirements.
- May not be advertised or actively promoted by the issuer.
- Trade electronically on PORTAL (a system managed by the National Association of Securities Dealers) pursuant to Rule 144a of the Securities Act of 1933.
- Are restricted to Qualified Institutional Buyers (QIBs) for purchase or trading.
- Are not registered with the US Securities and Exchange Commission.

At least two years from the last deposit of shares in the Rule 144A ADR facility, the ADRs issued under the Rule 144 program may be eligible to be merged into an unrestricted ADR facility.

Listed programs (Level II and Level III)

Listing of ADR means it will be traded on one of the three major US exchanges – the New York Stock Exchange (NYSE), The American Stock Exchange (Amex), or the National Association of Securities Dealers Automated Quotation System (NASDAQ). ADRs that are listed on the NYSE or Amex, or quoted on NASDAQ, have higher visibility in the US market, are more actively traded, and have increased potential liquidity.

In order to list company's securities, company must meet the listing requirements of your chosen exchange or market. Company must also comply with the registration provisions and continued reporting requirements of the Securities Exchange Act of 1934, as amended ("The Exchange Act"), as well as certain registration provisions of the Securities Act, which generally entail the following:

- Form F-6 registration statement, to register the ADRs to be issued.
- Form 20-F registration statement, to register the ADRs under the Exchange Act. This requires detailed financial disclosure from the issuer, including financial statements and a reconciliation of those statements to US GAAP (Generally Accepted Accounting Principles).
- Annual reports (on Form 20-F), filed on a regular, timely basis with the US Securities and Exchange Commission (SEC).
- Interim financial statements and current developments, furnished on a timely basis to the SEC on Form 6-K, to the extent such information is made public or filed with an exchange in the home country or distributed to shareholders.

Level II ADR: - A Level II ADR uses existing shares to satisfy investor demand and liquidity. New ADRs are created from deposits of ordinary shares in the issuer's home market. Because these securities are listed or quoted on a major US exchange, Level II ADRs reach a broader universe of potential shareholders and gain increased visibility through reporting in the financial media. Listed securities can be promoted and advertised, and may be covered by analysts and the media. In addition, listed securities can be used to structure incentives for an issuer's US employees, or could be used to facilitate US mergers and acquisitions.

Level III ADRs: - A Level III ADRs are a public offering of new shares into the US markets. These capital raisings have a high profile. They are followed closely by the financial press and other media, often generating significant visibility for the issuer. In addition to the requirements noted above, an issuer establishing a Level III ADR program:

- Is required to file Form F-1. This registers the securities underlying the ADRs that will be offered publicly in the US, including a prospectus informing potential investors about the issuer and any risks inherent in its business, the offering price of the securities, and the issuer's plan for distributing the ADRs. In certain circumstances, an abbreviated registration statement (Form F-3) may be acceptable.
- May substitute Form 8-A for Form 20-F registration to register under the Exchange Act. However, Form 20-F annual reports must be filed thereafter. This annual filing contains detailed financial disclosure from the issuer, financial statements and a full reconciliation of those statements to US Generally Accepted Accounting Principles (GAAP).

Level III ADRs can be actively promoted and advertised to increase investor awareness and market liquidity. As with Level II ADRs, the securities can be used to structure incentives for an issuer's US employees, and may be used to facilitate US mergers and acquisitions.

1.3.2   GLOBAL DEPOSITARY RECEIPTS:-

Global Depositary Receipts tap markets outside the US. Increasingly, issuers are looking beyond the US capital markets to raise capital. The Global Depositary Receipt (GDR) was created to satisfy that interest, allowing issuers access to new sources of funding and increasing their shareholder base. GDRs provide exposure to the global markets outside the issuer's home market, most commonly by combining two complementary structures: the Regulation S (Reg S) depositary receipt and the American Depositary Receipt (ADR)

GLOBAL DEPOSITORY RECEIPT OPTIONS			
Purpose	Outside US	In US	Comments
Raise capital in all markets	Reg S DR	Rule 144A DR	This is the most common GDR structure which is available to only qualified Institutional buyers in the US.
	Reg S DR	Level III ADR	This is allowed for public offering of shares in two markets.
Raise capital Expand shareholder base in US	Reg S DR	Level I ADR	Also called a "Side by side" DR program. Level I program is established 40 days after the initial Reg S offering.
	Reg S DR	Level II ADR	Infrequently combined, as regulatory/ reporting requirements are stringent and no capital may be raised in the US (although capital may be raised outside the US)

Source: - JP Morgan

Table 1.2: Global Depository Receipts options

Regulation S (Reg S) DRs: - These DRs allow issuers to raise capital in markets outside the United States. Reg S DRs are often listed on the London or Luxembourg stock exchanges, and clear through the Euro market clearing systems Euro clear and Clear stream.

The issuer must comply with the regulations of the markets on which their shares are issued, as well as the rules of the exchange where they are listed or traded. US investors may not purchase Reg S DRs. Pairing an American Depositary Receipts (ADRs) with a Reg S DR allows the issuer to access US markets.

- If the issuer seeks to raise capital, a Rule 144A DR or a public offering via listed, Level III ADR is utilized.
- If the issuer seeks to broaden their shareholder base in the US, they can establish a Level I ADR in the US forty days after a Reg S offering. This combination Reg S/ Level I ADR structure is called a Side by side depositary receipt program.

1.4   Corporate governance rules for ADR issuers: Sarbanes-Oxley

The Sarbanes-Oxley Act of 2002 (the Act), signed into law in July 2002, instituted a broad set of new reforms regarding the corporate governance of publicly held corporations. The objectives of the Act included: heightening the level of corporate accountability to shareholders; increasing the transparency of financial statements; and reforming the oversight of corporate accounting. The Act directed the SEC to issue enabling rules for certain provisions, and after the adoption of the Act the SEC engaged in an extensive rulemaking process. The Act applies to non-US issuers whose ADRs have been publicly offered in the US

(Level III ADRs), or are listed on a US securities exchange (Level II), but not to those whose ADRs trade only OTC (Level I) or privately via Rule 144A.

Overview of key provisions

Audit committee requirements: - The Act requires that the audit committee of a company's Board of Director's be composed entirely of independent directors. The audit committee's responsibilities include overseeing and approving outside auditors.

Audit committee financial expert: - The Act requires issuers to disclose in their periodic reports (i.e., for ADR issuers, annual reports on Form 20-F) whether or not at least one "financial expert" serves on the audit committee. The qualifications of an audit committee financial expert include an understanding of US GAAP, financial statements, audit committee functions and internal controls and procedures, as well as experience in financial statement preparation, auditing, analysis or evaluation.

Certification of financial reports: - In each periodic report filed with the SEC (i.e., Form 20-F filings for listed ADR issuers), the issuer's CEO and CFO must certify in writing to certain matters, including:

- that the issuer's financial statements fairly present its financial condition, cash flows and results of operations
- that certain disclosure controls have been established and followed and the certifying officers have evaluated their effectiveness
- That any significant changes to internal controls over financial reporting have been disclosed in the report and significant deficiencies and material weaknesses have been disclosed to the audit committee and the auditors.

Management assessment of internal controls: - The Act requires management to submit (along with the annual report on Form 20-F), an "internal control report" which evaluates the effectiveness of the company's internal controls and procedures followed in the preparation of the financial statements.

Improper influence of audits: - An issuer's officers and directors cannot take any action to coerce, manipulate, mislead or fraudulently influence any accountant engaged in an audit.

Prohibition on loans to officers and directors:-Issuers are generally prohibited from extending personal loans in any form to any executive officer or director. Loans made prior to signing of the Act are exempt, so long as they are not materially modified or renewed thereafter.

CEO and CFO reimbursement of issuer relating to an accounting restatement:-If a company's accounts need to be restated due to material non-compliance by the company with financial reporting requirements as a result of misconduct, the CEO and CFO must reimburse the issuer for all profits from the sale of the company's securities, and all bonus, incentive-based or equity-based compensation, received by such officers during the one-year period after the filing of the document that contained the information required to be restated.

Disclosure of material off-balance sheet transactions:- All off-balance sheet transactions, obligations and other arrangements that may have a material effect on the company's financial condition, results, revenues or expenses, liquidity, capital expenditures or capital resources, must be disclosed on an annual basis, filed on Form 20-F.

Disclosure of pro-forma, or non-GAAP financial information: - Where a company discloses non-GAAP financial information (e.g., use of EBITDA or results that exclude non-recurring items), the information must not be materially misleading, and all non-GAAP financial measures must be reconciled to the most comparable GAAP financial measure.

Correcting adjustment disclosures:-Financial statements must indicate any material correcting adjustments identified by outside auditors.

Code of ethics for senior financial officers: - On an annual basis, issuers must disclose whether or not they have a code of ethics (standards designed to deter wrongdoing and promote honest and ethical conduct, including proper disclosure and compliance with law) that applies to the CEO, CFO and chief accounting officer. If an issuer has no code of ethics, it must explain why. A copy of the code of ethics must be filed as an exhibit to an issuer's annual report.

Pension fund blackout periods:- During any blackout period of at least three business days during which at least 50% of the issuer's pension plan participants or beneficiaries are prohibited from trading, executive officers and directors are prohibited from trading equity securities acquired in connection with their service or employment as directors or executive officers. Non US issuers are subject to this provision if the total number of pension plan participants or beneficiaries located in the US who are affected by a blackout is greater than 50,000, or exceeds 15% of the total number of employees of the issuer.

SEC review of periodic disclosures: - The SEC is directed to conduct a review of the disclosures and financial statements of listed issuers at least once every three years. Factors that may determine the timing of a review include the issuance of a material restatement, significant volatility in the stock price, large market capitalization, disparities in price to earnings ratios, and the existence of operations that significantly affect any material sector of the economy.

Real-time additional disclosures: - The Act mandates that issuers are required to disclose to the investing public, on a "rapid and current basis," any information concerning material changes in the company's financial condition or operations. Based on this provision, the SEC issued several implementing regulations relating to current disclosure requirements under Form 8-K. Non US issuers are not subject to these regulations since they are not required to make Form 8-K filings. However, under existing regulations, material information including interim financial information and earnings releases of non-US issuers must generally be furnished to the SEC on Form 6-K, to the extent the information is made public in an issuer's home country or disclosed to shareholders.

Form F-6:- Simple, basic registration of DRs with the SEC for Level I, II and III ADRs. Under the Securities Act, any issuer establishing a publicly available ADR program in the US must register the DRs under the Securities Act. Form F-6 is used to register the DRs that represent the issuer's underlying securities. Under Form F-6, disclosure regarding a DR program is provided by attaching a copy of the Deposit Agreement that specifies the form of DR included therein. No other substantive disclosure is required.

Form 20-F: - Annual disclosure to SEC and registration document for Level II and Level III ADR programs. Form 20-F can be used to register securities under the Exchange Act and, for issuers that are already registered and are therefore subject to Exchange Act reporting requirements, Form 20-F is used to file annual reports with the SEC.

1.5 EVOLUTION & PERFORMANCE OF DEPOSITORY RECEIPTS:-

There was a great demand for foreign capital in some of the lesser developed countries, at the same time supply of capital was in excess in the countries like U.S.A & England. There was a need to bridge this gap and make a channel to enable the flow of funds from these countries to the countries that require the funds. Investing without such a channel was a challenge not just financially but also administratively. The transactions were complicated and the settlement of the transactions in was very difficult owing to currency values. In an effort to bridge this gap, JP Morgan introduced a system of depository receipts in 1927. JP Morgan intended to provide a channel that allows for easier flow of funds from developing countries like U.S.A to other countries by offering them investment option overseas. Globally markets for DRs are 90 yrs old. In 1927, the first DR program was launched by UK retailer "Selfridge Provincial Stores ltd" listed through ADRs on New York stock exchange. During this period, nearly more 18 DR programs were introduced. DRs are traded on major international stock markets with large investment banks running this program. The depositary receipts were intended as both an investment vehicle as well as an investment option.

The early growth came to an abrupt halt at the time when stock markets crashed in 1929, until early 1950, no fresh DRs were introduced. Present form of ADRs came into existence in 1955, when SEC introduced its Form S-12 for registering all ADR programs. Several Australian, South African mining companies started trading in DR programs. Same manner several Japanese companies issued ADRs during 1960s. In 1970's & 1980's, firms from all over the world started trading by adopting DR route for capital rising. DR as mentioned earlier has introduced to overcome problems faced for capital rising allover. New regulatory frame work was introduced by SEC 1985, leading to introduction of range of DR programs. The first global depository receipts (GDR) was introduced by Citi bank for Samsung Corporation to raise capital in US & Europe. Rule 144a was introduced to give rise to private placements resulting increased liquidity & marketability of privately placed ADRs.

Firms from developed capital markets such as Australia, Hong Kong, Japan, Netherland Sweden & UK dominated the DR market during 1990's. US investment in the foreign equity has increased in 1991 from US $279 to $ 1943 billion in 2001. Emerging markets experienced a reduction in funding from the official sources & a high economic growth rate. In order to overcome this situation, emerging markets were forced to rely on the private flows of funds though foreign private placements. Since 1992, a majority of capital raising of DR programs have been issued by emerging market firms. Many of the newly listed companies from emerging markets had their IPO in mature markets, by crossing the orders.

Issuers from emerging markets completed 96% of the years DR capital raising, out of which 71% of the DR capital raising were by companies from BRIC[3] in 2004. Issuers from India, Taiwan & Korea accounted majority of all DR capital raising in 2005. In 2006, nearly 47% of the DR capital raising was collected by issuers from Russia, Kazakhstan, Korea, China & India. BRIC countries have dominated the DR market for nearly 4 years. As such after introduction of GDR under private placements grab the market. For strengthen the US DR market, it introduced unsponsored DR programs for strengthening the US $ in 2005. In 2008, 56% of the DR capital raising & 54% of the trading volume was from BRIC.

---

3   BRIC: Brazil, Russia, India & China.

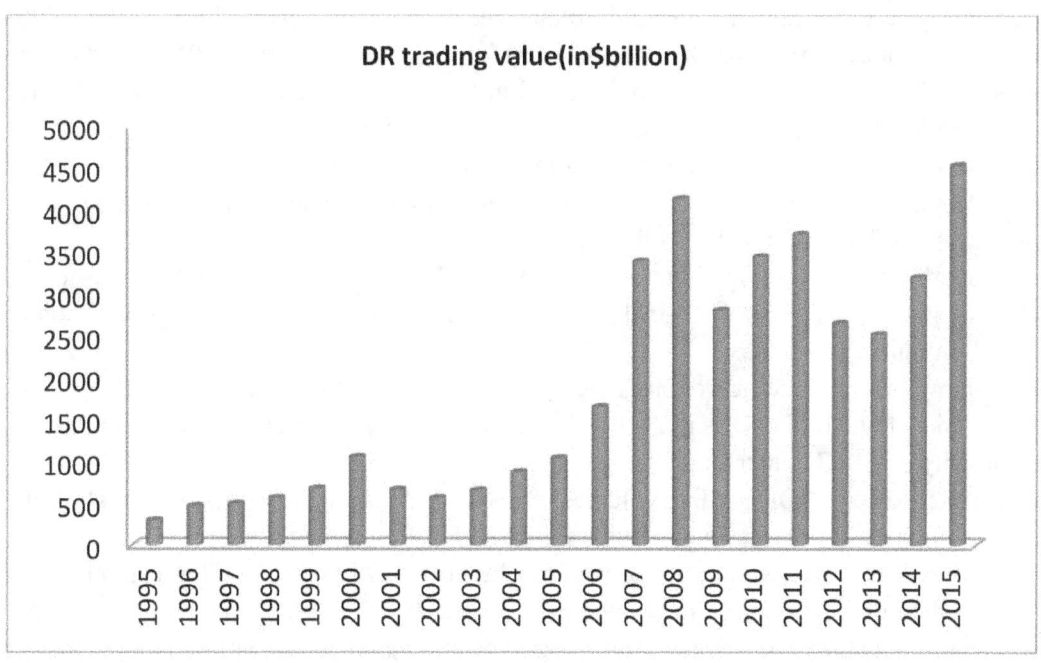

Source: - JP Morgan, BNY Mellon
Figure 1.2 ADR trading value in major stock exchanges (US $ in billions)

In the above graph, the ADR trading value increased from $300 billion to $4533 in 2015. The DR has all time high record in 2015, after 2008 with $4139. The ADR trading volume increased from $ 20 billion in 1998 to $ 147 billion in the year 2015. The ADR trading volume was all time high of $ 170 billion 2011.

1.5.1   PERFORMANCE RECORD OF DRS[4] :-

Growth records of DRs from year 2005 to 2016 are as follows 2005:-Depositary Receipts capital raising was $7.9 billion in 2005, which represents an increase of 121% over 2004 driven by all regions. DR trading value was $367.7 billion, while DR trading volume was 15.3 billion shares. Depositary Receipts capital raising approaches record high reaching $27.5 billion in 2005, a 194% increase over full year 2004. ADR trading volume hits new record of 38.4 billion shares, while DR trading value rises to $1.2 trillion.

2006:- Depositary Receipts IPO capital raised reaches $20.9 billion – a record high – and total DR capital raised reaches $28.2 billion. DR US$ trading value increases 31% to $1.55 trillion, which is also an all-time record, while DR trading volume rises 13% to 42.3 billion shares.

2007:- Depositary Receipts capital raised reaches $49.5 billion in 2007, all -time records set by key measures. IPO capital raised in DR form is $31.9 billion driven by Russia, China, India, Taiwan and Kazakhstan. DR US$ trading value increases to $2.61 trillion, while DR trading volume rises 34% to a record 55.9 billion shares.

---

4 https://depositaryreceipts.citi.com/adr/common/linkpageC.aspx?pageId=2 & subpageid=9

2008:- Depositary receipts trading value and volume reach all-time highs in 2008 – IPO value declines. DR trading value increases 27% to an all-time high of US$4.2 trillion; ADR trading volume rises to a record 120 billion shares. IPO capital raised in DR form is $3.8 billion – down 88% from 2007's record of $31.9 billion, due to the global economic slowdown.

2009:- Capital raisings increased 16% over 2008 to $15.9 billion: IPOs rebounded in second half of 2009 and accounted for 55% of total capital raising; DR trading volumes down 7% in 2009 to 124 billion shares versus 2008 all-time high of 133 billion.

2010:- Depositary Receipts trading volumes were up by 4.8 billion shares in 2010 to 147.4 billion shares, versus 142.6 billion in 2009. Capital raisings increased 26% over 2009 to $20.6 billion dominated by activity in BRIC countries.

2011:- Depository receipts trading volume reached a high by 22.4 billion shares in 2011 to170.7 billion DRs, versus 148.3 billion DRs in 2010. DR capital raising reached a total of $ 16.6 billion dominated by activity of BRIC countries.

2012:- Depositary Receipts (DR) trading volumes reached 139.9 billion in 2012. DR capital raisings totaled $12.4 billion driven primarily by issuers from Russia and Mexico.

2013:- Depositary Receipts (DR) trading volumes reached 141.7 billion in 2013. DR capital raisings totaled $10.5 billion driven primarily by issuers from Russia, Taiwan and China.

2014:- The market for non-US companies depository receipts capital raising reached a significant milestone with $ 37.3 billion of capital raised in 2014.

2015:- Depositary Receipts (DR) trading volumes totaled 163.7 billion in 2015. Non-U.S. companies raised $11 billion in DR form during 2015; Follow-on offerings in DR form represented $8.8 billion – or 80% – of the total, driven by transactions from the pharmaceutical, internet and banking sectors.

2016:- Depositary Receipts (DR) capital raisings totaled $6.8 billion dominated by activity from Chinese issuers. DR trading volumes were down 2% in 2016 to 155.1 billion shares, versus 157.7 billion shares in 2015.

1.5.2   PERFORMANCE OF INDIAN DRS:

DR scheme were introduced in April 1, 1991. Companies with good performance can get listed internationally. The first Indian DR was introduced by Reliance industries on Luxembourg stock exchange in 1992, followed by Grasim industries with GDR listed program. A high degree of foreign listing activity by the Indian firms increased during 1994 to 1996 period, attributed to the increased allocation of investible funds by the international investors to the emerging markets like India; & desire of many Indian firms to raise the funds during the boom phase of the domestic markets to get a better pricing for their DR programs. A major improvement in Indian stock market was in 1995, when the new electronic National stock exchange taken place. It generated renewed interest and increased trading volumes in the Indian stock market in 1995-1996. The government of India allowed financial services companies, non- bank finance companies & financial institutions to trade on international stock markets. The mandatory three year good performance track record criteria for listing norms was relaxed for financing investments in infrastructure sectors such as power generation, telecom, petroleum exploration, refining, ports & roads. This encouraged foreign listings by related firms like BSES ltd, VSNL (telecom) & MTNL (telecom) during 1996-97. During the same period, SBI & ICICI also foreign listed through private placement.

Year	Apr	May	Jun	July	Aug	Sep	Oct	Nov	Dec	Jan	Feb	Mar	Total
1	2	3	4	5	6	7	8	9	10	11	12	13	
1999-00	0	0	0	0	0	315	86	0	0	0	218	149	768
2000-01	275	146	0	172	75	11	17	0	0	3	0	132	831
2001-02	0	0	285	0	173	19	0	0	0	0	0	0	477
2002-03	0	20	0	0	0	0	117	0	400	30	0	33	600
2003-04	15	0	0	17	286	29	0	6	50	14	42	0	459
2004-05	35	135	0	0	0	0	0	224	0	48	0	171	613
2005-06	13	347	60	63	85	302	557	288	267	159	129	282	2552
2006-07	435	572	254	286	0	174	52	77	78	1578	245	25	3776
2007-08	11	5	300	2028	448	1	2731	158	2708	249	87	43	8769
2008-09	552	446	1	7	129	0	7	0	0	0	0	20	1162
2009-10	33	0	10	965	1603	96	0	381	94	46	0	100	3328
2010-11	156	532	426	364	0	128	74	110	49	116	0	94	2049
2011-12	105	125	48	20	24	161	84	0	0	30	0	0	597
2012-13	0	0	94	60	0	25	8	0	0	0	0	0	187
2013-14	0	0	207	0	0	0	0	0	0	-	-	-	207
2014-15	0	0	273	0	0	100	0	0	0	0	0	0	373

Source: SEBI hand book 2015

Table:1.3 Indian ADR/GDR issue

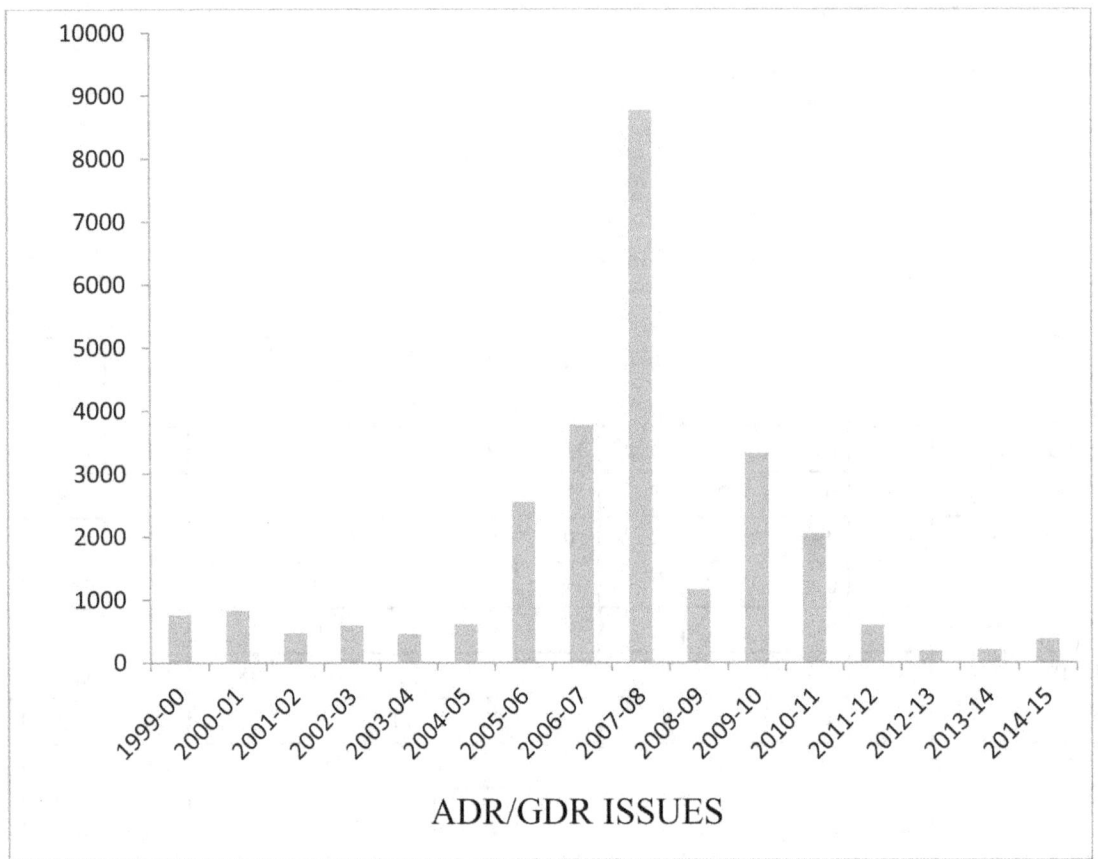

Figure 1.3 Indian ADR/ GDR issues

Due to changing economic & political conditions during 1997-98, witnesses a reduced foreign listings & issuance activity resulting economic crises in the south-east Asian markets. In early twenty century, the ministry of finance continues to liberalize the procedures & environment for the Indian corporate sector for acquiring capital from domestic & foreign sources reflected in the growth of the DR market. During this period, software companies were allowed to issue DR without reference to RBI up to US$ 100 million. First Indian firm to get listed on NASDAQ through ADR was Infosys Technologies 1999.

On Jan 20 2000, RBI gave general permission to Indian firms to issue DRs, by simplifying the procedures under the Foreign Exchange Regulation Act (FERA) 1973. Finance institutions were allowed to raise capital through GDRs or ADRs within limits prescribed for FDI by the government of India. In 2002, overseas business acquisitions were allowed through DR route under the automatic approval mechanism for Indian companies engaged in IT, software, pharmaceuticals, Biotechnology etc. During the year 2002-03, two - way fungibility[5] was introduced.

In 2004, RBI permitted to issue DR programs linked with ESOPs. The coverage was expanded to include employees of all companies. During 2005-06, there was a sudden increase in the DR listings with 2552

---

5 Fungibility means company can convert the DR program in to Indian company shares and vice versa. Before it was one way fungibility

issues. Unlisted companies were allowed to sponsor DR level programs. During 2007-08, India experienced all time high growth with remarkable 49.8% of capital raised from International capital markets with 8769 issues. India was the second country after Russia with 16 new sponsored DRs Offerings. In 2008-09, DR program reduced to 1162 issues, this may be because of recession. In 2009-10, DR programs again increased with 3328 issues. In 2014-15, the DR programs were performing better than previous years with 373 DR issues.

1.5.3   Evolution of the DR Scheme in India

Date	EVENTS
November 12, 1993	The Scheme was notified with effect from April 1, 1992. Companies required a track record of good performance.
May 22, 1998	Unlisted companies to comply with domestic listing conditions within three years of making profit.
June 23, 1998	DR linked employee stock options permitted for software companies.
March 2, 2001	Two-way Fungibility permitted subject to guidelines to be announced by RBI.
July 29, 2002	Companies permitted to sponsor DR issue at a price determined by lead manager. All shareholders of a company would get opportunity to offer shares against which the DRs would be issued. Such issues need to conform to FDI policy.
August 31, 2005	Companies ineligible to access capital markets made ineligible to issue DRs. Unlisted companies issuing DRs to simultaneously list underlying shares on Indian exchange. Introduced pricing guidelines for such DR issue based on prevailing price of the underlying share on the Indian exchange. Erstwhile Overseas Corporate Bodies (OCBs) prohibited from buying DRs. Pricing of DRs against shares of unlisted companies as per RBI regulations.
September 14, 2005	Exempted unlisted companies from simultaneous listing if they had taken verifiable effective steps and completed issue by December 31, 2005.
November 17, 2005	Pricing norms for issue of DRs aligned with pricing norms by SEBI for Qualified Institutional Placements (QIPs).
October 11, 2013	Unlisted companies allowed raising capital abroad by issuing DRs without undergoing simultaneous listing. Such DRs must be listed in IOSCO and FATF compliant jurisdictions. Such companies must comply with SEBI disclosure norms. Raising of capital abroad must be complaint with FDI norms.

Source : RBI

Table No 1.4: Evolution of DR scheme in India

Issue of eligible securities under DR Scheme 2014:-

Depository Receipts (DRs) are foreign currency denominated instruments issued by a foreign Depository in a permissible jurisdiction against a pool of permissible securities issued or transferred to that foreign depository and deposited with a domestic custodian. DRs may or may not be traded in an international exchange.

- In terms of Schedule 10 to Notification No. FEMA.20/2000-RB dated May 3, 2000, a person will be eligible to issue or transfer eligible securities to a foreign depository, for the purpose of converting the securities so purchased into depository receipts in terms of Depository Receipts Scheme, 2014 and guidelines issued by the Government of India there under from time to time. Depository Receipts issued under the Issue of Foreign Currency Convertible Bonds and Ordinary Shares (Through Depository Receipt Mechanism) Scheme, 1993 shall be deemed to have been issued under the corresponding provisions of DR Scheme, 2014 and have to comply with the provisions laid out in Schedule 10 of Notification ibid.

- A company can issue DRs, if it is eligible to issue eligible instruments to person resident outside India under Schedules 1, 2, 2A, 3, 5 and 8 of Notification No. FEMA 20/2000-RB dated May 3, 2000, as amended from time to time.

- The aggregate of eligible securities which may be issued or transferred to foreign depositories, along with eligible securities already held by persons resident outside India, shall not exceed the limit on foreign holding of such eligible securities under the relevant regulations framed under FEMA, 1999.

- The eligible securities shall not be issued or transferred to a foreign depository for the purpose of issuing depository receipts at a price less than the price applicable to a corresponding mode of issue or transfer of such securities to domestic investors under the relevant regulations framed under FEMA, 1999.

- The issue of depository receipts as per DR Scheme 2014 shall be reported to the Reserve Bank by the domestic custodian as per the reporting guidelines for DR Scheme 2014 are given in Section V of the Master Circular.

1.6   INDIAN DEPOSITORY RECEIPTS:-

The world has become global village due to advancement in technology in recent years and information can be shared very rapidly across the globe resulting stock markets have become international leading to easier trading on international markets. Large number of countries have opened their stock markets to foreign investors and abolished laws restricting their citizens investing abroad. Companies which trade locally on domestic stock market now can tap internationally foreign source of capital.

Indian companies' trades on foreign markets through various instruments are American depository receipts, global depository receipts & foreign currency convertible bonds on overseas stock exchanges like NYSE, Luxembourg stock exchange, London stock exchange & European stock exchanges. As the Indian securities markets have become deeper with BSE Sensex and NSE nifty giving higher returns as compared to other indices of the world. Foreign companies have started showing interest in the Indian securities market. India is becoming popular among foreign investors as a preferred investment destination for investment; the Indian government has introduced and modified various financial instruments through which investment can be made by different investors. Indian government has introduced the concept of Indian depository receipts (IDRs) to facilitate listings by foreign firms on Indian stock markets. An international company can now access Indian stock market by raising funds through issuance of IDRs. The government of India notified the companies issue of Indian depository receipts rules, 2004 (companies IDRs rules), amended till date, pursuant to section 642 read with section 605 A of the companies act, 1956 of India.

SEBI has defined as IDR "an instrument denominated in Indian rupees in the form of a depository receipt created by a domestic depository against the underlying equity of the issuing company to enable foreign companies to raise funds from Indian securities markets".

1.6.1   REGULATORY FRAME WORK OF IDR:-

The issue of IDRs is governed by Companies Act, 1956, SEBI (Issue of Capital and disclosure Requirements), Regulations 2009 and RBI Circular on the same. Apart from these the regular requirements applicable to any issue and listing of shares are applicable in this case also. Companies (Issue of Indian Depository Receipts) Rules,2004: There are some very relevant and mandatory provisions to be complied for issue, listing, transfer and disclosure purpose in case of an IDR. Some of important among them are as follows-

1. **Applicability:** These rules shall apply only to those companies incorporated outside India, whether they have or have not established any place of business in India. Thus these rules are extra territorial in nature.

2. **Eligibility for issue of IDRs:** Without prejudice to anything contained in the Securities and Exchange Board of India Act, 1992, an issuing company may issue IDRs only if it satisfies the following conditions.

   a) Its pre-issue paid-up capital and free reserves is at least US$ 50 million and have a minimum average turnover of at least US$ 100 million during the preceding 3 financial years of the issue in its home country.

   b) According to companies act 1956 section 205, a company which has been making profits for at least three years out of five years preceding the issue and has been declaring dividend of not less than 10% each year for the said period.

   c) Its pre-issue debt equity ratio is not more than 2:1.

   d) A continuous trading record or history on a stock exchange in its home country for at least three immediately preceding years.

   e) Listed in its home country and not been prohibited to issue securities by any regulatory body and has a good track record with respect to compliance with securities market regulations.

   f) It shall fulfill the eligibility criteria laid down by SEBI from time to time in this behalf.

3. **Procedure for making an issue of IDRs:**

   a) Company shall not raise funds in India by issuing IDRs unless it obtained prior permission from SEBI. An application taking permission shall be made to the SEBI 90 days prior to the opening date of the issue, in application form information should be furnished as may be notified from time to time with a non-refundable fee of US $10000 provided that when permission has been granted, an application shall pay an issue fee of half a percent of the issue value which is a minimum of

₹.10 lakhs where the issue is up to ₹ 100 crore. When the issue value exceeds ₹100 crore, for every additional value of the issue shall be subject to a fee of 0.25 percent of the issue value.

b) Issuing company shall obtain the necessary acceptance from the appropriate authorities from the country of its incorporation under the relevant laws relating to issue of capital, when required.

c) The issuing company shall appoint an overseas custodian bank, a domestic depository and a merchant banker for the purpose of issue of IDRs and deliver the underlying equity shares or cause them to be delivered to an Overseas Custodian Bank and the said bank shall authorize the domestic depository to issue IDRs.

d) The issuing company shall file through a merchant banker or the domestic depository a due diligence report with the Registrar and with SEBI in the form specified.

e) The issuing company shall, through a merchant Banker file a prospectus or letter of offer certified by two authorized signatories of the issuing company, one of whom shall be a whole-time director and other the Chief Accounts Officer, stating the particulars of the resolution of the Board by which it was approved, with the SEBI and Registrar of Companies, New Delhi, before such issue.

f) The draft prospectus or draft letter of offer shall be filed with SEBI, through the merchant banker, at least 21 days prior to the filing the prospectus or letter of offer. Provided that if within 21 days from the date of submission of draft prospectus or letter of offer, SEBI specifies any changes to be made therein, the prospectus shall not be filed with the SEBI/Registrar of Companies unless such changes have been incorporated therein.

g) The issuing company, seeking permission under sub-rule (i) above, shall obtain in principle listing permission from one or more stock exchanges having nationwide trading terminals in India.

4. **Not Redeemable:-**IDRs shall not be redeemable into the underlying equity shares before the expiry of one year period from the date of the issue of the IDRs.

5. **Paid up capital: -** IDRs issued by any issuing company in any financial year shall not exceed 15 per cent of its paid-up capital and free reserves.

6. **Disclosure by merchant banker: -** The Merchant Banker to the issue of IDRs shall deliver for registration the following documents or information to the SEBI and Registrar of Companies at New Delhi, namely:-

a) Instrument constituting or defining the constitution of the issuing company;

b) The enactments or provisions having the force of law by or under which the incorporation of the issuing company was effected, a copy of such provisions attested by an officer of the company be annexed;

c) If the issuing company has established place of business in India, address of its principal office in India.

d) If the issuing company does not establish principal place of business in India, an address in India where the said instrument, enactments or provision or copies thereof are available for public inspection, and if these are not in English, a translation thereof certified by a responsible officer of the issuing company shall be kept for public inspection;

e) A certified copy of the certificate of incorporation of the issuing company in the country in which it is incorporated;

f) Copies of the agreements entered into between the issuing company, the overseas custodian bank, the domestic depository, which shall inter alia specify the rights to be passed on to the IDR holders;

g) If any document or any portion thereof required to be filed with the SEBI/ Registrar of Companies is not in English language, a translation of that document or portion thereof in English, certified by a responsible officer of the company to be correct and attested by an authorized officer of the Embassy or Consulate of that country in India, shall be attached to each copy of the document.

h) The prospectus to be filed with the SEBI and Registrar shall contain the particulars as prescribed in Schedule and shall be signed by all the whole-time directors of the issuing company and by the Chief Accounts Officer.

7. **Conditions for the issue of prospectus and application are as follows:**

a) No application form for the securities of the issuing company shall be issued unless the form is accompanied by a memorandum containing the salient features of prospectus in the specified form.

b) An application form can be issued without the memorandum as specified in clause.

c) Above if it is issued in connection with an invitation to enter into an underwriting agreement with respect to the IDRs.

d) The prospectus for subscription of IDRs of the issuing company which includes a statement purporting to be made by an expert shall not be circulated, issued or distributed in India or abroad unless a statement that the expert has given his written consent to the issue thereof and has not withdrawn such consent before the delivery of a copy of the prospectus to the SEBI and Registrar of Companies, New Delhi, appears on the prospectus.

e) The person (s) responsible for issue of the prospectus shall not incur any liability by reason of any non-compliance with or contravention of any provision of this rule, if as regards any matter not disclosed, he proves that he had no knowledge thereof; or ii. As regards any matter not disclosed, he proves that he had no knowledge thereof; or

8. **Listing of Indian Depository Receipt:**
The IDRs issued under this Rule shall be listed on the recognized Stock Exchange (s) in India and such IDRs may be purchased, possessed and freely transferred by a person resident in India as defined in section 2(v) of Foreign Exchange Management Act, 1999, subject to the provisions of the said Act.

9. **Procedure for transfer and redemption:**

i. A resident holder of IDRs may transfer the IDRs or may ask the Domestic Depository to redeem these IDRs, subject to the provisions of the Foreign Exchange Management Act, 1999 and other laws for the time being in force.

ii. In case of redemption, Domestic Depository shall request the Overseas Custodian Bank to get the corresponding underlying equity shares released in favour of the Indian resident for being sold directly on behalf of Indian resident, or being transferred in the books of issuing company in the name of Indian resident and a copy of such request shall be sent to the issuing company for information.

iii. In case of redemption, Domestic Depository shall request the Overseas Custodian Bank to get the corresponding underlying equity shares released in favour of the Indian resident for being sold directly on behalf of Indian resident, or being transferred in the books of issuing company in the name of Indian resident and a copy of such request shall be sent to the issuing company for information.

10. **Continuous Disclosure Requirements:**

  i. Issuing company shall furnish to the Overseas Custodian Bank and Domestic Depository, a certificate obtained by it from the statutory auditor of the company or a Chartered Accountant about utilization of funds and its variation from the projections of utilization of funds made in the prospectus, if any, in quarterly intervals and shall also publish it or cause to be published in one of the English language newspapers having wide circulation in India.

  ii. The quarterly audited financial results should be prepared and published in newspapers in the manner specified by the listing conditions.

11. **Distribution of corporate benefits:** On the receipt of dividend or other corporate action on the IDRs as specified in the agreements between the issuing company and the Domestic Depository, the Domestic Depository shall distribute them to the IDR holders in proportion to their holdings of IDRs.

12. **Penalty:** If a company or any other person contravenes any provision of these rules for which no punishment is provided in the Act, the company and every officer of the company who is in default or such other person shall be punishable with the fine which may extend to twice the amount of the IDR issue and where the contravention is a continuing one, with a further fine which may extend to five thousand rupees for every day, during which the contravention continues.

13. **Repeal and savings:** On the commencement of these rules, all rules, orders or directions in force in relation to any matter for which provisions are made in these rules shall stand repealed, except as respects things done or omitted to be done before such repeal.

14. **Power of Central Government to decide certain Questions:** If any question arises on the applicability and interpretation, such question shall be decided by the Central Government.

Approvals for issue of IDRs:-

IDR issue require SEBI approval and application can be made for this purpose 90 days before the proposed issue opening date.

Fungibility: - Fungibility means the ability to convert IDRs into underlying shares. Companies are not automatically permitted to convert into underlying shares, however after mandatory lock-in one year period it can be converted & subsequent to obtaining RBI approval. In case of conversion, a listed company may continue to hold the underlying shares; any other Indian investor would have to dispose of the underlying shares within month of conversion.

Corporate action: - Once the dividends & other corporate actions are received on the IDRs, the domestic companies' depository shall distribute them to the IDR holders as per deposit agreement.

Tax aspects: - Any income earned by way of dividends, capital gains will subject to tax consequences on application of general provisions under the income tax act.

1.7   Statement of Research problem

To identify the research problem, the researcher was advised by many professors and scholars to go for a vast study, resulted to identify many areas. This study leads to select one Exploratory topic i.e., Impact of cross listings on the valuation of Indian stocks, conceptual basis of study, historical observations. It was found that, in India, there is lack of research in these areas when compared to international countries, and there is a need for research in cross listings through DRs in India.

An investigation into the existing literature (chapter 2) reveals that most of the earlier research is focused on cross listings in general, concentrating largely on direct listings. Indian markets are relatively less explored in depository receipts. Most of the research is on American depository receipts impact on the various factors. Observing this as a research gap, the objectives are framed for the study.

1.8   Objectives of the Study:

➢   To study the impact of cross listings on the Indian stock returns.
➢   To assess the role of cross listings on the Indian stock liquidity.
➢   To study the causality pattern between Depository receipts prices and Indian stock prices.
➢   To study the effect of cross listings on the Indian stock volatility.
➢   To study and compare the DR regulatory framework of selected capital markets.

1.9   Hypotheses of the study:

➢   Hypothesis 1 H_0: There is no significant difference in returns of Indian stocks listed on International stock exchanges.
➢   Hypothesis 2 H_0: There is no significant impact on liquidity of the underlying domestic Indian stocks due to cross listings.
➢   Hypothesis 3 H_0: The cross listings of Indian firms on the international stock exchanges has no abnormal effect on the prices in the home market.
➢   Hypothesis 4 H_0: Depository receipts listings do not significantly affect the volatility of underlying stocks.
➢   Hypothesis 5 H_0: There is no significant difference in the DR regulatory frame work of selected capital markets.

1.10   Need of the study:

Cross listings through Depository receipts is a new instrument emerged in India to promote firms to cross list their shares on international markets. Cross listings through depository receipts has become one of the avenues for integration of global market securities. A DR issuer may list its shares on an international stock market for gaining visibility, to increase international base, to improve liquidity, to expand business. The role of depository receipts is quite different and important for the firms who make decision to list their shares abroad. While dealing in these types of instruments, there are many dimensions or factors which will be affecting the local stock market. So, there is a need to study the dimensions or factors such as Returns, price, liquidity & volatility.

1.11   Structure of the Study:

Chapter I: Provides introduction about cross listings, statement of the research problem, objectives of the study, hypotheses of the study, need of the study and structure of the study.

Chapter II: Traces Review of Literature, Extensive body of literature deals with the impact of cross listings on the underlying stocks. The chapter includes the reviews done by various authors across the countries. The chapter is divided into five sections. (I) the impact of cross listings on the Indian stock Returns. (ii) The impact of cross listings on the Indian stock Liquidity. (iii) The impact of cross listings on the Indian stock Price. (iv) The impact of cross listings on the Indian stock volatility (v) Comparison of DRs regulatory framework of select capital markets.

Chapter III: Research Methodology, methodology includes research design, sample population & selection, sources of collection of data, research objectives & financial tools, scope & period of the study and Limitations of the study.

Chapter IV: Data Analysis and Interpretation, the analyses of five objectives are included in this chapter. The chapter is divided into six sections. (1) Impact of cross listing on the Indian stock Returns (2) Impact of cross listing on the Indian stock Liquidity (3) Impact of cross listing on the Indian stock Price. (4) Impact of cross listing on the Indian stock volatility. (5) Comparison of DR regulatory frame work of select capital markets. (6) Conclusions.

Chapter V: Findings, Conclusions & Suggestions.

Bibliography

References

REVIEW OF LITERATURE

Extensive body of literature deals with the impact of cross listings on the underlying stocks. The chapter includes the reviews done by various authors across the countries. The chapter is divided into five sections. (i) the impact of cross listings on the Indian stock Returns. (ii) The impact of cross listings on the Indian stock Liquidity. (iii) The impact of cross listings on the Indian stock Price. (iv) the impact of cross listings on the Indian stock volatility (v) Comparison of DRs regulatory framework of select capital markets.

2.1 The Impact of Cross Listings on the Indian Stock Returns

Alexander, Eun and Janakiramanan (1988) are among the first to test the theoretical propositions empirically. According to their hypothesis, expected returns should be at a lower level after the listing. Their research design tries to consider possible liquidity and signaling effects as well as selection bias, therefore choosing a 36-month period (from t=-72 months to t=-36) to estimate the expected return before listing. Thus, they avoid getting an upwardly biased estimate. They argue that using residual analysis in this way allows them to detect changes in expected returns following the event of international listing. Persistent abnormal returns in the post -listing period combined with the assumption of efficient markets may indicate a change in the expected returns upon international listings. The study includes a sample of 34 non-US companies which listed on an US stock exchange over the period 1969-1982. Furthermore, they split the sample into two sub samples of 13 Canadian and 21 non-Canadian firms to detect any differences of the integration among national capital markets. They also hypothesize that non- Canadian firms should have a larger decline in expected returns than Canadian firms because their capital markets are less integrated with US-market. Their results indicate a persistent decline of CARs in the post listing period. This decline starts two months before the listing date and is statistically significant for the overall sample and the non-Canadian subsample. Their tests on the paired differences of means returns also show significantly lower mean returns for the post-listing period in comparison to the pre- listing period for overall sample and the non-Canadian subsample. In their view, the empirical results support their hypothesis that a listing is accompanied by a reduction in expected returns, especially for non-Canadian stocks if markets were either mildly or completely segmented beforehand. This decline in expected returns was stronger and statically significant for non- Canadian companies. They suggested that non- Canadian stock markets are more segmented from the US market as the other stock markets but has a higher covariance with the US market. They found that there is a decline in the expected returns and cumulative average abnormal returns of 14%. The study concludes that there was a decline in the average abnormal returns of the Canadian firms & the decline is much smaller than non-Canadian firms.

Howe and Kelm (1987) were among the first to examine the effects of an overseas listings on shareholders wealth. The study includes a sample of 112 US firms which have listed on foreign stock exchanges with 165 listings out of which 67 listings were on Basle stock exchange, 60 from Frankfurt stock exchanges, 31 from Paris stock exchange and 7 from Tokyo stock exchange. The study was done for a period of 1962-1985. The study used a market model to estimate abnormal returns over a 90 day pre listing period (t=-90 to t=0) and the 40 days post listing period (t=+1 t=+40). Howe & Kelm (1987) found significantly negative abnormal returns for US firms listing on Basle and Frankfurt stock exchanges and negative abnormal returns for Paris stock exchange as well. These negative abnormal returns especially occur in the pre-listing period where as post listing period does not seem to be consistently associated with negative abnormal returns. They explain these wealth losses are due to the arising regulatory uncertainty which is an important cost for companies listed abroad. The study found that average abnormal returns turned significantly negative post listings.

Hermann A., Arauner (1996) studied the impact of cross listings on the cost of capital. The study examined whether an international listing on London stock exchange, NASDAQ, and the NYSE has an impact on the cost of capital of the firms. The purpose of the study was to investigate whether foreign firms that list on NYSE or NASDAQ experience more positive wealth effects in the pre- listing period and shorter decline in the expected returns in the post listing period than London listings. The study includes a sample of 233 international listings consist of 118 firms listed on the London stock exchange, 84 firms listed on New York stock exchange and 31 firms listed ADRs on NASDAQ for a period of 1980 to 1994. The majorly selected London listed firms were from US 58 companies are from Japanese companies 26 firms. The NYSE listed firms were from UK 21 companies and 18 from Canada. NASDAQ includes a sample of 10 UK companies listed through ADRs. To examine the stock performance event study has been used in the study. Cumulative average abnormal returns & holding period return approaches were used in the study. To check the return pattern surrounding the listing date, the study used abnormal returns and holding period returns with a 52 week as a pre- listing period and a 104 week as a post listing period. Arauner (1996) compared the CARs for London, NYSE and NASDAQ listings. NYSE listings experience positive CAR in the pre listing period reaching a peak of 11.37 %. CARs of London stock exchange are positive in the pre- listing period but are lower insignificantly. This pattern in the post listing period changes. NYSE listings starts declining from listing announcement onwards. CARs of NASDAQ listed firms increased in the post listing period and reached to 5.02 % in week 5. While NYSE with 0.22 % and NASDAQ with 2.83% experience a positive cumulative average abnormal returns (CAARs) in the pre – listing period. London stock listings experienced a negative CAAR of 3.46 %. The CARs of London stock exchange, NYSE and NASDAQ listings showed a negative CAAR, the decline is far more pronounced for NYSE (-36.09%) AND NASDAQ with -19.85% listings than London stock exchange with -12.83%. Over a 104 week post listing period. The study confirms that foreign firm's listings on NYSE or NASDAQ experienced a positive abnormal returns in the pre- listing period and negative abnormal returns in the post- listing period. These results were not similar to London stock exchange which did not experienced any significant changes in the pre- listing and post- listing period. These findings were attributed to the institutional differences in regulating foreign equities across both markets. The study also shows that the underlying share price becomes aligned to the ADR price after the listing. The substantial positive abnormal return of 12.185 on the listing day for firms that upgrade their OTC- traded ADR programme to a fully listed ADR programme provides strong support for the benefits associated with the listings. The study concludes that US listings experience positive average abnormal returns in the pre- listing period and a decline in the expected returns thereafter.

Varela and Lee (1993 a) examined their hypothesis that the integration effect of the listing decreases the expected rate of return. The study includes a sample of 68 US firms listing on the London stock exchange between 1984-87 and 43 US firms listing on Tokyo stock exchange between 1973-87. They observed a significant decrease in the SML's intercept. The results of the study support the theoretical implications in that international listings lead to a decrease in expected returns.

Varela and Lee (1993b) studied the sample of US firms listing on London stock exchange. The study also reports significantly negative deviations from expected returns for the sample. The study was for a period of 1965-1987. Inter temporal comparisons yield significantly negative deviations for the period 1965-1975. the 1984 and the 1984-1987 listings group while the deviation from expected returns for the period 1975-1983 group is negative but not statistically significant. Varela and Lee (1993b) perform inter beta- comparisons for the sample of US companies, listed on the London stock exchange. They base their investigations on Stehle's (1997) findings that low beta firms tend to have a higher non-domestic systematic risk because a higher degree of international operations and a larger in size than high beta returns. In order to determine the pre -listing return, Varela and Lee (1993b) used a black's modified asset pricing model in which barriers to international investments are represented by a proportional tax on holdings of foreign assets. The post-listing return is represented by the SL model. The difference between both equations results in u; which may be defined as the difference, between the listed firm's true required return and the required return corresponding to the pre-listing relationship. The expected value of u across firms should be zero if no segmentation exists between the domestic and the foreign markets. But the theoretical models, as described above, suggest a negative value for u assumed that the "super" risk premium for the segmented security vanishes upon dual listing. The cumulative value for u is estimated by employing a matrix format. A significant value for u would indicate a downward drift in returns in the post-listing period. Their empirical tests employ a sample of 168 US firms that listed on the London Stock Exchange comparisons between 1965-87. They perform inter temporal and inter-beta for their sample. Their testing period is from 0 to 30 days after the listing. They assign dummy variables to high beta securities (defined as $\beta>1$) to test their hypothesis that low beta stocks experience a larger decline in expected returns upon listings. This would be reflected by a negative deviation of the value of u. The finding of Varela and Lee (1993b) shows significant negative deviations for a pre-listings and the post listings for 84 groups for a low beta stocks. High beta stocks have generally negative but insignificantly deviations. These deviations may be due to changes in the pricing parameters of those firms. The results of the pre-listings 84 group are consistent with their hypothesis of a fall of the intercept and a rise in the slope. This suggests that low beta firms experienced significant integration effects in the 1965-83 periods through a listing on the London stock exchange. But the results for the 1985-87 groups do not show significant parameters changes although significant negative deviations exist. They conclude that some other unknown factors cause this deviation but see their results generally in support with the theoretical propositions. Their findings show significant negative deviations for low beta stocks but they are not able to explain the differing results in comparison towards high beta stocks.

Doukas & switzer (2000) stated that there are several factors that has an impact of DR returns, liquidity and risk. The study examined the impact of foreign listings on Canadian firms by taking a sample of 79 Canadian firms that were cross listed on NYSE, NASDAQ and AMEX for a period of 1977-1997. The study found that there was a positive stock market returns to the announcement of listings in US.

Baker, Khan and Edelman (1994) investigated 87 NYSE and AMEX stocks that dually listed on the pacific stock exchange (PSE). The study was for a period of 1984 and 1990. The study used event study for computation of their findings. Their results show that cumulative average abnormal returns (CAARs) declined (-3.29 %) during a 20-day period event window following the day of listing but it does not persist for the 100-day period. The findings also indicate that the low liquidity stocks, as measured by the amivest liquidity ratio, perform worse than high liquidity stocks. This suggests that market fragmentation has a grater negative effect on low liquidity stocks.

Foester & Karolyi (1999) lins, strick & zenner (2003) stated that international listings provides companies with greater access to global market leading to enhanced visibility, liquidity and has less risk exposure. The study expected that the firms from emerging countries with high market capitalization should experience larger average abnormal returns than firms from developed markets. The sample includes 153 firms from 11 different countries that listed through ADRs in US during the period 1976 to 1992. The study observed stocks earned a positive excess returns prior to listings. The study concludes that emerging countries firms experienced a positive average abnormal returns in the post listings period, on the contrary non capital raisings firms experienced negative average abnormal returns post listings.

Kumar(2001) investigated the impact of overseas listings by firms on the returns of the domestic stocks. Event study was conducted by taking an event window of 100 days. Sample constitutes 68 foreign listed firms from emerging market of India. The study done was separate for ADR & GDR on London stock exchange and Luxembourg stock exchange. The study observed that there was a significant average abnormal returns (AAR) of 0.09% per day prior to listings and a -0.64% of AAR on the listing date. The study evidenced a pre -listing run-up and post – listing decline in prices in underlying shares. The evidence of pre listing is some what weak as daily AARs, through positive, are not significant between days -100 & -1 (0.06% with a t-statstics of 0.93%). The study showed a significant positive AAR between days -49 and -10 (0.16 percent with a t-statistics of 2.12) which shows a pre listing run up in the prices of the underlying domestic shares. Daily AAR becomes significantly negative on and around the listing day (-0.38% with a t-statistics of -3.46). And in the post listing period between days +1 and +100 days, daily AARs continue to be significantly negative with (-0.19% with a t-statistics of -4.29). The CAARs of overall sample exhibit two clearly discernible patterns. The first is a pattern of price increases during the 78-days period prior to the foreign listing day. The peak value of CAAR is 9.90% attained at about 12 days prior to the listing day. The second is a downward drift from the listing day onwards. The CAARs between days +1 and +100 are significantly negative (-17.1 percent with a t-statistic of -4.23). First, the peak level CAAR figure for GDR listings (8.68 percent) is comparatively lower than that of overall sample (9.90 percent). Second, the post-listing decline in the prices of underlying shares in case of GDR listings is more abrupt compared to the overall sample. While for the overall sample CAARs turn negative from 18 th day onwards after the listing day, for the GDR listings CAARs turn negative from 13 th day onwards after the listing day. Third, the CAAR on the 100th day after the listing day for GDR listings (-11.96 percent) is comparably more negative than that for the overall sample (-10.13 percent). The study concludes that there was a decline in AAR for a post listing period.

Tripathy & Jha.K. (2014) examined Indian stock market reaction to international cross listings for a period of 2004 to 2009.25 days event window was taken to conduct an event study. The study found that there was a positive average abnormal return (AAR) of 1.58% pre listing period and a significant negative AAR of -0.206% post listing period. They observed that there was a gradual decrease in AAR after cross listings announcement. They evidenced that shares of cross listed stocks experienced abnormal higher AAR prior to foreign listings & shortly thereafter turned to negative AAR post listings.

Sarkissian and schill (2009) examine monthly stock returns during 120 days with an event window of (-120,+120 months) around foreign listings for more than 1500 listings placed in 25 host countries based on the listing status as of December 1998. Firstly, they control for the order of the firms foreign listings and report that the first listings is associated with unique effects on shareholders wealth while the multiple listings yield diminishing gains. Secondly, they report substantial stock price run-up prior to cross listing and a profound post listing decline in returns in the long run, which is consistent with market timing theory. Nevertheless, the study find a permanent change in a firms cost of capital of about 2 percent that can be predominantly explained by cross product market trade and investor familiarity. In other words, the long term gains from a foreign listing are grater for firms listing on foreign markets that are geographically, economically and culturally closer to their home market. Study concludes that listing on American stock exchanges does not offer unique benefits to foreign firms in terms of shareholders wealth.

Roosenboom and Van Dijk (2009) compared the stock market price reaction to cross listings on eight major stock exchanges controlling for country – specific and firm – level characteristics. The study reports that abnormal returns around the day of the announcement of cross listings is higher for American listings through ADR, followed by British and then by European listings while it is insignificant for Tokyo listings. This study identifies significant determinants for the effect on shareholders wealth that results from cross listing in the USA and UK but finds no significant determinants for either for Europe or Japan.

Dodd Olga (2011) examined the effects of international cross listings on shareholders wealth. The study computes average abnormal returns (AAR) & Cumulative average abnormal return (CAAR) over 21-day (-10,+10) around the cross listings announcement as a measure of the wealth effects of cross listings. Using robustness test, cumulative average abnormal returns (CAAR) were further estimated for alternative event windows (-5,+5)days, (-3,+3) & (-1,+1) days around the announcement of cross listings. The study investigates impact of cross listings on shareholders wealth for European companies listed in American, British & European stock markets & the determinants of these effects & their evolution overtime. Dodd Olga (2011) used a data of 254 cross listings announcements by 210 companies from 21 European stock markets during the period 1982-2007. The results of the study reports that European companies experienced a positive market reaction around the announcement of cross listings with an average statistically significant cumulative average abnormal return of 1.8% with an event window of (-10,+10) around the announcement of an international cross listings. The results for the alternative windows were also similar with an event window of (-5,+5)days CAAR was 2.0%, in the event window of (-3,+3) days CAAR was 1.5%, & finally in the event window of (-1,+1) days CAAR was 0.8%. These abnormal returns are contributed mostly by American & British cross listings firms with 3.3% & 2.7% respectively, while the European listings firms do not generate any significant average abnormal returns. The study concludes that introduction of the Euro had no impact on the wealth effects of the European cross listings. The study also provides a evidence that the impact of cross listings on shareholders wealth is affected by capital market developments like the introduction of AIM by London stock exchanges & the adoption of sox in the US. With respect to British cross listings, the significant abnormal returns can mainly be attributed to the AIM listings. In turn Small size companies listing on AIM offers higher abnormal returns around AIM listings.

Lee (1991) analyzed a sample of 141 US companies that listed on foreign stock exchange. Out of 141 US companies, 119 companies were listed on London stock exchange and 22 were listed on Toronto stock exchange. The study was for a period of 1962-86. Lee (1991) computed average daily residuals and cumulative average daily residuals over 131-day test period with an event window of (t=-90 to t=+ 40). CAAR for both the London & Toronto stock exchanges were not statistically significant which indicates that overseas listings do not harm shareholders wealth.

Lee (1992) studied about companies listings overseas. The study includes 16 Uk companies listed on Tokyo stock exchange and 9 Japanese companies listed on London stock exchange. The study was for a period of 1983-89. the study examined average abnormal returns and cumulative average abnormal returns over a 17 weeks period which includes 12 weeks before and 4 weeks after the listing using market model. The results are consistent with Lee (1991) as they do not observe any significant price movement before or after the listing.

Fry, Lee and Choi (1994) examined the valuation effects of overseas listings. The study used a sample of 71 US firms that listed on the Tokyo stock exchange between 1973 to 1989. The study includes a event window of 121 -days (pre listing period from t= - 100 to t=0, post listing period from t=+1 to t +20). The study used market model and computed average abnormal returns and cumulative average abnormal returns. The results of the study indicate no significant wealth effects for shareholders.

Lau, S. T., J. D. Diltz and V. P. Apilado (1994) studied the impact of firm's listings on foreign stock exchanges. The sample includes 346 US firms' listings on ten different stock exchanges for a period of 1962- 1990. For a reduced number of sample firms, they used three different event dates (1) the date of application for listing (42 firms); (2) the date of acceptance of the application (153 firms) and (3) the first trading day on the stock exchange (346 firms). The study showed a CAAR of 1.25% for an event window of (-5, +4). The study observed a positive abnormal returns around the date of acceptance & negative returns on the first day of trading (0.36)

Dharan, B. & Ikenberry, D. (1995) examine the post-listing behaviour of 2889 US listings which moved from the NASDAQ to either the ASE or NYSE, or exchange from the ASE to the NYSE between July 1962 and December 1990. They find that CARs of domestic exchange listings are significantly negative during a 36-month period subsequent to the listing. The post-listing drift is persistent for different sub- periods and industries. However, it varies over time across the three types of exchange listings. CARs of firms moving from NASDAQ to ASE show the most pronounced negative reaction, followed by NASDAQ to NYSE movers, and ASE to NYSE exchange listings. Although the magnitude of the post-listing drift is reduced, the results do not change when adjusted for size and book-to-market effects. Dharan and Ikenberry (1995) continue their analysis by examining the impact of equity offerings on the post-listing performance. While the presence of IPOs does not account for the post-listing drift, the presence of seasoned equity offerings explains some portion of the poor performance following the listing. Although particularly firms that offered equity prior to changing their listing location from NASDAQ to NYSE performed badly, the "equity issuance puzzle" does not fully explain the negative post-listing behavior. They proceed their analysis and examine a "timing"-related explanation. Their results show that the post-listing drift is more severe for smaller firms and firms with relatively low institutional holdings. Since these firms have generally more volatile earnings, they are more constrained by the listings requirements. Hence, they have to list at opportune times when they qualify for a listing.

Ritter J., (1991) examined 1526 US initial public offerings (IPOs). The study was for a period of 1975 to 1984, Levis (1993) investigated 712 IPOs which came to the market between 1980-1988. The results of both the studies are similar as both the studies find a poor aftermarket performance of IPOs. However, the studies also showed a substantial variation in underperformance across industries and time periods. Ritter (1991) finds that firms which issued in high-volume years have the worst performance.

Loughran, T., and Ritter, J., (1995) and Spiess and Affleck-Graves (1995) provide similar evidence for seasoned equity offerings. Spiess and Affleck-Graves (1995) examine the five-year post-offering performance of 1247 US equity offerings during 1975-1989. Their results show long-run underperformance of equity issuing firms when adjusting for size (-39.36 percent), industry- and size (-31.24 percent), and book-to- market (-30.99 percent). The underperformance also persists after controlling for trading system, offer size, and firm age. The evidence suggests that there are a number of different factors influencing the price behavior in the pre-listing and the post listing period. However, listing and in particular foreign listing does not appear to be a uniform event across companies and the stock exchange. Hence, a research design must also consider other factors as institutional characteristics and capital raising activity of a firm.

Marr, Trimble and Varma (1991) studied about US companies offering Euro equities through international listings. The study compared 32 Euro equity offering and 196 domestic equity offerings of US companies for a period of 1985-1988. The study found that equity offerings experience higher positive abnormal returns in the pre – listing announcement period, but only little insignificantly negative returns in the post – listing period. Their results show that the issue size has a significant influence on the choice of the corporations between a euro equity or domestic equity offerings. This means that a firm increases the issue sixe above their actual needs if it perceives favourable market conditions overseas.

Firstly, they estimate the probability of a firm choosing Euro equity financing which is a function of issue size and the size and the ownership structure of the issuing firm. This estimation procedure provides selection bias W which controls for the self- selection bias that may occur if Euro equity issuers actually have a comparative advantage in issuing offshore. Secondly, they regress the following independent variables on the abnormal returns for domestic equity and Euro equity issues; the firms beta coefficient, the size and the ownership structure variables, the selection bias variable and the percentage of issue in the offshore market. The results of the study indicate that the abnormal returns are influenced by selection bias, institutional holdings and issue percentage.

Domowitz, Glen & Madhavan (1998) examined Mexican DRs trading on international stock exchange for the period of 1989 to 1993. They divided the study into two sets of shares, one on Mexican citizens and other is on some foreign countries with some constraints. The study observed a CAAR of 14.4% for the second set of firms, and much lower CAAR of 4.86% for the first set of firms. The study concludes that the firms post listings was negative.

Miller (1999) examined firms that list internationally of emerging market firms and developed countries firms. Sample included 181 firms from 35 different countries for the period of 1985 to 1995. The event study was conducted by using both announcement dates & listing dates of cross listings. The study found positive average abnormal returns (AAR) around both the event dates. The study observed a strong market reaction to the cross listings were mutually correlated with increase in shareholders wealth. They found AARs were greater for the firms listed on US stock exchanges than firms listed on portal. The study concluded that AARs for emerging markets firms were higher than the developed firms.

Kiran & Arun (2003) examined the risk & return of Indian stocks through cross listings on US stock exchanges. The study found that with the introduction of ADR trading in the US market has no significant effect on the returns of the underlying stocks. The study concludes that CAAR increased two months prior to ADR listings & decreased thereafter.

Martell, T. F., Rodriguez, L. Jr., & Gwendolyn P.W. (2000) investigated the risk & returns of Latin American stocks listed through ADRs on NYSE for a period of 1990 to 1994. The study constitutes a sample of 25 ADRs with a 75 days event window of event study. The study concludes that CAAR increased prior to foreign listings & negative drifts have been observed after foreign listings.

Callaghan, J., R. Kleiman and A. Sahu.(1999) examined stock market reaction to short term & long term holding period of DRs. The study includes a sample of 66 ADR listings issued by firms in 18 different countries on NYSE, AMEX & NASDAQ from 1986-1993. Event study was conducted & found that cumulative average abnormal returns for NYSE traded stocks measured 19.6% for the first year. They found that ADRs performed brilliantly the stock market index during short & long term holding periods from the date of issue.

Errunza & Miller(1998) investigated changes in cost of capital post listing. The study includes a sample of 78 global stock listed on the US stock market. They found that there was a decline in the abnormal returns after announcement. Moreover, they found that the decline in the cost of capital is related to the degree to which the home country capital market is segmented & isolated.

Sanger and McConnell (1986) investigate the behaviour of stock returns of US companies that moved from the OTC market to the NYSE between 1966 and 1977. They divide their sample into a pre-NASDAQ and a post-NASDAQ period in order to examine the impact of the introduction of NASDAQ. Consistent with earlier studies they find positive abnormal returns in the pre-listing period before the introduction of NASDAQ. However, this pattern changes in the post-NASDAQ period because they only find a reduced and statistically insignificant reaction to the same event. These results support their hypothesis that the increase in value associated with exchange listings is attributed to the "superiority liquidity" of the new market. They define superior liquidity as following ".... a market is said to provide superior liquidity services if the cost immediately trading a given quantity of a security in that market is lower than the comparison market". However, this advantage of superior liquidity has been substantially reduced through the introduction of the new NASDAQ system which is demonstrated by change of pattern. The study found in the pre NASDAQ communication system, a positive & significant reaction by the capital market was there & in the post NASDAQ communication system observed a reduced & statistically significant capital market reaction to initial announcement of exchange listings.

Perotti & Cord (1997) investigated the impact of foreign listings on local stock returns. The study includes a sample of 53 foreign listings by Dutch firms on 16 international stock exchanges in Belgium, Germany, France, UK, Japan, Luxembourg, Australia, US & Switzerland. The study observed firms experienced positive average abnormal returns (AAR) of 0.68% for a pre-announcement of foreign listing period & decreased thereafter.

Maaji, M, Abdullah S,R. (2014) investigated market reaction to international cross listings. The study used event study methodology with (day -60 to day -15 as an event window) to analyze market reactions to the international cross listings and the impact of it on the value of the firm. The sample of the study include 6 cross listed Nigerian stocks listed on foreign stock exchanges. Study observed abnormal returns around the date of cross listings are positive and statistically significant. This shows that cross-listing does not increase firm value therefore we reject the null hypothesis that cross listing increase firm value. The returns at the event itself are insignificant but positive. For day −1 the average abnormal return is 0.057 percent (CAAR = 5.3 percent) with a z-statistic of -0.151. The average abnormal return for day 0 is 4.24 percent (CAAR = 9.59 percent) with a z-statistic of 1.12. For day +1 the average abnormal return is 0.0008 percent (CAAR = 9.59 percent) with a z-statistic of 0.002. However the market reacted positively to the announcement of the cross-listing. The study shows that cross-listing does not increase firm value.

Jayaraman, N., Shastri, K., & Tandon, K. (1993) examined the impact of ADR listings on selected stock exchanges. The study included 95 US ADRs listings by firms from Japan, UK, Australia, France, Germany, Italy & Sweden for the period of 1983 to 1988. The study observed an increase of average abnormal return (AAR) by 0.33%. The study concludes that returns increased significantly after the DR listings.

Smirnova,.E (2004) examined the impact of ADR listings on the returns of local Russian stocks. Event study has been conducted with 25 days event window with ADR listings as an event date. The study concludes that there was a significant negative average abnormal return on an ADR listing announcement date & post listings.

Viswanathan, K. G. (1996) examined the performance local stocks listed on US stock exchanges. The study includes a sample of 20 firms of Canada, Australia, Japan listings on US stock exchanges. The study observed a surprisingly negative pre listing period return of -3.85% & a decline in post listing period of -2.44%. The study concludes that there was a decrease in AAR in the post listing period.

Karyoli (1998) studied various implications of the corporate decision to list shares on an overseas stock exchange. One of the objectives of the study is to find the impact of foreign listings on the local stock returns. The study includes a sample of non-US companies' listings on US stock exchanges for the first time, regions like Australia, Canada, Europe, Asia & UK were considered for the study. The study concludes that up to one year on an average there was a negative post listing performance but highly variable depending on the local stock market & the listed stock exchanges.

Chakrabarti (2003) investigated the impact of issuance of ADR listings on the issuing companies' shares in domestic market. The study attempts to identify the drivers of market returns of these DRs & investigates their relationship with the underlying securities. The study considered a sample of 10 ADRs listings of Indian origin trading on NYSE. The study observed ADR returns appear to have unanticipated movers & return on the underlying stock US, BSE as well as movement on the two S & P 500 & NASDAQ together provide less than half of the total volatility in most cases. The study concludes that there was a increase in abnormal returns of the stocks compare to US market.

Costa, N. D. Jr., Leal, R. P., Lemme, C. F., & Lambranho, P. (1997) investigated the impact of cross listings of Brazilian firms on US stock exchanges. The sample consist of 7 firms which issued their level II and level III ADRs on US market during a period of 1996. The study found that there is a small but insignificant positive ADRs around the listing date.

Sanvicente (2001) examined the effect of foreign overseas listings on Brazilian firms. Sample constitutes 26 Brazilian firms trade on US market for a period of 1997 to 2000. The study observed an increased an increase in CAAR before the listings and after the listings. The study concludes that the listings of the firms from the developed economics had a negative impact on the return after the listings.

Ng, Yong & Faff (2012) examined the long run and shared run performances of Australian cross listed stocks related to the rivals. Event study was conducted by taking an event window of (-15, +15) days. The study found that during the short run it was evidence a small listing gain ranging from 0.65% to 1.02%, on the contrary in the long run analysis there was no significance abnormal returns. The study concludes that both cross listing stock and rival stocks had a significant negative abnormal return in the long run, with rival stock displaying a great text of negative abnormal return.

Mazouz K, Alrabadi D & Yin S., (2012) investigated the impact of international cross listings on the firstly listed stock exchange by focusing on the experience of Hong Kong & Chinese cross for a period of 2000-2009. Event study was conducted with 150 days event window. The study observed positive cumulative average abnormal returns (CAAR) of 5.9% during the period of listings & an 8.15% positive average abnormal return (CAAR) during the one month period prior to listings & a decrease of 2.7% of CAAR during a post listing period. The study concludes that there was a negative AAR post listing period.

Onyuma, Mugo & Karuiya (2012) examined whether cross border listings has an impact on firms financial performance in eastern Africa. The study constitutes financial data of three years before & after cross listings of 3 Kenyan firms which were listed on US, Dutch & Russian stock exchanges between the periods 2001 to 2011. Financial ratio analysis were computed, ratios such as liquidity, profitability & investors ratio were computed for three years pre & post cross listings. The study found that profitability & liquidity ratio of cross listed firms improved after its cross listings. The firms current & quick ratios outperformed after the cross listings. The study concludes that there was an increase in returns ratios post listings.

Bris, Cantale & Nishiotis (2006) examined the impact of foreign listings on the firms listed on US stock exchanges such as NYSE, NASDAQ & AMEX. The sample consist of listed & unlisted firms of 2053 foreign firms, of which 314 firms are listed on NYSE, 448 firms on NASDAQ, 373 are rule 144A private placements & 918 were of OTC issues. The study found average abnormal returns (AAR) of domestic class is 1.32% & 0.62% before cross listings period & 0.40% & 0.14% post listing period. The study concludes that AAR showed a positive range pre listing period & statistically reduced post listing period both for listed & unlisted stocks.

Bianconi, Tan (2010) tested the valuation effect of cross listings on major Non- US & UK markets. These markets were compared to US market & analysis was done for the period of 2003-2004. The study focused on six Asian-Pacific countries including Australia, China, India, Japan, Korea & Taiwan. The study found that using OLS regression, firms that list US stock exchange gets a premium significantly positive with an increase of 17% & UK cross listing firms were also positive. The study concludes that cross listings premiums in US markets are significantly larger than those in the UK & non US markets.

Melvin, Valero (2007) examined the stock price impact of US firms cross listing on home market rival firms. The study analysed the spill over effect of cross listings on a specific group of firms from both developed & emerging markets & explored their differences. Sample consists of 146 rival firms from 21 countries during period 1986 to 2002. Event study was conducted by using a 11 day event window to find the impact on returns both pre listings & post listings period. The study observed that rival firms from developed countries experience a -2.35% mean cumulative average abnormal returns (CAAR) & emerging market rival firms have a CAAR of -1.44%. The study concludes that abnormal returns from emerging market firms are insignificant & smaller compared to their developed market counterparts.

Chopade, P & Sisodia, G. (2012) investigated if the returns of the GDR effects the underlying stocks of Indian stock market & vice versa. The study includes a sample of 35 GDR returns of Indian companies which were listed on NYSE, LUXSE, LSE & NASDAQ for a period of 2009 to 2011. The study concludes that the return of underlying stock affects the returns of the respective GDR but not vice versa.

Gheaus (2010) examined impact of cross listings on stock return of local stock market. Sample includes 54 companies from central & Eastern Europe for a period of 1990 to 2009. Event study was conducted with 25 days event windows for finding the effect of cross listings on stock returns. Companies from Russia, Hungary, Ukraine & Poland countries that were listed on US stock exchanges were considered for the study. The study observed a positive average returns & a skewness of 0.4635 in a pre-listing period & tend to became negative & a negative kurtosis of -0.7349 in the post listing period. The study concludes that cumulative average abnormal returns (CAAR) of both samples drifts downward indicating a negative excess returns.

Jong, A., Mertens, G. & Poel, M. (2010) studied the impact of cross listings on Dutch firms returns listed in the US or the UK stock exchanges. The study examined the influence of cross listings on management forecast decisions by taking a sample of 168 Dutch firms. The study observed that US exchanges listed firms had shown a positive CAAR of 0.31% & UK exchange listed firms had shown a negative abnormal returns of

-2.52%. The study concludes that firm's listed US stock exchanges had a significant higher announcements return which signals net effect of cross listing is positive.

Yun, Zhu (2013) examined the impact of cross listings on the valuation of Chinese firms. One of the main objectives of the study was to find whether there exists a positive average abnormal return after cross listings. Event study was conducted for a period of 10 years (2003 to 2012). Sample constitutes 17 companies listed on Chinese stock market such as Shanghai stock exchange, Shenzhen stock exchange, Hong Kong stock exchange & Taiwan stock exchange with different event windows for different exchanges. The study concludes that the Chinese firm returns during cross listings declines in a post listing period.

Kim, O., examined the impact of cross listings through ADRs & GDRs programme on the cost of capital of local stock returns. CAPM model was used to compute the cost of capital in pre & post listing periods. Sample consists of 98 cross listed ADR listed firms & 41 cross listed GDR listed firms. The study found that cost of capital decrease for both the samples post listing period.

McConnell and Sanger (1986) examined several explanations for the observed negative post listing returns behavior but none of them gives a sufficient answer. Explanations related to data peculiarities, as (a) negative returns are due to a few peculiar sub periods ; (b) negative returns are to a few outlier observations; and (c) negative returns are due to biases in the first trading price, do not provide an answer. They also name a number of other explanations (a) negative post listing stock returns are due to the loss of market maker support. This explanations are based on the difference in the market structure between the NYSE and NASDAQ. (b) Negative post listing stock returns are due to peculiarities of the NYSE. (c) Negative stock returns are due to new stock issues shortly after the listing (d) Negative stock returns are due to insiders dumping the stock. Insiders postpone their sales of large blocks until listing occurs. They hope to get a better price in the supposedly more liquid market than in the relatively illiquid market before the listing. This excess supply creates downward pressure on the stock price (e) negative stock returns are due to a correction of an initial market overreaction. For the purpose of this study, only their test of the new issue explanation will be discussed briefly. McConnell and Sanger (1987) classify the companies into two subsamples, one for companies having issues within the following 12 months and those not having any issues. However, only 10% of all companies had issues within the following 12 months and they experience positive average abnormal returns compared to those without new issues which experience significantly negative returns. Thus, their evidence is strongly contrary to the conjecture that new issues of common stock explain the negative post listing performance3 in stock returns.

Elliott, Schaub (2009) examined whether Brazilian ADRs newly listed on NYSE performs well on the S & P 500 index for a period of 36 months (1990-2002). Event study was conducted with a 21 days event window. Sample includes 31 Brazilian ADRs listed on NYSE for a period of 1990 to 2002. The study observed that 28 out of 36 months there was a significant positive return ranging from 11.97% to 44.61%. The study concludes that Brazilian companies' listings through ADRs significantly outperform the S & P 500 in both short & long term holding period.

Gerasymenko (2009) analyzed the cross listing impact on Ukrainian stocks listed through ADR on NYSE. Sample constitutes 14 Ukrainian stocks listed on NYSE for a period of 1998 to 2008. Event study was conducted with 175 days as an event window. The study observed positive average abnormal returns (AAR) of 0.6% & at post listing a negative AAR. The study concludes that there was negative average abnormal return posts cross listings.

Damodaran, Liu and Harlow (1993) investigate a sample of 276 NYSE stocks that listed on the Tokyo and London stock exchanges between 1965 and 1990. The study compared raw and excess returns in the pre and post listing period using a sample 500 days of returns before and after the listings. They find some evidence of lower mean returns after the listings. However, they did not find any price effects in the listing period starting 10 days before and ending 10 days after the listing date.

Sundaram and Logue (1996) examine valuation effects of companies that list ADRs on the NYSE and the American Stock Exchange. To measure valuation effects associated with international listings, they employ price-to- book, price-to-cash-earnings, and price-to-earnings valuation ratios. Although their approach differs from previous studies, their findings are consistent with the implications of the models of international market segmentation.

Kadlec and McConnell (1994) examine the stock price reaction of 273 US-domiciled OTC firms that listed their stock on the NYSE between August 1980 and December 1989. Their findings are consistent with previous studies of domestic exchange listings. They report statistically significant positive abnormal returns from four weeks prior to the listing week through to the listing week. They continue their analysis by investigating the potential sources of value from exchange listings such as liquidity benefits and an increase in the shareholder base. Therefore, they jointly test Metrons (1987) investor recognition factor and Amihud and Mendelson's test (1986) liquidity factor by regressing the specified proxies for the asset-pricing factors on the listing period abnormal returns. Their results indicate that post-listing relative and absolute bid-ask spreads are lower than pre listing spreads. The change in the bid-ask spread for each security is examined further by controlling for the change in Merton's and regressing both proxies on the listing period abnormal returns to test for differences across securities. They find that firms experiencing a reduction in their bid-ask spreads exhibit higher positive abnormal returns. However, their results provide even stronger support for Merton's (1987) model as firms experiencing the greatest increase shareholders exhibit the highest abnormal returns.

Sadeghi (2001) investigated the impact of dual listings of Australian shares on the New Zealand Stock exchange. The study used event study methodology to study the effect of dual listings on the stock returns by using a event window of 200 trading days (-50 to +150 days) for a period of 1986 to 2000. Study shows a negative market reaction of -0.428 percent on the dual listing day. However, this figure is not statistically significant at the conventional levels. The study suggests that dual listing has no significant effect on the value of shares in the event day. The average daily return is 0.654 percent for the week before and –01.30 percent after the listing date. These figures were not statistically significant. The result of Z-tests shows that only percentage of companies with positive or negative excess returns are not statistically different from the average of 50 percent. However, a low level of t-statistics indicate that dual listing of Australian shares on the NZSE have no considerable impact on the value of shares on the day of listing, a week before and a week after. The present study investigates the impact of dual listing of Australian shares on the NZSE. The results suggest that the average excess return on the day of listing is negative but is statistically insignificant. The negative excess return starts to accumulate before the day of listing and becomes statistically significant several weeks after this date to the end of the period (day +150).

Bris, Catale & Nishiotis (analyzed the abnormal reaction to the foreign listings reflected in the prices of the two classes of shares, in the domestic market. The study includes an event period of (-250,+100)days around announcement of foreign listings. The results of the show that the average daily abnormal returns across all firms in the pre listing period is positive and statistically significant and it is reduced significantly in the period after cross listings for both the listed and unlisted shares. The study finds an AAR for the domestic class of 1.32 percent and AAR of 0.62 % for the listed stocks.

Mello, Junior, T., P & Lima F,G & Gaio, L,E. (2010) analysed the impact on liquidity profitability and volatility of Brazilian stocks that were listed on the NYSE through American Depository Receipts. The sample of the study includes return and liquidity data from all Brazilian ADRs programs listed on the NYSE for a period of 2001 and 2009 with 18 programs for 14 companies. Event study was used to find the impact with an estimation window of (-52, -4) & (+52,+4). Study considered 18 listed stocks and reported that there was no difference between returns before and after DR listings. Data on average returns before and after ADR listings for each asset and the statistical significance was found. During the study several alterations in stock returns were observed. A possible explanation was given in the study that Brazilian stock market has undergone transformation over the past few years. The study concludes that Brazilian stock market is not segmented, ADR listing is not contributing to the process without changing the expected returns.

Apak, Eda (2007) examined the impact of American Depository Receipts on the return of the underlying British stocks. The sample of the study includes 65 companies domiciled in the UK that announced their first ADR program for a period of 1993-2007. An event study methodology was used to analyze the impact on firm value around the listing date by comparing actual returns to expected returns. A fifty one day event period (-25, 0,+25) from twenty five days prior to and twenty five days after the listing dates were employed. Estimation period used for the study was -175 days prior to and 26 days to the event date. On the event day, 36 out of 65 stocks cross listed had a positive abnormal returns, the day after cross listings this number decreased to only 28 out of 65 stocks showed a positive average abnormal returns. 30 stocks had a positive average abnormal returns above 2% and above 5% there were 12 stocks. On the last day of event window, only 17 stocks exhibits a positive cumulative abnormal returns above 2% and 16 stocks above 5%. the study concludes that none of the abnormal returns are statistically significant. On the event date t -test reports a value of 1.85373 with a p- value of 0.06380 which was not statistically significant. The average cumulative abnormal returns for equally weigthed portfolio of 65 British stocks around the listing date were negative with a value of -4.5% then it reached to -7.31% towards the end of the event period suggesting that market reflects weaker than expected demand for the ADR program. The study concludes that ADR listings have no impact on the underlying British stock returns.

The study contributes to the literature by examining the impact of cross listings on the stock returns. More specifically, the main research question would be: Does cross listings affect the local stock returns? Several measures are considered to capture various dimensions of stock returns. The impact of cross listings is evaluated in a multivariate framework after controlling the other factors such as company size, accounting practices, analyst and trading activity which potentially affect the stock returns.

2.2   The Impact of Cross Listings on the Indian Stock Liquidity

In the literature, liquidity has generally computed by three different measures; (1) volume (2) bid – ask spread (3) depth (defined depth as the size of an order flow innovation that is required to change prices at an given amount means that in a highly liquid market almost any amount of stock could be bought or sold immediately without moving the current market price). Previous research has showed a relationship between these different measures of liquidity and other related variables.

Stoll (1978), Barclay and Smith (1988) provide empirical evidences that price level, return volatility, and volume explain a significant fraction of the cross-sectional variation in bid- ask spreads. Jagadeesh and subrahmanyam (1993) confirms these similar findings by examining the change in bid-ask spreads of the underlying shares after the introduction of the S & P 500 index future contracts, and price control, return volatility and volume. It is generally discussed that a greater volume should result in lower spreads because it offers market makers greater flexibility to offset inventory differences. Larger volatility will lead to higher spreads because it implies higher inventory risk. Snell and Tonks (1995) develop a model that measures the impact of inventory control, adverse selection, and anticipated liquidity trade effects on price quote revisions of market makers on the London Stock Exchange. Their dataset allows for stronger tests of inventory control effects since all trades on the London Stock Exchange must pass through the market makers' inventory and can be unambiguously classified as buys or sells. They find that market makers set their price quotes to maintain their inventory around a desired level. Although there is some evidence of adverse selection, they conclude that asymmetric information is not very widespread in highly liquid stocks. Freedman (1989) and chowdry and Nanda (1991) analyzed the impact of multi trading locations on the liquidity of assets. The study predicts that multimarket trading increases liquidity.

Previous research has investigated the cross listings impact on liquidity, issues related to liquidity listings and liquidity for the domestic US market in various context. Research for example, includes studies that examine the impact of international listings on liquidity (Foerster & Karyoli (1998), Cooper & Kaplanis (1994), Groth and Dubofsky (1984), Sanger and McConnell (1986) Makhija & Nachitmann (1990), Kumar (2004), Edelman and Baker (1994), Kadlec and McConnell (1994), Noronha, Sarin & Saudagaran (1996), holicka (2004) Chan S.P J., Hong J & Subrahmanyam M G (2006).

Kadlec and MCConnell (1994) Sanger and McConnell (1986) provide a empirical evidence that a major stock exchanges listings improves liquidity. They compared the liquidity ratio and ups and down betas of 1515 NYSE, 801 AMEX and 964 OTC stocks. The study finds that smaller stocks and less liquid stocks are affected by institutional buying and selling behavior if swings in the market place. Their result suggests that security performance becomes more sensitive to market upswings as liquidity increases. OTC stocks appears to be more liquid than AMEX stocks of the same size which suggests that exchange listing is of little benefit to the companies.

Beneish and Gardner (1995) examine stock price and trading volume effects of changes in the composition of Dow Jones Industrial Average (DJIA). The sample of the study includes 37 listings and 31 delisting's for a period of 1929 to 1988.They find that the inclusion of stocks in DJIA does not affect their stock price and volume behavior. However, delisting's experience negative abnormal returns and a decrease in trading activity. These findings are consistent with an information cost. Since bid-ask spreads decrease with trading volume, the decline in trading volume for delisted stocks is consistent with an increase in transaction costs and a reduction in information for these stocks.

Freedman (1991) develops a theoretical trading model which examines the impact of international cross-listing on the variability of prices, the volume of trading, the in formativeness of prices, and the costs of trading for different types of traders. The study assumes that the foreign and the domestic market do not operate simultaneously. The study includes three different types of traders:

1) "Informed traders" trades on their long-lived private information about the value of the stock. This value information becomes the public information at the end of the 2nd period. There are several informed traders who compete with each other. Since this information is long lived, information traders must decide how to optimally allocate their trading between the domestic and foreign market.

2) "Uninformed traders" are traders who trade randomly. The study further assumes that most of the liquidity traders prefer to trade on the domestic stock exchange.

3) "Market makers'" receives submitted orders from liquidity and informed traders' and sets prices so that his expected profits of the given order flow are zero.

Freedman examines the effects of international cross-listing on trading costs, price variance. in formativeness of prices, and trading volume in the domestic and the foreign market under different scenarios by comparing the results of a dually listed stock with a singly listed stock. Freedman measures trading costs using the market depth parameter (lambda) which is an inverse measure of market depth. Trading costs for liquidity traders on the domestic market are a decreasing function of the number of informed traders in the case of a dually-listed stock as well as for a single-listed stock. However, the decline in trading costs is stronger than for dually-listed as long as there is the more one informed trader. An increasing number of informed traders causes more competition in the earlier round of trading in the foreign market, thereby forcing traders to reveal more information. Therefore, informed traders make less profit in the second round of trading in the domestic market. Liquidity traders who are assumed to prefer trading on the foreign markets always face higher trading costs. But this result has to be treated with some caution as the assumed benefits of trading earlier are not modeled. The expected profits of the informed traders equal the costs of the liquidity traders since the market makers profits are expected to be zero. This implies that dual listings can increase informed traders profits because they move opportunity to trade upon their inside information, however provided the number of informed traders are relatively small. The result of the study shows that the variance on the domestic stock exchange increases after the dual listings because traders are provided with more opportunities to trade. This leads to an increase in the revelation of information by time the price is set on the domestic stock exchange.

Chowdhry and Nanda (1991) and Admati and Pfleiderer (1988) to investigate the effects of multiple trading locations on trading volume. They model a market with different participants who have different strategies. "Small" liquidity traders are assumed execute all their trades in one market. "Large liquidity traders split their trades across markets to minimize costs. The informed traders' and the large traders' order sizes are perfectly correlated across different markets. Therefore, an increasing proportion of liquidity trading leads to an increase in the total trading volume. If trading costs differ between markets the cost-minimizing liquidity trader is forced to concentrate his trading in the cheapest market. This will also attract the information traders because their profitability of trading on the information is maximized in the most liquid market. Furthermore, the presence of "small" liquidity traders implies that the aggregate size of a typical trade becomes smaller if there is only a single market.. However, informed traders need liquid markets which enable them to camouflage their trades.

While Freedman's model predicts an increase in liquidity for internationally cross- listed stocks, other studies have suggested that an additional trading location may lead to a decline in the liquidity of a stock. Three different hypotheses concerning the effect of an additional trading location on the market quality of the primary market (or domestic market) have been suggested by previous literature: fragmentation, competition, or segmentation.

"Fragmentation"' assumes that international listing diverts order flow away from the domestic market, thus resulting in less efficient pricing and lower market quality.

"Competition" assumes that international listing increases the number of traders. This increased competition enhances the liquidity and the efficiency of the market.

"Segmentation" presents an intermediate view combining aspects of both theories. Segmentation assumes that the effect on liquidity depends on the structure of the local market, especillay if there is segmentation between domestic and foreign customers. Therefore, segmentation may lead to narrow bid-ask spreads accompanying by a lower depth.

Empirical studies on these areas of international cross listings examine the theoretical predictions in a number of ways and for different markets. Foerster and Karyoli (1993) analyzed changes in trading volume from pre-listing period to the post-listing period for Canadian stocks listed in the US,Noronha, Sarin and Saudagaran (1996) investigated changes in bid-ask spreads and depth for US firms. Domowitz, Glen and Madhavan (1995) tested, where one of the first to examine changes in liquidity for ADR listings of Mexican firms. Kleidon and Werner (1996) used a different approach find the effect of liquidity on international cross listings. The study compared the intra-day pattern of cross listed stocks with the firms which were not cross listed.

One of the major motivation for managers to list their company shares internationally is improvement in liquidity. Mittoo (1992) uses a survey approach to address the question of managerial perceptions of the net benefits of foreign listings. His sample consists of 78 Canadian companies which are listed in the US and UK. The results show that managers' perceptions of benefits from foreign listings are associated with the increased liquidity of their firms' stock A further examination utilizing unvaried tests between the perceived net benefits and the percentage of a firms stock trading on the foreign stock exchange supports this relationship. Multivariate tests used to control other variables such as percentage of sales in foreign countries, percentage of equity issued, firms size, and listing location. This indicates that trading volume on foreign exchanges is the only factor that influences the net benefit significantly. These reports that managerial perceptions of net benefits from foreign listings are strongly linked to the level of trading activity in their firms shares on international stock exchange.

Foerster & karolyi (1998) investigated the effect of cross listings on the underlying stocks bid – ask spreads listed on US stock exchanges. Sample of 49 Canadian firms listed on US stock exchange was considered for the study. They found that underlying spread of companies listed experienced a decline in the liquidity post listings. The study concludes that there was a slight negative but non-significant shift in beta was there with regard to Canadian market.

Karyoli (1998) studied various implications of the corporate decision to list shares on an overseas stock exchange. One of the objectives of the study is to find the impact of foreign listings on the local stock liquidity. The study includes a sample of non-US companies' listings on US stock exchanges for the first time, regions like Australia, Canada, Europe, Asia & UK were considered for the study. The study concludes that shares liquidity improved post overseas listings overall, but also depends on the total trading volume, listing exchanges & the foreign ownership restriction in the local market.

Holicka (2004) investigated the effect of DR listings on local underlying stocks. Sample of 19 stocks form Czech Republic, Hungary & Poland were considered for the study. The daily trading volumes were increased on an average by 21% in the year post listing of shares. The study concludes that liquidity improved significantly on an average & declined largely in case of 3 stocks.

Hermann A., Arauner (1996) studied the impact of cross listings on the liquidity. The study examined whether an international listing on London stock exchange, NASDAQ, and the NYSE has an impact on the liquidity of the firms. The purpose of the study was to investigate whether the effect of international cross listings on the trading volume of the domestic market differs for firms listed on the London stock exchange, NASDAQ, and NYSE. An US listing may lead to a larger increase in trading volume from pre-listing to the post- listing period since it increases the total number of traders. The study also states that an increase in the number of traders is generally associated with an increase in competition and pricing efficiency. While it is assumed that trading costs are typically low in the US market, this may provide even stronger competition for traders in the firms domestic market. The increase in the trading volume in the firms domestic market stems from the increased trading by liquidity traders who concentrate their trading activity in the market with the lowest transaction costs. Liquidity can potentially be measured by a number of different variables. Commonly used measures are (1) trading volume (2) the bid-ask spread and (3) market depth. Since quoted bid-ask spreads are not available for a large number of sample firms. The study examined trading volume effects associated with international listings. Moreover, volume has been shown as a significant fraction of the cross – sectional variation in bid-ask spreads. The study measured abnormal trading volume, mean adjusted model and a market volume adjustment. The study includes a sample of 233 international listings consist of 118 firms listed on the London stock exchange, 84 firms listed on New York stock exchange and 31 firms listed ADRs on NASDAQ for a period of 1980 to 1994. The study used a 52 week estimation period from -78 to -26 prior to listing week. The average volume ratio (VR) for NYSE listings increases from 1.14 (t=3.33) in the pre – listing period to 1.32 (t= 8.89) in the post listing period. The respective medians are 1.09 (p= 0.006) and 1.27 (p=0.000). The results show that VR of London stock exchange and NASDAQ listings was lower in the post listing period than in the pre-listing period. While the median (1.07) and mean (1.06) volume ratio for London listings in the pre- listing period is significant different from 1, the post-listing does not seem to be associated with abnormal volume effects. Study shows that NYSE listings experience high abnormal trading volume in the listing week (mean VR=1.79 and median VR=1.45) which is statistically significant (t=2.75 and p=0.001). But the VR for London and NASDAQ listings is not statistically different from 1. NYSE listings (mean VR=1.34 and median VR=1.33) and London listings (VR=1.13 and median VR=1.12) experience significantly positive abnormal volume effects in the 16-week period preceding the listing week. The mean VR for NASDAQ listings is 0.89 but not significantly from 1 (t=-1.52). However, the median VR is 0.76 with a p-value of 0.028. The study shows that public offerings have a liquidity advantage over private placements in the 144A, market. This has suggested that internationally listed firms are rewarded for complying with the stringent registration requirements of the SEC. The study also observed that internationally listed firms have lower bid -ask spreads, which holds when adjusting for size effects and controlling for other spread determinants. The lower bid-ask spread for listed firms has been explained by a larger potential shareholder base and the permission to be traded on a regulated marketplace. The study concludes that liquidity benefits outweigh the higher costs of a public offering which leads to a reduction in the cost of capital.

Noronha, Sarin and Saudagaran (1996) investigated liquidity effects of internationally listed US companies using intraday data. The sample of the study includes 126 US compaines which were listed on London stock exchange and Tokyo stock exchange. The pre listing period starts 125 days prior to listings and ends 26 days prior to the date of listing. Comparing bid ask spread and depth from the pre- to the post-listing period their results show no change in bid-ask spreads but an increase in depth after the listing. The increase in depth is around 10%, and is statistically and economically significant. They also report an increase in daily trading volume. They proceed their analysis by regressing other microstructure related variables such as price, trading volume, daily return variance, and a dummy variable indicating spread changes on bid-ask spreads and depth. Their results for the spreads are consistent with earlier findings' raw spreads should be higher for higher priced stocks, larger volatility implies higher spreads, and a higher trading volume leads to lower spreads. Return variance and volume have the opposite effect on depth than on spreads. The effects of the price on depth are the same as for spreads. These results indicate that all changes in depth can be explained by changes in other micro structure variable. The study includes a sample of NYSE listed stocks which are simultaneously listed on LSE & Tokyo stock exchange for the period of 1983 to 1989. The study observed there was no change in bid-ask spread for either of them in the whole sample. On the contrary, spreads of Tokyo stock listings increased in the post listing period.

Noronha, Sarin and Saudagaran (1996) further analyse the impact of international listing on informed trading. Their results suggest that trades in the underlying stock become more informative after the listing. This is consistent with Freedman (1991) who argues that more informed traders are attracted to the market after the listing because they can trade for extended hours and with a greater degree of anonymity. They argue that this increase in informed trading is responsible for the lack of improvement in spreads in spite of increased competition among traders. The study observed there was no change in bid-ask spread for either of them in the whole sample. On the contrary, spreads of Tokyo stock listings increased in the post listing period.

Kumar (2001) examined an impact of overseas listings on Indian stocks liquidity. The study includes a sample of 85 DR listings done by 72 Indian firms for a period of 1992 to 2001. Event study was conducted to study the impact of listings on foreign exchanges on the liquidity of the underlying domestic stocks. The study observed the overall volumes of the market had decreased in 62 % cases of the post listing period. The study was conducted separately for ADR & GDR programs. The study concludes that impact of listings on Indian stocks through GDR had an increase in liquidity & through ADR had a decrease in liquidity of the domestic stocks.

Chan S.P J., Hong J & Subrahmanyam M G (2006) examined the liquidity effect in asset pricing by studying the liquidity premium relationship of an ADR & its underlying shares. The sample comprises of 401 ADRs from 23 different countries for a period of 1981 to 2003. The study concludes that change in ADR premium is positively correlated with the change in ADRs liquidity & negatively correlated with the change in home share liquidity.

Kiymaz H., Alon I, Veit, E,T (2009) the liquidity effect of DRs on emerging markets. The sample consists of 628 firms listed through DRs on NYSE & LSE for the period of 1980 to 2007. The study covered Brazil, Russia, India & China along with Asia, East Europe, Middle East countries & Africa.The study concludes that DR program established by firms added significant value & improve home Market liquidity to benefit of both issuer & investor.

Bacidore, J. M., R. Battalio, N. Galpin and R. Jennings (2005) used a model of bid-ask spreads based on the theory of constable markets to examine the impact of multi-listed options on spreads. This model relates the bid-ask spread to trading volume, price, volatility and competition and predicts lower spread for a market with potential competition. The competition variable is constructed as a multiple listing dummy variable which is zero if the option listed on a single exchange and one for multi-listed options. The results of the shows that multi- listed options have lower bid-ask spreads than options which are listed on a single stock exchange.

Moel, Alberto, (2000) investigated the impact of ADR listings on the local stocks liquidity. The sample consists of 28 firms from various emerging markets. The study observed due to ADR there was an increase in transparency & a decline in liquidity & also there was a growth in home equity market. The study concludes that foreign listings abroad have an adverse impact on the local market liquidity.

Ng, Yong & Faff (2012) examined whether liquidity change is one of the determinant of cross listing performance. The study concludes that cross sectional regression suggest that liquidity gain is not a significant factor in explaining abnormal returns for cross listing in either short run or long run period.

Mazouz K, Alrabadi D & Yin S., (2012) investigated the impact of international cross listings on the liquidity of the Hong Kong & Chinese cross listed stocks for a period 2000 to 2009.The study consist of 30 stocks listed on Hong Kong & Chinese stock exchanges. The study found that, if markets are segmented, cross listings are associated with an increase of liquidity in Hong Kong stock exchange. The study concludes that an increase in liquidity happened on the   Hong Kong stock exchange subsequently to cross listings.

Stoyan, Novozhilova, Kartashov, Lemasson & Noronha (1996) examined the effect of foreign listings on firm's liquidity. The sample includes 126 American firms listed on London & Tokyo stock exchanges for a period of 1983-1992. The study concludes that there was no significant change in liquidity post listing period.

Bris, Arturo and Cantale, Salvatore and Nishiotis, George (2006) measured the relative liquidity effect before & after the listing date for both listed & unlisted shares in the domestic market & US. The study used event study by taking 200 days event window. The study concludes that liquidity of both stocks listed or unlisted in domestic market increases significantly after the cross listings.

Domowitz, Glen and Madhavan (1998) examine the impact of Mexican companies' ADR listing in the US on the market quality of their primary Mexican stock market. The study includes a sample of 16 Mexican firms listed through ADRs on US stock exchange for a period of 1989 to 1993. The data comprised of 26 different time series. They argue that inferences about market quality can be made by examining underlying market liquidity and base level volatility. In a market where transitory order imbalances generate price movements, price volatility and volume are positively correlated. They develop an econometric model to examine the effects of ADRs on price volatility and liquidity. Price volatility consists of two elements. The first component arises from changes in fundamentals and imperfect information signals. The second component is due to order flow shocks that arise from non- information based trading. The volatility induced by order flow shocks increases with greater risk aversion, greater variance in public beliefs, and fewer market participants. The second component can also be expressed as the product of volume and a market liquidity matter. This implies that liquidity increases with the number of traders, and decreases with greater risk aversion and a greater variance in public beliefs. Their empirical results show an increase in the base level of volatility and an increased sensitivity of price variability to volume. They argue that their results are consistent with the fragmentation hypothesis. Their test of changes in spreads reveals a decrease in 17 of their 23 series. This indicates that there may have been trade-off between depth and spreads which is seems to be consistent with the segmentation hypothesis.. However, their analysis of average ADR and domestic market returns.

Kleidon and Werner (1996) use a different approach to examine the liquidity effect of international cross-listing. They sample comprises of 23 firms which were listed in the form of ADRs from a period of Jan 1991 to Dec 31 1991. They compare the intraday pattern of cross-listed firms with other firms which are not cross-listed. Kleidon and Werner (1996) compare the intraday pattern of volatility of prices, trading volume, and bid-ask spreads of a sample of UK firms that are cross-listed on the NYSE or AMEX to FT-SE 100 firms which are not cross-listed and S & P 100 firms. Firstly, they estimate time-of-day-effects using regression analysis for the S & P 100 firms. Their results show a U-shaped pattern of volatility with significantly higher variances in the first hour of trading. Trading volume is also U-shaped since it is significantly higher at the open and at the close. Bid-ask spreads are also U- shaped being significantly higher from the open up to 11: 00 and rising again above the mid-day-level during the last 35 minutes of trading. This observed intraday pattern is generally explained by Admati & Pfleiderer's (1988) model which focuses on asymmetric information between traders. Informed traders choose to trade in periods of high volume because this enables them to disguise their trades. Competition among informed traders reveals sufficient information to the market to induce liquidity traders to trade at the same time because their trading costs are lowest when volume is heavy. Therefore, informed and uninformed traders trade simultaneously.

The volatility pattern for UK cross-listed securities in the UK is similar to the results for FT-SE 100 firms. The volume pattern is also similar; however, volume is significantly higher between 14: 40 and 16: 30. Spreads also show the same intraday behavior but they generally decline between 15: 30 and 16: 25. This might be an indication of increased competition at a time when the US market and SEAQ simultaneously operate. The results for UK cross-listed securities in the US are generally similar to those of S & P 100 firms. Trading volume shows a U-shaped higher the morning. However, spreads are not U-shaped and are significantly higher in the morning and significantly lower in the last hour of trading. Kleidon and Werner (1994) conclude that their results suggest some degree of segmentation between the two markets. Furthermore, the results indicate distinct intraday patterns in prices and volumes for different market structures.

Frino A., Marco E., & Lepone A., (2009) studied the impact of ADR listings on liquidity. The study includes a daily trade listings of 122 Australians stocks issued ADRs in US for a period 1983 to 2008. Study shows a development in liquidity, turn over for ADR listed stocks increased by 0.129991 standard deviations compared to 0.05884 standard deviation for the control stocks in the 6 months following the first trading date of the DR programs. Analysis of pre- listings and post listings date and first trading date reveals that liquidity improves in the period around the date ADR first trades in the USA. The overall result of the study suggests that listing an ADR improves the liquidity and increased the visibility of the firm.

Dhara, Jewtha (2014) analyzed the effect of international listings on liquidity and profitability. The study includes two Indian internationally listed companies Satyam computer ltd and Dr. Reddy's laboratories ltd. To study the liquidity researcher has considered current, cash and liquidity ratios where as to study profitability net profit, return on capital employed and return on equity ratios. The current ratio increased for companies after DR listings with 6.33 and 5.96.Liquid ratio also increased with 6.26 and 4.61 after DR listings. Cash ratio increased with 4.36 and 2.48 after DR listings. Net profit ratios increased after by 25.52 % and 27.58 % for Satyam and Dr. Reddy Laboratories. Return on capital employed increased by 22.95% and 24.55 % for two companies. Return on Equity decreased for Satyam by 18.84% whereas for Dr.Reddy Laboratories. The study concludes that there is no any direct effect of international listing on Liquidity and profitability of the company but it will certainly affects the company image in the global front which indirectly says that international listing increases the company value in the domestic as well as foreign market which helps in expanding the business operations and increases the possibility of improvement in profitability in future.

Avdic, Lana & Resulovic and Emina (2006) studied cross listing of Swedish stocks in London and New York stock exchanges. The study examined whether Swedish firms on the Stockholm stock exchange with a cross listing in the London or New York stock exchange exhibit any differences in volatility and liquidity is there after the listing date. The study include a sample of 19 Swedish stocks, listed on the Stockholm stock exchange, with foreign listings on the London stock exchange, the New York stock exchange, NASDAQ with issued ADRs in the United states. The study includes a period of 1989 and 2004. Quantitative approach is used to examine the fluctuations in volatility and liquidity of Swedish stocks during a certain time period before and after cross listings on the U.S and U.K markets. By using a minimum of -171 to a maximum of + 250 daily observations study captured both short term and the long term effects of cross listings by using squared daily price changes. For computing liquidity impact, the study used daily trading volume before and after cross listings. The mean values for the volume coefficients λ_0 and λ_1 are 0.092 and 0.015 implying a decrease in price sensitivity to trading volume, liquidity of the stock increases. The study observed that volume increases in 15 out of 19 cases following the listings, 13 of these are statistically significant. The remaining 4 cases demonstrated a decrease in volume. The study concludes that liquidity increases for Swedish stocks after the listings in London or New York.

Olga (2010) examined the impact of cross listings and multi market trading on the stocks information environment, measured by stock liquidity and price volatility. The impact of the stock presence on a foreign exchange on the stocks information environment is evaluated in a multi variate framework. The study includes 509 stocks from 20 European countries that were listed and traded in various foreign markets during the period from 1990 to 2007. The study used three measures for stock liquidity 1) proportional bid-ask spread that reflects the difference between ask and bid home market prices, monthly average bid ask spread. 2) turnover ratio that is monthly average daily turnover ratio & 3) total turnover ratio i.e the monthly average of the daily total turnover ratio which is a ratio of the total trading volume in GBP (British Pound) to the stocks market capitalization. Bid ask spread of 0.54 % was noticed in the study, stating that bid ask spread of companies with foreign presence is almost half of the domestic companies even before cross listing. The study reveals that there was a significant downward trend in the bid ask spread following both cross listing and cross trading signifying that the reduction in bid ask spread after foreign listings. The next proxy of stock liquidity, turnover ratio, takes into account the number of shares outstanding. Relative mean turn over ratios of cross listings was more than one, and was steadily increasing following the cross listings.

Gheaus (2010) examined impact of cross listings on stock liquidity of local stock market. Sample includes 54 companies from central & Eastern Europe for a period of 1990 to 2009. Event study was conducted with 25 days event windows for finding the effect of cross listings on stock returns. Companies from Russia, Hungary, Ukraine & Poland countries that were listed on US stock exchanges were considered for the study. Three proxies were used in the study, trading volume of daily traded shares in the home market, share turnover ratio as the ratio between the total number of traded shares and natural logarithm of the number of daily traded shares in the home market and foreign market. To determine the overall impact of an event, study compared the mean values before (-200,-7) and after (+7, +200). The companies listed on the NYSE experienced the highest increase in home market trading volume (0.3876) followed by portal (0.2871) and OTC (0.1997). Panel B companies cross listed on the NYSE experience highest increase in trading volume of daily traded shares in home market and foreign market with 0.4465, followed by portal with 0.3902 and OTC with 0.2029. Panel c of the study reports that only firms that listed on the NYSE experience a statistically significant increase with 0.013 in turnover ratio and portal increase of 0.134 and over the counter increase of 0.713. The study concludes that cross listing leads to an increase in trading volume in the home market and firms cross listed on NYSE experience greatest increase in trading volume.

Makau S.,M, Onyuma S.,O & Okumu A.N., (2015) studied the impact of cross listing on share liquidity for for cross listed firms within the East African community, with domestic market being the Nairobi stock exchange. In order to find the liquidity impact, event study has been used in the study. Study focused on stocks cross listed in other EAC markets from the Nairobi Stock Exchange in the last five years where data on traded volume was used. After the event that is cross listings the volume traded increased from a mean of 9.6 million shares to a mean of 41.1 million shares one year after cross listings representing a percentage change of 351% for equity bank. The increase is statistically significant at p- value of 0.0002 which is less than the level of significance level of 0.05. Volume traded increased after cross listing with a mean of 477550 shares for the year before cross listing and a mean of 770,652 for the year after cross listing, representing a percentage change of 61.4% for nation media group company. The increase is not statistically significant with a p value of 0.236942 which is greater than 0.05. Traded volume increased after cross listing with a mean of 1.76 million shares to over 4.47 million shares after cross listing representing a change of 150 % for Centum Investments. The increase in volume traded is statistically significant with a P- value of 0.000469 which is less 0.05. Volume traded declined after cross listing from a mean of 24.6 million shares to 16.6 million shares after cross listing representing a percentage change of -32% for Kenya Commercial Bank. The decrease in traded volume is not statistically significant with a P value of 0.286324 which is greater than the 0.05. Turn over for the four firms in the study increased from a mean of 9 million shares year before cross listing to a mean of 16 million shares year after cross listings, representing a percentage change of 77.8%. This increase in shares traded was statistically significant with a p- value of 0.0049 which is less than a level of significane of 0.05. On the other hand, Turn over for the four firms had declined from a mean of 369 million year before cross listing to a mean of 317 million year after cross listing, representing a percentage change of -14.1%. The decrease in turnover after cross listing is not statistically significant with a p- value 0.000086 which is less than 0.05. Study concludes that traded volume increased for Centum, Equtiy Bank and Nation Media group, and decreased for Kenyian company. Share liquidity improved for NMG and Centum when measured by turn over and for Equtiy Bank, NMG and Centum Investment measured by traded volume. The study also concludes that improvement in liquidity of shares also depends on the increase in total trading volume, the listing decision and the scope of foreign ownership restrictions in the primary market. The study concludes that cross listing generally impacts a firms shares liquidity both positively and negatively.

2.3   The Impact of Cross Listings on the Indian Stock Price.

Karyoli (1998) studied various implications of the corporate decision to list shares on an overseas stock exchange. One of the objectives of the study is to find the impact of foreign listings decisions on the local stock price. The study includes a sample of non-US companies' listings on US stock exchanges for the first time, regions like Australia, Canada, Europe, Asia & UK were considered for the study. The study concludes that share price react favourably to cross border listings initially.

holicka (2004) investigates the impact of DR listings on the local underlying stocks price. Sample of 19 stocks from different countries such as Czech Republic, Hungary & Poland were considered for the study. The study found that the prices of DRs by Central Europe companies & their underlying stock prices are very closely correlated & the opportunity of arbitrage is therefore very limited. The study concludes that the share price of the underlying stocks & the DRs of the central Europe companies effect each other.

Ghosh(2014) investigated the relationship between the ADR prices with the local underlying equity prices of the national index. The study includes a sample of eight companies listed on S & P 500 through ADR. The study observed a relationship between the different Indian stock market indices (CNX Nifty & BSE Sensex) to the US stock market index to S & P 500. The study concludes that there was a significant correlation between the ADR prices & their underlying stocks.

Kato, Linn, and Schallheim (2008) investigate the underlying share and ADR prices of 8 Australian, 7 English, and 8 Japanese firms. Their findings show no significant differences between the prices, and thus no arbitrage opportunities seem to exist. Rosenthal and Young (1990) examine two Anglo-Dutch groups (Unilever and Royal/Dutch Shell) which trade on the London Stock Exchange, on the Amsterdam Stock Exchange, and as ADRs on the NYSE. Although they report persistent deviations from the theoretical pricing relationships, the direction and the magnitude of the mispricing is not sufficiently large enough to formulate profitable intra- or inter market trading rules. Kim, Mathur, and Szakmary (1995) examine 21 Japanese, 21 British, 5 Dutch, 5 Swedish, and 4 Australian companies which trade as ADRs in the US. To investigate informational efficiency and the dynamics of information transmission of ADRs and underlying shares, they perform multivariate cointegration tests and a vector autoregressive analysis (VAR). Their results show that ADRs respond to unexpected movements in the underlying shares, the S & P 500 index, the domestic index, informationally and the exchange rate, implying that ADR markets are efficient. Moreover, their findings show that currency shocks have become a more important factor for pricing ADRs in recent years.

To explore the transmission of pricing information for identical assets trading in different markets, Garbade and Silber (1979) develop a model that examines short-run relationships for dually- traded securities on the NYSE, the Midwest Exchange (MSE), and the Pacific Stock Exchange (PSE). Their results indicate that regional market prices always adjust to NYSE prices. Hence, the NYSE is the dominant market while the regional stock exchanges are satellites of NYSE. The "Garbade Silber approach" is also used by Pagano and Roell (1991) to investigate whether the London market for Italian equities and the Milan Stock Exchange are integrated. Their examination of the direction of information flows between both markets shows that a mutual feedback relationship over time between prices exists but in most cases Milan seems to lead London.

Quan.J. (1992) examines the price discovery of crude oil and futures markets. They find that the spot price and one- and three-month-ahead futures prices are co integrated which suggests there is a long-run relationship between the spot and futures price. The results of an error correction model, which is used to study the dynamics of the relationship between futures and spot prices, show that the spot price leads the futures prices.

Wahab and Lasghari (1993) examine the daily price change relation between stock index and stock index futures markets for the Standard and Poor 500 (S & P 500) and the Financial Times-Stock Exchange 100 share index (FT-SE 100). To test the causal relationship between time series, they employ the theory of cointegration, as developed by Engle and Granger (1987). The estimation procedure consists of two steps. In a first step, a levels regression is performed to generate residuals which may be thought of as equilibrium pricing errors. These residuals are then subjected to a variety of tests for cointegration. In the second step, the lagged values of the residuals enter into the error correction model as the last period equilibrium error. The error correction coefficients serve to purposes: they help to identify the direction of causal relation between two time series and show the speed with which departures from the equilibrium are corrected in the short run.

The results from Wahab and Lasghari (1993) indicate that a feedback relationship between spot and futures markets seems to exist. Similar to previous studies the spot appears to lead the futures market. The equilibrium adjustments are not fully completed within one day. They argue, however, that the presence of causal linkages is consistent with a variety of market imperfections and realities that prohibit market participants from responding to every single deviation between both markets. Fleming, Ostdiek, and Whaley (1996) also argue that in practice frictions exist and trading costs differ across markets. Hence, price discovery will tend to occur first in the lowest cost market, as information-based trades are executed where they produce the highest net profit. Their empirical results show that the S & P 500 index futures and S & P 100 index options appear to lead the S & P 500 stock index and the underlying S & P 100 index respectively since trading in index futures and index options is cheaper than trading an equivalent stock portfolio. This trading pattern, however, is reversed for individual stocks since the stock market offers lower trading costs and is deeper than any particular option price series.

Chakrabarti (2003) investigated the impact of issuance of ADR listings on the issuing companies' shares in domestic market. The study attempts to identify the drivers of market returns of these DRs & investigates their relationship with the underlying securities. The study considered a sample of 10 ADRs listings of Indian origin trading on NYSE. The study empirically investigated how much of variation ADR prices may be explained by different variables affecting them. The study concludes ADR issuance often has a temporary positive impact on underlying stock price, but usually does not materially alter the stocks relationship with the US & Indian market.

Chan S.P J., Hong J & Subrahmanyam M G (2006) investigates the impact of foreign listings liquidity on the asset pricing by studying the liquidity premium relationship of an ADR & its underlying shares. The sample consists of 401 ADRs from 23 countries for a period of 1981-2003. The study concludes that there was impact of liquidity on the asset price of the underlying securities.

Ray, P., Madhavan V., (2014) investigates the relationship between Indian GDR prices traded in Luxembourg & their underlying shares prices traded in Mumbai with appropriate exchange rates. VAR & DCC Garch model was used for the study. The study constitutes sample of 12 companies listed on Luxembourg & London stock exchanges. The study found that there was a high correlation between the Indian GDRs listed on Luxembourg & their respective underlying stock traded in Mumbai. The study concludes that there was a quite bit similarity between the two prices of Mumbai scrip & that of scrip listed on Luxembourg.

Saxena, S., (2006) investigated the relationship between the ADR premiums & the movement in underlying stock price levels for a period of 2001 to 2005. The study found a correlation between the prices of the ADR prices & the prices of underlying equity prices. The study concludes that ADR prices do not move in lockstep with the underlying equity prices.

Madura, Armand & Tucker (1991) examined the impact of overseas listings on local stock prices. The sample comprises of 26 ADR listings listed across the various stock exchanges from countries like Europe, Japan & Australia. The study observed firms prices are driven by US & domestic market movements overall.

Eun, Sabherwal (2003) examined the extent to which the US stock exchanges contribute to the price discovery of Canadian stocks listed on Toronto & US stock exchanges. The study observed price adjustments due to cross market information flows takes place not only on US stock exchange & Toronto stock exchange, but also on majority of the stock exchanges. The study concludes that US prices adjust more to the Toronto stock exchange & vice versa.

Kadlec, McConnell (1994) analysed the effect of market segmentation & illiquidity on asset prices of selected stock exchanges during 1980's. The study observed each stock earned an abnormal return of 5 to 6 % in response to the announcement of listings on NYSE. The study concludes that the introduction of the NMS had a little effect on the stock price increase on companies those which were listed on NYSE.

`Eun, Cheol S., and Sangdal (1989) construct portfolios of firms that are cross-listed on three major markets (New York, London, and Tokyo), Hauser(1998) investigated international transfer of pricing information between dually listed stocks. The sample of Eun, Cheol S., and Sangdal (1989) is comprised of 29 US, 9 UK, and 18 Japanese firms which are simultaneously listed on the New York, London, and Tokyo Stock Exchange. Using daily price series they construct three portfolios (US portfolio, UK portfolio, and Japanese portfolio) to examine the pattern of international price transmission. They find that the home market returns always cause the foreign market returns. While the New York market provides significant feedback for the UK and Japanese portfolios to their domestic markets, it does not receive feedback from both markets for US stocks. The study of Hauser (1998) takes account of the different trading days in Israel and in the US since trading in Israel takes place from Sunday through to Thursday. While the domestic market emerges as the dominant market, they find, as expected, a different pattern for middle of the week days and beginning/ end of the week days. Only in one case a feedback relationship seems to exist. They argue, however, this is not surprising since this company is a large international company.

Mazouz K, Alrabadi D & Yin S., (2012) investigated the impact of international cross listings on the firstly stocks listed on Hong Kong & Chinese stock markets. The sample constitutes 30 firms cross listed for a period of 2000 to 2009. The study found that stock prices rise by 2% over pre listing period, 4.4% rise during the announcement week & a decrease of 2.69% in stock prices for a post listing period. The study concludes that there was a decrease in the stock prices post listing period.

Janakiraman (1987) investigated the impact of listing decisions on the stock price performance. The study constitutes 34 foreign listings on US stock exchanges during a period 1969-1982. The sample was divided into two groups Canadian & non-Canadian firms. The study examined a relationship between market segmentation & stock price performance. Event study was used in the study. The study concludes that there was a decline in cumulative average abnormal returns (CAAR) after information of cross listings became public.

Chopade, P & Sisodia, G. (2012) examined the prices generated from depository receipts are affected by the market. The study comprises of 35 samples listed on both LSE & NASDAQ, Luxembourg & NYSE for a period 2008 to 2009. Granger causality test was conducted for checking whether the prices of Indian GDRs are affected by the prices of underlying stocks or vice versa. The study concludes that security prices have an impact on the respective GDR returns but not vice versa.

Gurgul L., Omerovic S., Syrek R., (2015) examined a dependence analysis of the log-levels & returns of Australian stocks listed in Frankfurt & Vienna stock exchanges for a period of 2010-2014. The main objective of the study is to provide empirical evidence on the price effects of dual listings on the Frankfurt & Vienna stock exchanges. The study observed the stock prices of Australian companies listed on Frankfurt & Vienna stock exchanges are quite similar. The study concludes that Australian firms listed on Frankfurt stock exchange do not cause any significant & permanent change in domestic stock price; on the contrary prices of Australian stocks are caused by the prices of these stocks listed on Vienna stock exchange.

Visalakshmi and Lakshmi (2013) investigated the short run and long run relationship of cross listed Indian stocks traded in US stock market for a period of 2007 to 2009. The interrelations between the portfolios of three American Depository receipts and their underlying stocks were examined by using cointegration test, Granger causality test and vector correlation model. The study reports there is a long run cointegration relationship among the prices of Indian ADRs and their underlying shares, short term dynamics of the ADR portfolio are influenced by the deviation from the long run equilibrium.

Hansda S K., Ray P., (2003) studied the price interdependence of 10 Indian stocks listed through ADRs on NYSE & AMSE. The idea of the research was to find the relationship between the prices of ADRs & the prices of the domestic scrip's. The study observed a very high & positive coefficient of correlation between ADR price & the corresponding domestic stock price. The study found stock wise close quote at BSE is found to granger cause the respective open quote of ADR for each & every of the 10 stocks dually listed at the BSE & NASDAQ. The study concludes that there exist bidirectional causality between the quotes of Indian ADRs at NASDAQ, NYSE & the quote at BSE.

Patel (2015) investigated the linkages between ADR price & their respective underlying stock prices of the Indian stock market for a period of 2013. Dicker – fuller unit root test, Johansen cointegration test, granger causality test, vector error correction model & impulse response function methods were used for the study. The study found that both underlying stocks & ADR listings are at stationery level & long term equilibrium exist between them which signifies both underlying stocks & ADR listings positively affect each other.

Wang J.,(2014) examined whether the price discovery takes place between domestic market & US stock exchange such as NYSE, AMEX & NASDAQ. The study constitutes a sample of 642 cross listed companies with 771 cross listings from 39 home countries during a period 1981-2010. Augmented dickey-fully test, Johansen cointegration test & error correction model was used for the study. The study found price adjustment from the US share price responses & domestic sides, the US share price responses to domestic share price by 0.700, where as domestic share price responses to US share price by 0.280. The study concludes that the higher the US to domestic stock market turnover, the more domestic share price adjusts towards to US share price.

Punitham M., (2015) examined the dynamic linkages between ADRs & their respective underlying stock prices of Indian stock market. Sample includes 6 companies listed on BSE and simultaneously listed on NYSE for a period of 2010 to 2014.   Vector error correction (VECM) & GARCH test was conducted for the study. The study concludes Indian ADR prices are depending upon the share price prevailing in Indian markets but not vice versa.

Roschow S., (2013) investigated the average and conditional price discovery relationship between Moscow equity market and London market. The sample consists of 8 Russian cross listed securities in six overlapping & continuous trading hours. MICEX, RSE & LSE were considered for the study in order to know the price discovery relationship between multiple markets. Cointegration/error correction model (ECM), VECM, Granger causality test methods were used for the study. The study concludes that conditional price discovery relationship suggest that volatility is positively correlated with higher price discovery contribution of the higher volume trading market.

Majumdar S., (2007) examined the movements of stock prices & premia levels in the American & the Indian stock market. The main objective of the study was to examine whether Indian companies experience any significant increase in their domestic stock price or their domestic trading volumes following their foreign listings. Sample of eight companies included. The study observed a correlation coefficient was found to be very high of 0.9 between ADR price & NSE price. The study observed ADR price trading day was higher than prevailing price of the same stock on NSE. The study concludes that ADR premia levels of each & every stock in sample shows a positive relation with the S & P 500 index of US stock exchange which signifies the relationship is strong & significant.

Hales (2015) examined the price discovery for Latin American equity cross listed internationally through ADRs in US. Vector error correction model (VECM) was used to know the relationship. Samples comprises of non-financial stocks listed on ADR programs for a period of 2003-2010. The study concludes the exchange rates in Latin America are sensitive to innovations in stock market prices.

Gupta, Yuan & Roca (2016) investigated dynamics of information flows between the ADRs & its respective underlying stock prices in both the short run & long run period. Sample consist of BRICS (Brazil, Russia, India & China) for a period of 2003 to 2012. Vector auto regression & error correction model has been used for the study. Data includes 25 Brazilian, 1 Russian, 9 Indian & 11 Chinese ADR. The study observed a cointegration tests which shows a long run equilibrium relationship of ADR & their underlying stock prices. The study concludes that except china all stocks listed through ADRs have a long run relationship between ADRs & its respective stock prices.

2.4   The Impact of Cross Listings on the Indian Stock Volatility

Jayaraman, Shastri and Tandon (1993) investigated the impact of ADR listings on the underlying Asian & European stocks. Basing their investigation on several theoretical models which examine the linkage between information arrival, trading volume and the variance of return on a security, they hypothesize that international cross listing should result in an increase in the variance. According to the freedman model, they assume that international cross listing allows informed traders to optimally allocate their trading of dually listed stock between two separate markets to take advantage of information differentials in the markets. Informed traders are provided additional opportunities to trade on and profit from their long lived information. Thus, cross listing leads to an increase in the revelation of information which causes the variance of stock prices to increase. The study includes 95 foreign stocks (ADRs) listings listing for a period of 1983-1988. The empirical analysis of Jayaraman et al. (1993) compares pre- and post-listing variances of returns on the underlying stock. They compute pre-and post-listing variances from daily close-to-close returns on the underlying security. The pre-listing period starts 150 days and ends 26 days before the listing, while the post-listing period starts 26 days and ends 150 days after the listing date of the ADR. They report a 55.7% increase in the variance for their sample of ADRs. A breakdown into subsamples shows that the magnitude of the variances change differs with nationality of the companies. UK firms experience a significant change of 98.8%, while the variance of Japanese stocks only changes 34.6%. Their results are consistent with the Freedman-hypothesis but inconsistent with noise trading because they do not observe changes in the autocorrelation structure after the listing. The increase in volatility is also inconsistent with the hypothesis of a listing. Their results support the proposition that the increased trading time associated with the cross listing allows for more revelation of information. The study found that variances of the local stocks are significantly higher after ADR listing than pre listings. The study interpreted as consistent with informed trade hypothesis.

Makhija & Nachtmann (1989) analysed impact of cross listings on London stock exchange & Tokyo stock exchange by US firms. The study examine the variance effect of 37 NYSE stocks listed on the Tokyo stock exchange between 1973-1988. They compared pre-listing and post listings daily variances for various windows. However, the change in the variance is not significant for the 50, 100 and 200 day periods. But they report significant increases in the variance when using different windows after dropping 100 trading days before and after the listing date. They conclude that the variance of NYSE stocks increased after their Tokyo listing. Their results, however, need to be treated with some caution because 50% of the companies in their sample listed in 1986. After dropping 100 trading days the reported values of their post-listing periods are probably strongly influenced by the occurrence of the crash in October 1987. This might explain their findings that the variance increases as the period is extended away from the listing dates. Makhija and Nachtmann (1990) interpret their results as being consistent with the private information theory. This states that the flow of information is increased when exchange hours are extended. Makhija and Nachtmann's (1990) results, however, are in contrast to Barclay, Litzenberger and Warner's (1990) findings which indicate no changes in the overall level of return variance for dually listed US stocks on the Tokyo Stock Exchange. They perform time-series and matched pair tests to examine the ratios of open-to-close to close-to-close variances. They match 21 internationally listed US firms with 21 only domestically traded US companies on the basis of size and industry but find no differences in their US companies on the basis of size and industry but find no differences in their ratio of variances. Their average ratio of within-day (open -to-close) to 24 hours (close-to-close) return variances is almost identical and shows that approximately 80 % of the 24 hour variances occurs during the trading day in the domestic market. Furthermore, they compare the variance ratio of 16 listed stocks before and after the listing. The results do not show any changes and indicate again stock-return variance is more closely related to the level of normal trading volume than to the number of trading hours. Thus, the variance only increases if the international listing increases the trading volume. They found that there was a significant increase in the NYSE close-to-close variance of returns on stocks.

Howe, J,. Madura, J., & Tucker, A. (1993) examined impact of cross listings on UK firms volatilities listed on various stock exchanges. Sample includes firm's listings on Basel, Frankfurt, Paris & Tokyo stock exchanges for the period of 1973-1983. The study found there was a little change in volatility post listings.

Smirnova E., (2004) examined the impact of ADR listings on local Russian stocks. The study consists of 16 companies domiciled in Russia during the period of 1995 to 2001. Event study was used for the study by taking 16 companies to find the volatilities differences before & after cross listings. Eleven out of 16 companies experienced increased volatility of local Russian stocks post listings.

Lowengrub & Melvin (2000) investigated volatility before & after international cross listings. Sample of 23 German firms listed through ADRs on NYSE for the period of 1991 to 1997 were considered for the study. The study concludes that intraday volatility pattern became flatter post cross listings.

Barclay, M., R. Litzenberger and J. Warner (1990) examined the effect of cross listings on US firms local stocks volatility listed on Tokyo stock exchange. The study includes a sample of 16 American stocks listed on London stock exchange & Tokyo stock exchange for a period of 1973-1989. The study concludes that cross listings had no impact on the variances of the NYSE close to close returns on stocks.

Damodaran, A., Liu, C., & Harlow, W. V. (1993) investigated the impact of firm's listings on its variances when it is listed internationally. Study includes a sample of 276 firms listing on Tokyo stock exchange & LSE. The study concludes that volume increased but no change in variance after dual listings.

Howe & Madura (1993) examined changes in stock price volatility of US firms listing on various overseas listings. The study found there was a significant increase in volatility post overseas listings.

Agarwalla and Pandey (2012) investigated the impact of various stocks specific & market wide events on intraday volatility dynamics in the Indian markets. The study covers high frequency trading data of 500 most liquid stocks at NSE over the 9 years period during 2001 to 2009. Sample also consisted of Indian 96 stocks listed on London, New york & Luxembourg stock exchanges. The study found cross listed stocks exhibit higher volatility during the first 45 minutes of trading at open and a gradual reduction thereafter.

Howe and Madura (1990) investigated the effect of international listings on common stock volatility. The study findings are markets already reasonably were integrated and also listings cannot reduce segmentation.

Athanasius, constantirs and Nicholas (2006) examined the impact of cross listing on stock price volatility in specific European markets such as Amsterdam, London, Zurich, and Vienna stock exchanges. The research includes five companies cross listed on various stock exchanges. The result of the study are spill over effects appear to the more common from foreign listing.

Tripathy & Jha.K. (2014) examined Indian stock market reaction to international cross listings for a period of 2004 to 2009. Sample of 9 companies listed through ADRs with 25 days event window was taken to conduct an event study. The study concluded that there was a increased variances of local stock returns after cross listings.

Howe (1993) analysed the impact of foreign listings on volatility of local stocks. Sample of 40 companies listed on Basel, Frankfurt, Paris & Tokyo for a period of 1973 to 1983 was considered. The study found a little change in post listing period.

Kumar (2004) investigated the impact of Indian overseas listings on the volatility of the underlying stocks by taking a mixed samples of ADRs & GDRs of Indian stock market securities listed on LSE, Luxembourg & NYSE for a period of 1992 to 2001. Event study was conducted by taking an event window of 100 days. The study observed that 41 out of 68 companies' variances were less than one signifies that there is a decrease in volatility of the underlying stocks post listings. The study concludes that the volatilities of local domestic stocks of foreign listed Indian companies have declined after listings.

Foester & Karolyi (1999) stated that international listings provides companies with greater access to global market leading to enhanced visibility, liquidity and has less risk exposure. The study expected that the firms from emerging countries with high market capitalisation should experience larger average abnormal returns than firms from developed markets. The sample includes 153 firms from 11 different countries that listed through ADRs in US during the period 1976 to 1992. The study concludes that there was a decline in the volatilities of local stock price significantly post listings.

Domowitz, Glen & Madhavan (1998) examined the impact of overseas listings on local stocks volatilities. The sample included Mexican companies' listings through ADRs on NYSE for a period of 1984 to 1993. The study concludes that the nature of volatility change from one security to another.

Ray, P., Madhavan V., (2014) investigated the relationship between Indian GDRs volatility traded in Luxembourg & London stock exchange & their underlying shares volatilities traded in Mumbai. VAR & DCC GARCH model has been used for the study. Sample consists of 12 companies traded on Luxembourg, LSE & simultaneously listed on NSE/BSE. The study found that volatility linkages between GDR listed on Luxembourg stock exchange & underlying stocks traded in Mumbai have a high volatility persistence in all DCC GARCH model. The study concludes there was a high dynamics correlation between Luxembourg stock exchange traded through GDR & their underlying stocks traded in Mumbai.

Costa, N. D. Jr., Leal, R. P., Lemme, C. F., & Lambranho, P. (1997) investigated the impact of on Brazilian firms volatilities listed on US stock exchanges. Sample includes 7 Brazilian firms which were listed on US market during the period 1996. The study concludes that there was a decline in volatility of underlying Brazilian stocks post listing period.

Mazouz K, Alrabadi D & Yin S., (2012) investigated the impact of international cross listings on the volatility of the local Hong Kong & Chinese stock market. Sample of 30 companies trading for the period of 2000-2009 were considered for the study. The study investigated the differences in volatility of returns for pre & post listing period. The study concludes there was a slight upward shift in volatility was detected.

Gheaus (2010) examined whether ADR listing has an impact on the volatility of stock in their local markets. The study computed the standard deviation of daily stock returns & used it as a proxy for volatility. The study includes a sample of 54 companies listed on various exchanges for the period of 1990-2009. The study done a comparison of mean volatilities of two sub periods (1990 to 1999) & (2000 to 2009). Parametric paired sample mean t test & non parametric Wilcoxon rank test was used for the study. The study observed volatilities experienced a significant reduction of from 0.0317 to 0.0309. The study concludes that there was a decrease in volatility following cross listings.

Punitham M., (2015) examined the volatility of share price movements in NSE & NYSE with respect to Indian listed companies. Sample of six companies for a period of 2010 to 2014 were considered for the study. Vector error correction model & GARCH model were used for the study. The study found that average volatility spill over from NSE to NYSE was 0.412 & NYSE to NSE was 0.121. The study concludes that volatility spill over from NSE TO NYSE is higher than that of NYSE TO NSE.

Gerasymenko (2009) investigated the cross listings impact on Ukrainian stocks volatility listed through ADRs. Sample constitutes of 14 Ukrainian stocks listed on Russian stock exchanges for a period of 1998 to 2008. Event study was conducted by taking (+26,+175) days event window. The study observed out of 14 listings, 5 companies' ratios are more than 1 signifying volatilities increased after listings & 9 companies ratio was less than one but statically insignificant volatilities signifying decreased volatility post listing period.

Avdic, Lana & Resulovic and Emina (2006) studied cross listing of Swedish stocks in London and New York stock exchanges. The study examined whether Swedish firms on the Stockholm stock exchange with a cross listing in the London or New York stock exchange exhibit any differences in volatility and liquidity is there after the listing date. The study include a sample of 19 Swedish stocks, listed on the Stockholm stock exchange, with foreign listings on the London stock exchange, the New York stock exchange, NASDAQ with issued ADRs in the United states. The study includes a period of 1989 and 2004. Quantitative approach is used to examine the fluctuations in volatility and liquidity of Swedish stocks during a certain time period before and after cross listings on the U.S and U.K markets. Study observed 8 significant decreases post listings while t-test provides 6 statistically significant decreases. For the base level volatility coefficients before and after cross listings, Study observed a mean values of 0.085 and -0.020 implied a decrease in base level volatility after cross listings. The study concludes that eleven of the nineteen studied companies showed a decrease in base level volatility after listing in London and New York stock exchanges, remaining eight were statistically significant.

Olga (2010) examined the impact of cross listings and multi market trading on the stocks information environment, measured by stock liquidity and price volatility. The impact of the stock presence on a foreign exchange on the stocks information environment is evaluated in a multi variate framework. The study includes 425 cross listing announcement by 210 companies from 17 European countries that took place on three US stock exchanges (AMEX, NASDAQ and NYSE) during the period from 1982 to 2007. The study used three measures that reflects different aspects of volatility, stock return volatility, volatility ratio & high low ratio. Study reports that mean and median volatility ratios of cross listed and cross traded stocks are more than one or are not statistically different from one based on t-test and wilcoxon test. This indicates either an increase or no change in return volatility after the change in the listing status. Less than half of the stocks in the sample that is (48.9% for return volatility ratio, 47.3% for market adjusted volatility ratio and 42.4% for high- low ratio) have volatility measures ratios of less than one, or in other words, less than half of the stocks experience a decrease in volatility after cross listing. The study concludes that based on univariate analysis there is no evidence that foreign listings reduces stock volatility. Stocks from developed markets experience more substantial improvement in liquidity and reduction in volatility than stocks from emerging markets.

Apak, Eda (2007) examined the impact of American Depository Receipts on the variance of the underlying British stocks. The sample of the study includes 65 companies domiciled in the UK that announced their first ADR program for a period of 1993-2007. An event study methodology was used to analyze the impact on firm value around the listing date by comparing actual returns to expected returns. A fifty one day event period (-25, 0,+25) from twenty five days prior to and twenty five days after the listing dates were employed. Estimation period used for the study was -175 days prior to and 26 days to the event date. 35 out of 65 of the variance ratios are greater than one, and 26 of them are statistically significant at the 5% significance level and 27 of them are statistically significant at 10% significance level based on F-ratio test with a null hypothesis of variance ratio equals to 1. Only 41.5% of the companies in the sample experienced a greater volatility in their stock returns after the cross listings. 31 companies experience a ratio less than one. 23 of these ratios are statistically significant at 5% significance level and 26 of them are statistically significant at the 10%. The study reports that 40% of the companies in the sample experienced a reduction in the volatility of their stock returns after cross listings. The study result indicate that there was no increase in the variance for an equally weighted portfolio of British stocks. The study concludes that the variance in the pre- listing period does not diverge from the variance in the post-listing period.

Bayar and Önder (2005) examine the volatility and liquidity of French stocks before and after cross-listing on the German Stock Exchange, Xetra. The study also involves testing the integration of the Paris Bourse and the Xetra and identification of how trading and non-trading hour volatility is affected by cross-listing. The study is based on French stocks since there are more French companies listing on the German market compared to the number of German companies listing on the French market. This decision is also based on a research made by Pagano et al. (2001) which states that European companies prefer to cross-list on more liquid and larger markets and on markets with more investor protection and more efficient legal systems. Since there are many other factors besides cross-listing that can affect volatility and liquidity of stocks several restrictions are made in order to adjust for these. For example, in order to eliminate the effect of cross-listing on other stock markets, the stocks that are listed on other markets within a range of 100 days before and 50 days after cross- listing are excluded from the sample. Also stocks that have paid out dividends within 5 days before and 10 days after their cross-listing are excluded. The reason behind this is that investors tend to reinvest their dividend income in the stock. The results show there is an increase in volatility in many stocks during trading and non-trading hours after cross-listing. Also when controlling for the impact of market volatility, the results show an increase in volatility after cross-listing. Finally the stocks liquidity is found to decline for many stocks, which implies that investors tend to migrate to the Xetra after the cross-listing. Based on these results, the authors draw the conclusion that there is a lack of integration between the French and the German capital markets.

The study contributes to the literature by examining the impact of cross listings on the stock volatility. More specifically, the main research question would be: Does cross listings affect the local stock volatility? Several measures are considered to capture various dimensions of stock returns. The impact of cross listings is evaluated in a multivariate framework after controlling the other factors such as company size, accounting practices, analyst and trading activity which potentially affect the stock returns.

2.5   To Compare DR regulatory framework of select capital markets.

Berg (2012) examined cross listings and valuation differences between Hong Kong and the Chinese stock markets. The main focus of the study was to find whether cross listings add & their share classes in Hong Kong reach the valuation of Hong Kong peers. The study found that Chinese stock markets are found to be more highly valued when compared to pure Hong Kong companies in the Hong Kong stock exchange. The tests give support the hypothesis and there is evidence for cross listings discount in china & Hong Kong frame work.

Tsai, Hsing Li (2004) examined the effect of foreign ownership restrictions on the price dynamics of depository receipts, evidence from the Taiwan and Hong Kong markets. The study investigated the depository receipts prices in regulated markets and free- entry markets. The study focused on the difference in the long term price relationships between depository receipts and underlying securities in free- entry and regulated areas, the incremental information content of the qualified foreign institutional investor ownership ratio for the depository receipts issued by Taiwanese firms. The study report revealed that long term equilibrium relationships between DRs and underlying security prices exist for firms listed in Hong Kong, a free entry market, but do not necessarily exist for firms listed in Taiwan with foreign ownership restrictions. The study concludes that in the absence of equilibrium, the lagged returns of depository receipts or underlying securities and the local market conditions become important.

Padhi & Pallavi (2012) examined & compared the regulatory frame work of depository receipts of India, Taiwan, and Hong Kong & Brazil. Author categorized the capital markets of the respected countries into two: strictly regulated & sparsely regulated markets. In the study, Indian norms were considered as more stringent in terms of issue, trading & listing of IDRs. DR program of Brazil & Hong Kong were found to be sparsely regulated. Taiwan was found to have a strictly regulated DR program. The study suggests that capital markets should adopt a middle path in the DR regulations with reasonable issuer friendly to encourage issuer participation & to ensure investor protection.

Hwang, JD (2013) investigated valuation and operating performance gains from international cross listing. By using a sample of 55 Taiwanese firms that instituted DR programs in the US, UK and Luxembourg from 1992- 2009. The study used Tobin's q; stock returns and operating performance of DR issuer's deteriorate and under- perform their bench marks substantially after issue. The findings of the study suggest that potential benefits of international cross listings might not be as significant. The study reports Taiwan being an emerging market is not very accessible for foreign investors and DR issuers from Taiwan should be in a better position to reap valuation gains and benefits by listing their shares in more prestigious markets.

Demirer, Lien and Shaffer (2005) examined the performance of short and long hedgers using four stock index futures contracts traded at Taiwan futures exchange. The study compared the optimal hedge ratios and hedge performances based on three risk measures: variance, extended gini and lower partial moment. The study found that long hedgers achieve greater hedging performance than short hedgers.

Hong (1996) examined the cultural relations of China and Taiwan & its policy change. The study discussed the three stages of policy changes, motivations for the changes, implications of the changes & trends of the two's future cultural relations. The study observed in the early, 1980's for nearly forty years there was no media, cultural exchanges between China & Taiwan. The study reports that with the exchanges of media/ cultural products have become an indispensable part of the two societies economic, political & cultural lives, Taiwan's material, especially the entertainment imports has produced a serious challenge & a big concerns among Chinese leaders.

Loures, Goncalves and Pardini (2017) examined relevant facts and acts occurred, disclosed by the Brazilian companies issuing DRs. The study was based on 1125 information extracted from CVM's website, the regulatory commission organization empowered to regulate, standardized and supervise the activities of trade agents of public securities in Brazil. The study was for a period of 2006-2012. The study investigates the knowledge of content, frequency and timing of disclosure of relevant information by Brazilian organizations in international equity markets. The study concludes that companies who trade their depository receipts in the markets with high standards of corporate governance practices do not disclose a larger amount of information than the lower other governance practices.

Elliott, Schaub (2009) examined the long term and short term returns of Brazilian equities traded on the New York stock exchange listed as DRs & they performance on S & P 500 Index. The study finds that the entire sample of Brazilian DRs outperforms the S & P Index market in both short term & long term holding periods. Evidence suggests that market timing is a key factor in Brazilian DR performance.

Goldfajn, Minella (2005) examined the relationship between capital account liberalization and macro volatility using Brazil as a case study. The study discloses several facts regarding evolution of capital flows & control in Brazil. The study reports the financial crises & macroeconomic volatility, capital account liberalization and the floating exchange regime have led to more resilient economy.

Leao, Montezano, Lameira, Baptista and Harris (2016) examined determinants of the adoption of good governance practices by Brazilian firms on the Sao Paulo Stock exchange for a period of 2003 to 2008. The study investigated firm level of corporate governance measured by an index comprising a set of good governance prescriptions. The study concludes that firm- level corporate governance is positively related to growth opportunities and external financing needs.

Klann, Beuren and Hein (2015) investigated canonical correlations among performance indicators calculated from a base of accounting statements prepared in accordance with U.S GAAP, Brazilian accounting standards and International Financial Reporting Standards (IFRS). The study includes a sample of 50 companies, including 17 Brazilian companies listed on the Bovespa's Board of Corporate Governance and 33 companies listed on the London Stock Exchange. The study observed that no company listed on Bovespa was found in the lists of European stock exchange. The study concludes that performance indicators of Brazilian and English companies were not affected in any way, despite divergence between BR GAAP and US GAAP and between IFRS and US GAAP.

Vaatanen, Podmetina, Pillania (2009) investigated the effect of internationalization process of Russian enterprises and its implications on foreign direct investment paradigm, their performance. The study reports that international operations have a significant effect on company performance indicators such as profitability & labor productivity. The positive effects grow gradually with an integration of Russian companies to the world markets.

Barry, Richard, Derek and Kirill (2002) studied corporate governance practices in Russia. The study covered the contributing factors for the success of Russian economic performance. The recent reforms in Russian corporate and securities laws, regulations and practices show a growing importance of improved corporate governance during 1998 & 1999.

Black (2001) examined corporate governance behavior and market value of Russian firms. The study investigated the relationship between corporate governance behavior and market value of a sample of 21 Russian Firms. The study used fall 1999 corporate governance for ranking these firms, developed by a Russian investment bank. The correlation between in and governance ranking is statistically strong. The study suggests that corporate governance behavior has a powerful effect on market value in a country where legal and cultural constraints on corporate behavior are weak.

Kumar, Venkateswara, Sripathi (2013) studied new Indian policy framework. The study aims at understanding the conceptual framework of IDR programs & studying the evolution of IDR markets. The paper examines the structure and status of IDRs along with the simplified listing norms given by SEBI. The study identified the legal implications, exchange control issues and tax aspects, the factors responsible for the slow growth of depository receipts in India, which still needs to be crystallized. The study suggests certain steps which can help to activate the IDR market and to become an important source of finance.

Kaur, Dhillon(2012) analyzed the relationship of Indian Depository receipts with their underlying Indian equity shares and the causes behind existence of premium on DRs. Sample of daily data of 14 Instanex companies of Indian depository receipts index from 2001 to 2010 was considered for the study. The study observed the underlying equity returns and returns on DRs move in the same direction. The study reports sectors have exhibited a decline in premium over the period of the study, but this decline has almost been traced after 2004. The coefficients of exchange rate return and return on Sensex and were positive and significant, coefficients of S & P 500 index is insignificant. The study concludes that the rupee depreciation in the past few years and booming Indian stock market performance which was a main cause behind Indian DR premium.

Raj (2011) compared the ADRs & IDRs regulatory frame work. The study covers ADR regulations in India, IDR regulation, eligibility of the investor, issuers eligibility, requisites for making an issue. The study concludes the Indian capital market comprises of stringent eligibility norms, disclosure and corporate governance norms resulting in higher compliance costs. The author reports that IDR is not having automatic fungibility; there is no clarity on tax issues. The study concludes that US being a developed country has less political flux, resulting stability in its financial markets, Indian markets are rumor driven leading to heightened volatility.

Rajib studied international equity market and Indian ADRs and GDRs. The study reports Cross listings of shares through issuance of depository receipts have become a common occurrence. The study covers ADRs, GDRs scorecard of Indian companies, arbitrage between DR and underlying shares, performance of Indian DRs, Indian depository receipts. Study observed that Indian companies have issued the maximum number of DRs while Russian companies have issued a highest volume of capital. Indian companies have listed more in number on London & LUXEMBOURG stock exchanges, this may be due to easy listing and accounting reporting requirements set by them. Till 1999, the Indian government allowed one- way fungibility, after that two way fungibility was allowed to avail arbitrage opportunities. The study also discussed about IDRs issued by Standard Chartered Bank, issue was oversubscribed two times with 240 million IDRs issued including 36 million shares of anchor investors. The study explains the benefits that investors get from cross listings.

Rustamov (2013) discussed about the legal problems of depository receipts. The research covers ADRs, forms and levels, GDRs. The study observed that DR as legal institution was launched and improved in the US legal system and spread through Europe to all over the world. The study explained the legal relationship between an issuer and depository bank, investor. Until now neither scholars nor governmental agencies have determined whether DR is domestic or foreign shares. The study reports it is not clear from few court cases that legal nature of DR was not defined properly yet, investors can put their investment under risk that incase of insolvency or such kind of other situation cannot get guarantee that their receipt will be in enforcement. US tried to resolve the problems arising from DRs, but congress by making amendments also, not able to resolve problems. The study concludes that the problems are not completely resolved or attempted to be resolved because DR institution is very expensive & therefore not widespread.

Licht. N (2004) explains cross listings entails more than just subjecting the issuer to the host market's regulatory regime; it is also subjected to potentially adverse effects coming from the issuers home country to host market. The research focuses on cultural and cross cultural psychology. The study concludes that in a multimarket environment, the home market is more likely to retain its informational advantage, and insiders are able to make better profits.

Li (2008) covered the three competing approaches to international securities regulation- harmonization, regulatory competition and cooperation. The focused on these three approaches and addressed the following questions, which regulatory approach is the proper and best way to govern securities regulation in the new international market? Are there areas which need to be improved? Harmonization is the idea that rules & regulations should be standardized across countries. Under regulatory competition model, countries do not coordinate with one another. International cooperation is conscious policy coordination among states. The study concludes that major problem in the international arena is that there are no international law- making institutions vested with legal authority to address these issues.

Sharma (2012) explained the Indian legal regime regulating IDRs. The author reports the government and regulatory authorities have taking progressive steps to facilitate issue of IDRs by taking away several stringent requirements, which are applicable to certain category of investors such as Mutual funds, NRIs and FIIs from investing in IDRs, by introducing simplified procedure for listings of IDRs. The study suggests from investor perspective, appropriate guidelines are necessary protecting the interest of investors. With progressive regulatory regime and immense pool of untapped capital, the Indian markets are bound to get the attention of foreign companies as a favorite destination to raise capital.

Chakraborty, Anindita, Holani and Umesh(2011) examined the impact of American depository receipts listings on the return of domestic stocks of six emerging markets from Asia and Latin America (India, Korea, Hong Kong, Brazil, Argentina and Mexico). The study used event study methodology and computed Average abnormal return and cumulative average abnormal return by taking an event window of 100 days. The study reports significant positive average abnormal returns of local market return in the pre listings period & ADR listing date, the entire sample adversely effects, positive turns to negative in a post listing period. The study also compared the long term performances of domestic and international market returns of the underlying shares and found insignificant difference between the returns of two markets. The study concludes that market segment hypothesis holds good in all the stocks of six countries, because of differences in the prices of the ADRs and underlying domestic shares.

RESEARCH METHODOLOGY

This research begins with four issues: which questions to study, which data is relevant, what data to collect & how to analyse the results. A careful, systematic, patient study & investigation in corporate field of knowledge that is applicable. The research attempts to study the impact of cross listings on the valuation of Indian stocks. The study includes the Indian stocks traded internationally. The methodology includes research design, sample population & selection, sources of collection of data, research objectives & financial tools, scope & period of the study and Limitations of the study.

3.1 Research Design:

The research design employed in the study includes the historical research design method to analyse the impact of cross listings on the valuation of Indian stocks. Historical research design was employed because by using past data helped the researcher to gain more knowledge on the subject and it prevented the researcher to make any mistakes. Historical research design was used to collect, confirm & combine evidence establishing facts that support the study. Thus to quantify the qualitative information, these research design method facilitated collecting large data & helped in answering the research questions.

3.2 Sample Population & Selection:

Sampling is defined as the selection of some part of an aggregate or totality on the basis of which a judgement or inference about the aggregate or totality is made. The target population includes Indian companies that cross listed across countries stock exchanges. The population is derived from 138 DR programs listed on different international stock exchanges by Indian companies for a period of 1999 to 2016. Study considered 64 companies sample size which listed on foreign stock exchanges like NYSE, LSE, LUXEMBOURG stock exchanges. 64 companies are again divided into 40 for each objective. For objective 1, to find the return impact & volatility impact 40 companies were chosen & while using the same companies for finding the liquidity impact, some companies volume was not available which made me to select another more companies. While finding the price impact, the companies trading from 2011- 2016 were selected for the study.

There were different aspects in selecting the sample. Firstly, the Indian company should primarily list on local stock exchange, then on a foreign exchange. And it should be listed through American Depository receipt & Global Depository Receipts. DRs are divided into two, listed programs (LEVEL II & LEVEL III,

Regs S), Unlisted programs are traded over the counter and privately placed (LEVEL I & Rule 144A DRs). The study takes into consideration Level II, III & Regs S programs as there are listed programs. Another aspect that plays an important role in sample selection is determined by the availability of home market trading data. Further, the study also eliminated those DR programs which were not listed before on any of the Indian stock exchanges prior to their DR program. The study used event study methodology for finding the impact with 175 days as an event window. The study used event study methodology to find an impact of cross listings on return, volatility & liquidity of Indian stocks listed on local stock exchanges. Study used an event window of (-0 to -175 days) prior to an announcement of cross listing and (+0 to +175 days) after the cross listing. The company should primarily be listed on Indian stock exchange (NSE) and after six months trading on local stock exchange it should get listed on International stock exchanges through DR program. Filtering of the companies was based on these observations. While considering these points, 64 companies were finalised for the study. The selection of the capital markets for the comparison of DR regulatory frame work was taken randomly.

3.3   Sources of Collecting Data:

Secondary source of data has been used for the study. The companies' historical data was collected from different websites such as Yahoo finance, NSE website, BNY Mellon depository receipts, Google finance, and Depository receipts from deutsche bank, Company websites, and Citi bank depository receipts.

3.4   Research objectives & financial tools:

The study comprises five objectives. For each objective different financial tools have been utilised.

Objective: To study the impact of cross listings by Indian firms on the local exchange stock returns, liquidity, price & volatility.

OBJECTIVE 1:-To study the impact of cross listings on the Indian stock returns.

Hypothesis 1 H_0: There is no significant difference in returns of Indian stocks listed on International stock exchanges.

The study adopts an event study methodology to analyze the impact of international cross listings on the firm's value, liquidity & volatility around the event date announcement. Since cross listing is a decision made at the firm level, the impact on firm value will influence the firm's decision to cross list or not. In order to find the impact cross listings on the firm's value, event study methodology have been used. Event study methodology has been used extensively in economics, finance and political economy literatures to empirically estimate market reaction to certain specific events by studying the reactions of relevant variables around the event window. The methodology is in an assumption that capital markets are efficient and the impact of an event will be visible immediately on the stock prices.

The study includes companies that were listed on a foreign stock exchange & continued trading in the home market. The impact of cross listing on stock returns, volatility & liquidity has been captured using event study methodology.

Figure.2.1 Event study for the Cross-listing Study

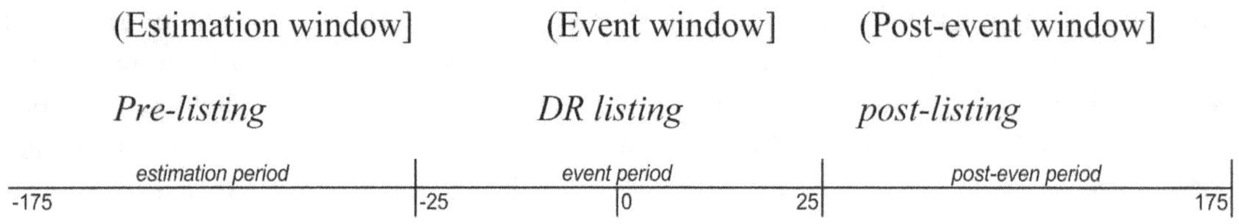

(Estimation window]   (Event window]   (Post-event window]

Pre-listing   *DR listing*   *post-listing*

estimation period	event period	post-even period
-175	-25 | |0 25|	175|

Abnormal returns in the event window are determined by the prediction errors from the market model. Coefficients from the pre-listing model are used to calculate abnormal returns from day –25 to day+25. Abnormal returns are then averaged across firms (average abnormal returns) and across time (cumulative abnormal returns).

According to Brown and Warner (1985) the return for the security can only be considered as abnormal relative to a certain expected level. Thus, we need to specify the model that generates the normal returns before we calculate abnormal returns. In this research we use mean adjusted returns technique for generation of normal returns. For this technique, the abnormal returns for certain stock for any time is defined as difference between the observed returns in the event period and that which is predicted under our generating process. The coefficients of the model estimated for the estimation period are used for calculation of abnormal returns during the event period.

To conduct an event study, the following terms need to be understood, event of interest, event window[6], the length estimation window[7], and estimation model[8].(Mehta, Jain & Yadav, 2014) The event of interest for the present study is the announcement of listing on a foreign market. The event window has been chosen 0 to -175, to +175, 0 depicts the announcement date, -175 is the 175th day time period prior the announcement date & +175 is the 175 days' time period after the announcement date. The choice of event period is a critical question because the length of the estimated reliable parameters is weighted against the other events probably affects the data & parameter estimates.40 companies have been taken for the study. To get announcement dates for the companies different news websites & finance websites have been used. Listing dates for the calculation were taken from the website BNY MELLON DR directory. The daily stock trading return data of the companies used in this study are calculated from the data available from yahoo finance & Google finances. Index values were downloaded from National stock exchange.

In the present study both ADRs & GDRs has been included for research. The traditional single factor market model has been applied to estimate the expected returns. It involves the computation of regression of a stock returns against a stock market index. For the present study, the value weighted market index, NSE has been used for regression. The regression equation is

$$R_{i,t} = \alpha_i + \beta_i R_{m,t} + \varepsilon_{i,t}$$

---

6 Event window is the period in which event occurs, during this period the security prices of the relevant stocks are examined.

7 Estimation window is the period used for estimating the expected returns. The estimation window is chosen prior to the event window.

8 Estimation model is used to estimate the estimated returns.

Where α_i & β_i are the estimated parameters, $R_{i,t}$ is the return on stock i at time t, $R_{m,t}$ corresponding return on NSE. The abnormal returns are

$$AR_{i,t} = R_{i,t} - (\alpha_i + \beta_i R_{m,t})$$

The average abnormal return AAR_t is the sample mean of abnormal returns on a particular day

$$AAR_t = \frac{1}{N}\sum_{i=1}^{N} AR_{it}$$

N is the number of companies in the sample. To get the accumulated impact of the event during a time period, Cumulative average abnormal returns (CAARs) are computed. CAAR means sum of the daily average abnormal returns over the time period starting at τ_1 through time τ_2, also called the event window.

$$CAAR_i(\tau_1, \tau_2) = \frac{1}{N}\sum_{t=\tau_1}^{\tau_2} AAR_{i,t}$$

The test statistics for AAR on day t during the event period & CAAR for the event window is

$$t\text{- statistics} = \frac{CAAR_t}{(\tau_2 - \tau_1 + 1)^{\frac{1}{2}} S(AAR_t)}$$

In the above equation S is standard deviation.

OBJECTIVE 2: To assess the role of cross listings on the Indian stock liquidity.

Hypothesis 2 H_0: There is no significant impact on liquidity of the underlying domestic Indian stocks due to cross listings.

In order to compute the cross listing impact on liquidity, three measurement tools have been used trading volume, mean trading turnover & Amivest Ratio.

Trading volume: - Trading volume in the home market is a common trade proxy for stock liquidity computation. It is measured by the average daily number of shares traded on the home market in each month (Foester and karyoli, 1998, Dodd, Olga, 2011)

Turnover ratio: - Turnover ratio is the monthly average daily turnover ratio of stock computed as a ratio of the trading volume by value i.e. the product of the number of shares traded and the stock price.

Amivest Ratio: It is a measure of liquidity to determine the rupee volume of trading associated with a 1% change in the price of a security. (Mehta, Jain & yadav, 2014). It was originally developed by Amivest Corporation and has been considered a good proxy for liquidity & market.

The ratio of Amivest Ratio[9]:-

$$\text{Amivest Ratio:- } 1/N \sum (VOL_d)/ R_d$$

---

9   N is the number of days for which data are available (trading volume is not zero), R_d is the absolute return on day d & VOL_d is rupee trading volume on day d.

A more liquid market should have a larger Amivest Ratio.

OBJECTIVE 3: To study the causality pattern between Depository receipts prices and Indian stock prices.

Hypothesis 3 H$_0$: The cross listings of Indian firms on the international stock exchanges has no abnormal effect on the prices in the home market.

Granger Causality test is used to find out whether the prices of Indian DRs are affecting the prices of underlying stocks listed in local stock markets or vice versa. For comparison purpose DRs Prices listed on international stock exchanges and closing prices of NSE indices are converted into Indian rupees. Table represents the list of 40 DRs employed for the study and provides the DR ratio, respective industries along with the listed international stock exchanges. Data of the companies & NSE index are collected from NSE website and BNY Mellon, JP Morgan; Citi depository bank, Google finance & yahoo finance. The assumption behind running granger causality is the stationery of time series. All the prices of underlying securities and respective indices were checked with the help of Augmented Dickey fuller test for stationery. The prices are found to be stationery. The main purpose the objective is to find out if the prices of the DR affect the underlying securities prices or vice-versa. E- Views software has been used for arranging the data & implementation of econometric analysis.

Granger (1969) proposed a time-series data based approach in order to determine causality. In the Granger-sense x is a cause of y if it is useful in forecasting y 1. In this framework "useful" means that x is able to increase the accuracy of the prediction of y with respect to a forecast, considering only past values of y.

To analyze causality patterns[10] we apply linear and non-linear tests. Although all series are integrated of order, we do not difference them when testing linear causality. Instead, we follow the procedure of Toda and Yamamoto (1995) which can by applied for possibly non stationary and co integrated series. We consider the bivariate var (k) model:

$$y_t = \Phi_0 + \sum_{i=1}^{k} \Phi=1 \; \Phi_i \, y_{t-i} + \varepsilon_t,$$

Where $\Phi 0$ is the vector of intercept parameters, $\Phi_i =$

$$\Phi_{11,i} \quad \Phi_{12,i}$$
$$\Phi_{21,i} \quad \Phi_{22,i}$$

are the matrices of parameters and the εt vector stands for white noise process. Appropriate lags are chosen by the Akaike information criterion (AIC) and Schwarz criterion (SC). We choose lowest lag which ensures the lack of autocorrelation of residuals. In all cases var models with at most four lags fit the best. Then we estimate var models for $k+1$ lags (the additional lag comes from the degree of integration of series) and use the Wald test (Toda and Yamamoto 1995), applied only to first k lags. Under the null hypothesis of the Granger non causality the test statistic is asymptotically $\chi 2 \, k$ distributed.

Definition 1: Assuming to have an information set Ωt with the form (x,..x−j, y,.....yt−i), we say that X is Granger causal for Y. Ωt if the variance of the optimal linear predictor of yt+h, based on Ωt, has smaller variance than the optimal linear predictor of yt+h based only on lagged values of yt, for any h. Thus, x

---

10   Causality pattern means an impact of one price on the other.

Granger-causes y if and only if $\sigma 2\ 1$ (yt : yt−j, xt−i) $< \sigma 2\ 2$ (yt : yt−j), with j and i = 1, 2, 3,....n and $\sigma 2$ representing the variance of the forecast error.

There are three different types of situation in which a Granger-causality test can be applied:

- In a simple Granger-causality test there are two variables and their lags.
- In a multivariate Granger-causality test more than two variables are included, because it is supposed that more than one variable can influence the results.
- Finally Granger-causality can also be tested in a VAR framework; in this case the multivariate model is extended in order to test for the simultaneity of all included variables.

The empirical results presented in this objective are calculated within a simple Granger-causality test in order to test whether underlying securities prices "Granger cause" prices of the depository receipts and vice versa.

Hence by obtaining these results it seems possible to detect the causality relationship between underlying stock prices and the prices of the depository receipts (DRs).

OBJECTIVE 4: To study the effect of cross listings on the Indian stock volatility.

Hypothesis 4 H_0: Depository receipts listings do not significantly affect the volatility of underlying stocks.

For calculating the volatility of stocks, variance is used as a proxy. Variances are calculated by dividing the post listing period return by that of pre listing period. To compare volatilities of security returns for the period before and after cross-listings, abnormal returns of Indian stocks has been calculated using event study methodology. Abnormal returns are used to measure the magnitude of volatility caused by cross listings. We calculate variance ratios as:

$$R = \frac{\text{var } after}{\text{var } before}$$

Where var *after* is calculated for the +25 day to +175 period and var *before* is calculated for -175 day to -26 day period.

3.5   Number of Indian Companies Listed on Foreign Exchanges

Table 3.1 reports Indian companies listed on different stock exchanges with different DR program as on date 6th SEP 2016.

Type	Stock Exchange	No. of DR Program
ADR	NYSE	8
ADR	NASDAQ	4
GDR	LSE	26
GDR	LUXSE	98
GDR	SINGAPORE	3

NOTE: - LUXSE: Luxembourg Stock Exchange, LSE: London Stock Exchange, NYSE: New York Stock Exchange, NASDAQ: National Association of Securities Dealers Automatic Quotation. GDR listed on Luxembourg Stock exchange constitutes the most frequent listings followed by London Stock Exchange and others (NYSE, NASDAQ).

3.6   List Of Indian Companies Listed Through DRs Selected For The Study:

DR ISSUE	SYMBOL	EXCHANGE	RATIO DR:ORD	COUNTRY	INDUSTRY	EFF. DATE
Ambuja Cements - Reg. S	–	Luxembourg Stock Exchange	1:01	India	Construct. & Materials	May 03, 1994
Anant Raj Industries - Reg. S	–	Luxembourg Stock Exchange	1:01	India	Real Estate Inv & Serv	Feb 29, 2008
Apollo Hospitals - Reg. S	APHG LX	Luxembourg Stock Exchange -Euro MTF	1:01	India	HealthCare Equip. & Ser	Jul 07, 2005
Aptech (Lux Listed) - Reg. S	–	Luxembourg Stock Exchange	1:04	India	Software & ComputerSvc	Sep 18, 2007
Arvind ltd		Luxembourg Stock Exchange	1:01	India	Personal Goods	Feb 01, 1994
Axis Bank - Reg. S	AXB	London Stock Exchange	1:05	India	Banks	Mar 16, 2005
Bajaj Holdings & Investment - Reg S	BAUD	London Stock Exchange	1:01	India	Automobiles & Parts	Mar 14, 2008
Ballapur ltd Reg. S		Luxembourg Stock Exchange	1:05	India	Forestry & Paper	Nov 18, 2003
Balrampur chilli mills ltd		Luxembourg Stock Exchange -Euro MTF	1:01	India	Food Producers	Jan 20, 2006
BSEL Infrastructure Realty - Reg. S	BSELG LX	Luxembourg Stock Exchange -Euro MTF	1:10	India	Real Estate Inv & Serv	Apr 10, 2006
CESC - Reg. S	CESCG LX	Luxembourg Stock Exchange -Euro MTF	1:01	India	Electricity	Apr 14, 1994
Cipla - Reg. S	CIPLG LX	Luxembourg Stock Exchange -Euro MTF	1:01	India	Pharma. & Biotech.	Apr 18, 2006
Cox & Kings - Reg. S	COXK	Luxembourg Stock Exchange	1:01	India	Travel & Leisure	Jan 20, 2015
Crompton Greaves - Reg. S	CGVD	London Stock Exchange	1:05	India	Electron. & ElectricEq	Jul 03, 1996
Dish TV India - Reg. S	–	Luxembourg Stock Exchange	0.736111	India	Electron. & ElectricEq	Dec 01, 2009

DR ISSUE	SYMBOL	EXCHANGE	RATIO DR:ORD	COUNTRY	INDUSTRY	EFF. DATE
Dr. Reddy's Laboratories		New York Stock Exchange	1:01	India	Pharma. & Biotech.	24-Apr-01
Elder- Reg. S pharmaceutical		Luxembourg Stock Exchange	1:02	India	Pharma. & Biotech.	Apr 30, 2004
Electrosteel Castings - Reg. S	–	Luxembourg Stock Exchange	1:01	India	Industrial Engineer.	Oct 05, 2005
Federal Bank - Reg. S	FEDS	London Stock Exchange	1:01	India	Banks	Jan 31, 2006
Financial Technologies (India) - Reg. S	FTIS	London Stock Exchange	1:07	India	Software & ComputerSvc	Oct 11, 2007
GAIL India - Reg. S	GAID	London Stock Exchange	1:06	India	Oil & Gas Producers	Nov 01, 1999
Gammon		Luxembourg Stock Exchange		India	General Industrials	
Gitanjali Gems - Reg. S	GITG	London Stock Exchange	1:01	India	General Retailers	Dec 14, 2007
Granules India - Reg. S	GRAN LX	Luxembourg Stock Exchange -Euro MTF	1:01	India	Pharma. & Biotech.	Jan 20, 2005
Great Eastern Energy - Reg. S	GEEC	London Stock Exchange	2:01	India	Mining	Dec 13, 2005
Gujarat narmada valley fertilizers – Reg. S		Luxembourg Stock Exchange	1:05	India	Chemicals	Oct 13, 1994
HDFC Bank - Reg. S	N/A	Luxembourg Stock Exchange	2:01	India	Banks	Jan 21, 2014
Hexa ware tech		London Stock Exchange	1:2	India	Computer software	Apri 14, 2003.
Hinduja Foundries - Reg. S	HVLX LX	Luxembourg Stock Exchange -Euro MTF	3:01	India	Indust.Metals & Mining	Apr 25, 2008
Hindustan Construction - Reg. S	–	Luxembourg Stock Exchange	1:01	India	Construct. & Materials	Mar 31, 2006
ICICI Bank	IBN	New York Stock Exchange	1:02	India	Banks	Mar 31, 2000
India cements		Luxembourg Stock Exchange		India	Construct & Materials	18-Oct-94
Indusind Bank - Reg. S	IBL LX	Luxembourg Stock Exchange -Euro MTF	1:01	India	Banks	Mar 30, 2007

DR ISSUE	SYMBOL	EXCHANGE	RATIO DR:ORD	COUNTRY	INDUSTRY	EFF. DATE
INFOSYS		New York Stock Exchange	1:01	India	Software & Computer Svc	21-Nov-06
Jindal Cotex - Reg. S	–	Luxembourg Stock Exchange	1:04	India	General Industrials	Jun 10, 2010
JINDAL STAINLESS LTD		Luxembourg Stock Exchange	1:02	India	Metals/Mining	sep16, 2005
Karuturi Global - Reg. S	KARG	Luxembourg Stock Exchange	1:03	India	General Industrials	Oct 21, 2010
Kotak Mahindra Bank - Reg. S	KMBG LX	Luxembourg Stock Exchange -Euro MTF	1:01	India	Banks	Apr 27, 2006
Larsen & turbo Reg. S		London Stock Exchange	1:01	India	Construct. & Materials	28-Nov-94
LIC Housing Finance - Reg. S	–	Luxembourg Stock Exchange	1:02	India	Financial Services	Sep 07, 2004
Lloyd Electric & Engineering - Reg. S	LLD	London Stock Exchange	1:02	India	Electron. & ElectricEq	Oct 10, 2005
Mahindra & Mahindra - Reg. S	MAHMG LX	Luxembourg Stock Exchange -Euro MTF	1:01	India	Industrial Engineer.	Dec14, 1993
Neha International - Reg. S	–	Luxembourg Stock Exchange	1:01	India	Food Producers	Apr 27, 2011
Nissan Copper - Reg. S	NCOP LX	Luxembourg Stock Exchange -Euro MTF	1:05	India	Indust.Metals & Mining	May 20, 2010
Noida Toll Bridge - Reg. S	NTBC	London Stock Exchange	1:05	India	Industrial Engineer.	Mar 21, 2006
Oriental Hotels		Luxembourg Stock Exchange	1:01	India	Hotels	16-Dec-94
Ranbaxy Laboratories - Reg. S	RBXYG LX	Luxembourg Stock Exchange -Euro MTF	1:1	India	Pharma. & Biotech.	Jun 29, 1994
Rei Agro - Reg. S	REA	London Stock Exchange	1:20	India	Food & Drug Retailers	Nov 17, 2005
Reliance Capital - Reg. S	–	Luxembourg Stock Exchange	1:01	India	Financial Services	Aug 21, 2006
Reliance Communications - Reg. S	–	Luxembourg Stock Exchange	1:01	India	Mobile Telecom.	Jul 21, 2006
Reliance Infrastructure –Reg. S	RIFS	London Stock Exchange	1:03	India	Electricity	7-Mar-96

DR ISSUE	SYMBOL	EXCHANGE	RATIO DR:ORD	COUNTRY	INDUSTRY	EFF. DATE
Rolta India - Reg. S	RTI	London Stock Exchange	1:01	India	Tech.Hardware & Equip.	Apr 07, 2006
SAIL		Luxembourg Stock Exchange		India	Indust.Metals & Mining	29-Sep-05
SBI		London Stock Exchange		India	Banks	3-Oct-96
SEL Manufacturing - Reg. S	SELMA LX	Luxembourg Stock Exchange -Euro MTF	0.111111	India	Personal Goods	May 04, 2010
Sterlite Industries		New York Stock Exchange	1:04	India	Indust.Metals & Mining	jun12, 2007
Subex - Reg. S	SUBX	London Stock Exchange	1:01	India	Software & ComputerSvc	Apr 07, 2006
Suzlon Energy - Reg. S	–	Luxembourg Stock Exchange	1:04	India	Electron. & ElectricEq	Jul 27, 2009
Tata Global Beverages - Reg. S	–	Luxembourg Stock Exchange	1:01	India	Beverages	Mar 15, 2004
Tata Motors	TTM	New York Stock Exchange	1:05	India	Industrial Engineer.	Sep 27, 2004
United Spirits - Reg. S	WSY	Luxembourg Stock Exchange -Euro MTF	2:01	India	Beverages	Mar 30, 2006
Videocon Industries - Reg. S		Luxembourg Stock Exchange	1:01	India	Oil & Gas Producers	Sep 29, 2005
Wipro	WIT	New York Stock Exchange	1:01	India	Software & ComputerS	Oct 24, 2000
Zylog Systems - Reg. S	–	Luxembourg Stock Exchange	1:03	India	Software & ComputerSvc	Apr 29, 2013

Table no.3.2 List of Indian companies listed through DRs selected for the study

3.6.1   Stock Exchange Wise DR's included in the Sample

TYPES OF DR PROGRAM	GDRs		ADRs	
Listing venue	LXSE	LSE	NASDAQ	NYSE
No of samples included	41	17	00	6
TOTAL	64			

Table No. 3.2.1 Stock Exchange Wise DR's included in the Sample

Out of 64 DR program, a majority belongs to GDR which includes 41 program listed on Luxembourg stock exchange, 17 program listed on London stock exchange. Remaining 06 ADR program listed on New York stock exchange.

3.6.2   DRs Included In the Study to Find Returns, Volatility Impact

ANANT RAJ	FEDERAL BANK	KARURTURI GLOBAL	ROLTA INDIA
APOLLO HOSPITAL	FINANCIAL TECH	KOTAK MAHINDRA	SEL MANUFA CO
APTECH	GAIL LTD	LIC FINANCING	SUBEX
AXIS	GEETANJALI	LLYOD ELECTRIC	SUZLON ENERGY
BAJAJ HOL	HDFC	NEHA INTERNATIONAL	TATAGLOBAL BEVERAGES
CIPLA LTD	HINDUJA FOUND	NISSAN COPPER	TATA MOTORS
COX & KING	HINDUSTAN CON	NOIDA TOLL BRIDGE	UNITED SPIRITS
CROMPTON GREAV	ICICI BANK	REIGRO	VIDEOCON INDUST
DISH TV	INDUSIND BANK	RELIANCE CAPITAL	WIPRO LTD
ELECTRO STEEL	JINDAL COTEX	RELIANCE COMM	ZYLOG LTD

Table No: 3.3 DRs Included In the Study to Find Returns, Volatility Impact

Stock Exchange Wise DR's included in the Sample to Find Return, Volatility Impact

TYPES OF DR PROGRAM	GDRs		ADRs	
Listing venue	LXSE	LSE	NASDAQ	NYSE
No of samples included	26	11	0	3
TOTAL	40			

Table No.3.3.1 Stock Exchange Wise DR's included in the Sample to Find Return, Volatility Impact.

Out of 40 DR program, a majority belongs to GDR which includes 23 program listed on Luxembourg stock exchange, 13 program listed on London stock exchange. Remaining 3 ADR program listed on New York stock exchange.

3.6.3   DRs Included in the Study to Find Liquidity Impact

Aptech	Hinduja Foundries	Neha International	Tata Motors
Bajaj Holdings & Investment	Hindustan Construction	Nissan Copper	Videocon Industries
Cipla	ICICI Bank	Noida Toll Bridge	Wipro
Dr. Reddy's Laboratories	INFOSYS	Rei Agro	Zylog System
Dish TV India	Jindal Cotex	Reliance Communications	Anant Raj Industries

Federal Bank	JINDAL STAINLESS LTD	Sterlite Industries	Apollo Hospitals
Financial Technologies	Karuturi Global	SEL Manufacturing	Indusind Bank
GAIL India	Kotak Mahindra Bank	Subex	Reliance Capital
Gitanjali Gems	LIC Housing Finance	Suzlon Energy	United Spirits
HDFC Bank	Lloyd Electric & Engineering	Tata Global Beverages	Rolta India

Table No.3.4 DRs Included in the Study to Find Liquidity Impact

Stock Exchange Wise DR's included in the Sample to Find Liquidity Impact

TYPES OF DR PROGRAM	GDRs		ADRs	
Listing venue	LXSE	LSE	NASDAQ	NYSE
No of samples included	24	13	0	3
TOTAL	40			

Table No.3.4.1 Stock Exchange Wise DR's Included in the Sample to Find Liquidity Impact

Out of 40 DR program, a majority belongs to GDR which includes 24 program listed on Luxembourg stock exchange, 10 program listed on London stock exchange. Remaining 6 ADR program listed on New York stock exchange.

3.6.4   DRs Included in the Study to Find Price Impact

Axis Bank	Ballapur ltd	Hindustan Construction	Videocon Industries
Cipla	Balrampur chilli mills ltd	India cements	HDFC Bank
Financial Technologies	BSEL Infrastructure Realty	Larsen & turbo	ICICI Bank
Kotak Mahindra Bank	CESC	LIC Housing Finance	Wipro
Jindal Cotex	Crompton Greaves	Lloyd Electric & Engineering	Dr. Reddy's Laboratories
Apollo Hospitals	Elder pharmaceuticals	Mahindra & Mahindra	Sterlite
Ambuja Cements	Gammon	Oriental Hotels	Tata Motors
Anant Raj Industries	Granules India	Reliance Infrastructure	Infosys
Arvind ltd	Great Eastern Energy	SBI	Ranbaxy Lab
Bajaj Holdings & Investment	Gujarat narmada valley fertilizers	SAIL	Hexa ware technologies

Table No.3.5 DRs Included in the Study to Find Price Impact

Stock Exchange Wise DR's included in the Sample to Find Cross Listings Impact on Indian Stock Price.

TYPES OF DR PROGRAM	GDRs		ADRs	
Listing venue	LXSE	LSE	NASDAQ	NYSE
No of samples included	24	9	0	7
TOTAL	40			

Table No.3.5.1 Stock Exchange Wise DR's Included in the Sample to Find Cross Listings Impact on Indian Stock Price.

Out of 40 DR program, a majority belongs to GDR which includes 24 program listed on Luxembourg stock exchange, 09 program listed on London stock exchange. Remaining 07 ADR program listed on New York stock exchange.

Objective 5: To study and compare the DR regulatory framework of selected capital markets.

Hypothesis 5 H$_0$: There is no significant difference in the DR regulatory frame work of selected capital markets.

Sample of five capital markets has been considered for the study. Countries like Brazil; Taiwan, Hong Kong, Russia & India DR regulatory frame work has been examined & compared. Emerging markets were considered for the study. The study focuses on analyzing the performance of each of them. The study also attempts to categories these capital markets into strictly regulated or sparsely regulated markets by examining their regulatory frame work.

3.7   Scope & Period of the study:

The present study focuses on the Impact of cross listings on the valuation of Indian stocks. The scope of the study encompasses of Indian firms listed on foreign stock exchange through depository receipts. DRs Characteristics, their success and the problems faced by firms listed abroad. Study includes impact factors affecting Indian stocks. Though many factors are incorporated to find impact of cross listings, the study is confined to only few dimensions of cross listings which were considered as significant. Study covers four dimensions namely, return, price, liquidity & volatility. One more dimension included in the study was comparison of DR regulatory frame work of five capital markets (India, Brazil, Hong Kong, Russia & Taiwan). The population is derived from 138 DR programs listed on different international stock exchanges by Indian companies for a period of 1999 to 2015. To find the impact of cross listing on Indian stock price, the period considered for the study is 2011- 2016. The study is restricted to indirect listings of DR route.

3.8 Limitations of the study:

- The sample taken for the study is limited to Indian companies listed on foreign stock exchanges (ADRs, GDRs). For finding the effect of cross listings, four factors return, price, liquidity & volatility has been considered.

- The population is derived from 138 DR programs listed on different international stock exchanges by Indian companies for a period of 1999 to 2015. Another aspect that plays an important role in sample selection is determined by the availability of home market trading data. Further, the study also eliminated those DR programs which were not listed before on any of the Indian stock exchanges prior to their DR program. Therefore, study includes a sample of 64 DR program traded by 64 Indian companies.

- The study is limited five capital markets (India, Brazil, Hong Kong, Russia & Taiwan) & hence the inferences drawn are pertaining to these selected capital markets.

- Hypotheses are framed on secondary data pertaining to research objectives "To find the cross listing impact on Indian stocks".

- Though there are various financial tools to find the performance of Indian stocks listed on foreign stock exchanges. The study uses event study methodology & granger causality test to find the impact. This study is limited only to the usage of few financial tools, namely, variances, returns, turnover, volume.

- Results of the study are subjected to the reliability of the secondary data.

DATA ANALYSIS AND INTERPRETATION

The chapter comprises of data analysis & interpretation. The analyses of five objectives are included in this chapter. The chapter is divided into six sections. (4.1) Impact of cross listing on the Indian stock Returns (4.2) Impact of cross listing on the Indian stock Liquidity (4.3) Impact of cross listing on the Indian stock Price. (4.4) Impact of cross listing on the Indian stock volatility. (4.5) Comparison of DR regulatory frame work of select capital markets. (6) Conclusions.

4.1 Impact of Cross Listing on the Indian Stock Returns

Indian securities market plays a crucial role in financing the growing needs of various sectors of the economy. Investors are looking for investment opportunities globally beyond the boundaries of their countries. Listings through DRs in foreign countries has given opportunities for companies looking to trade into new markets, get new customers, get new investments and raise more capital in international markets through listing and trading.

Cross listing of shares means a firm lists its shares on foreign stock exchanges in addition to its domestic local stock exchange to get maximum cost of capital. Returns are the income which will be received over the period of time and the change in the value of investment, the rate of return which the firms are going to earn over the period of investment made. Returns that an investor receives from the security are the cost of that security to the company that issues it. Returns are measured in terms of cost of capital, capital yield, capital asset pricing model, securities market line.

According to Berg (2012) the fragmentation of the capital market motivated corporate managers to consider whether offering stocks to foreign investors through cross listings enhances the stock value. Still there is a doubt among the corporate people whether cross listings creates the value.

International cross listings have inspired a great deal of academic research over the years. Most of the earlier studies is on either abnormal returns, cumulative abnormal returns, around the cross listings announcements, valuation effect of cross listings (Foester and Karolyi (1999), Doidge, 2004. Mostly studies were done on comparing valuation of cross listed firms with non-cross listed stocks. Most of the studies mostly focused on ADRs valuation listed on US stock exchanges. This effect is basically cross listing premium.

While considering impact of cross listing, the degree of integration between local and foreign markets plays a vital role. Alexander & Janakiramanan (1988) investigated by taking the sample of Canadian and non-Canadian firms whose stocks were listed internationally. The study observed a decline in expected returns of Canadian firms & the decline is smaller than in non-Canadian firms. Tripathy & Jha.K. (2014) examined impact of cross listings of ADR on the Indian stock market. The shares of cross listed stocks experienced abnormally higher returns prior to cross listing & less returns thereafter. Forester & Karolyi, (1993), Strickland, Lins & Zenner (2003), Karoyli, Andrew (2004) stated international listings provides companies with greater access to global markets, leading to enhanced visibility, liquidity & simultaneously has less risk exposure. There results indicate that there is a decline in the abnormal returns after foreign listing. Doukas & Switzer (2000) found that there is a positive stock market reaction to the announcement of listings in the US stock market by 79 Canadian firms. On the contrary, Cetorelli, Nicola, Peristiani & stravros (2010), Howe & Kelm (1987) stated there is an increase in the cost of capital post listing. Callaghan, Kleiman & Sahu (1999) states that ADRs perform brilliantly the stock market index during short & long term holding periods from the date of issue. Explicitly, one of the objectives of the study is to examine the impact of cross listings on the stock returns. The study adopts an event study methodology to analyze the impact of international cross listings on the firm's value around the event date announcement. Using event study methodology, Average abnormal returns & cumulative abnormal returns are computed (explained in chapter 3). Since cross listing is a decision made at the firm level, the impact on firm value will influence the firm's decision to cross list or not. The impact of cross listings is evaluated in a multivariate framework after controlling the other factors such as company size, accounting practices, analyst and trading activity which potentially affect the stock returns. For fulfilling the objective the following hypothesis has been framed.

Hypothesis: There is no significant difference in returns of Indian stocks listed on International stock exchanges.

Results:

4.1.1   Impact of cross listings on Indian stock returns listed on select stock exchanges:

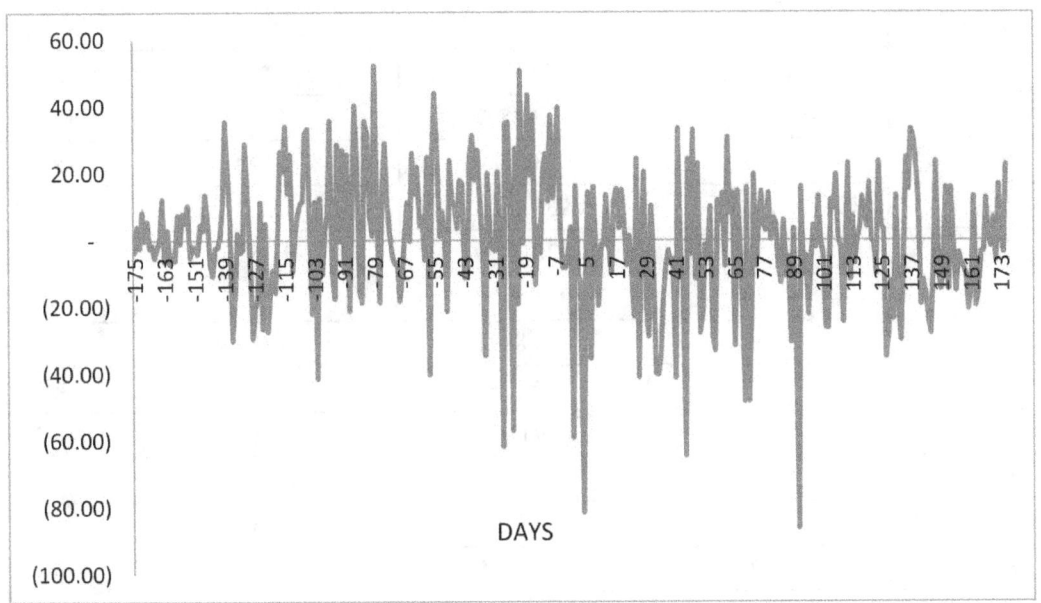

Figure 4.1.1 Average Abnormal Returns during the event window of 40 companies

Table 4.1.1 Average abnormal returns (AARs), Cumulative average abnormal return (CAARs) and test statistics on and around the cross listings

Days	AAR	CAAR	AAR t stat	CAAR t sta
-175	-3.52	-3.52034	-2.57	-2.57
-170	5.62	12.08151	-2.61	-3.93
-160	-4.12	-1.658	-4.42	-3.27
-150	-4.10	8.900467	-2.05	-5.47
-140	10.49	24.57779	1.80*	3.60***
-130	11.73	76.02805	1.77*	12.24***
-120	-8.96	-60.6171	1.74*	5.70***
-110	7.36	46.40433	-4.32	-12.25
-100	-10.35	84.46872	-1.14	5.43***
-90	25.70	174.6618	13.01***	15.67***
-80	1.40	269.7474	-3.05	-1.98
-70	-6.76	346.5708	2.20**	-0.07
-60	7.02	403.4754	12.64***	16.11***
-50	-21.35	465.2529	-13.08	-24.25
-40	31.32	584.2127	19.58***	29.41***
-30	20.28	638.2861	9.66***	7.18***
-20	-0.89	655.7302	-0.73	-4.11
-10	11.67	820.4996	7.48***	9.43***
-9	37.32	857.8154	7.68***	15.15***
-8	12.54	870.3536	7.99***	15.66***
-7	23.51	893.8597	7.29***	15.27***
-6	39.72	933.5784	5.63***	12.92***
-5	1.53	935.1106	2.22**	7.85***
-4	-8.33	926.7829	-9.66	-7.44
-3	-8.20	918.5804	-9.87	-19.53
-2	-3.69	914.8921	7.04***	-2.83
-1	3.82	918.714	1.51	8.55***
0	-59.11	859.6016	-8.98	-7.48
1	16.13	875.727	-0.85	-9.83
2	-11.15	864.5742	-4.36	-5.21
3	-12.26	852.3185	-3.67	-8.04
4	-81.38	770.9389	-8.77	-12.44

Days	AAR	CAAR	AAR t stat	CAAR t sta
5	-8.89	762.0498	-8.64	-17.41
6	14.25	776.3038	-1.21	-9.86
7	-35.42	740.8815	-15.60	-16.82
8	15.98	756.8572	9.72***	-5.88
9	-6.90	749.9568	-0.76	8.96***
10	-19.66	730.2958	2.15**	1.39
20	5.84	780.0125	0.19	3.51***
30	-28.82	696.8868	0.26	-5.12
40	-5.83	543.3707	3.72***	8.19***
50	22.89	518.3248	11.75***	2.81***
60	14.01	440.916	-4.86	-13.37
70	15.63	421.9602	10.04***	2.93***
80	0.18	403.6944	8.32***	16.40***
90	-28.13	329.2483	-11.01	-7.65
100	-0.25	231.9738	-12.93	-26.81
110	-1.70	188.1801	6.16***	3.76***
120	17.17	245.4237	7.26***	-1.19
130	-23.57	166.5729	0.12	-0.62
140	11.69	265.709	-8.30	-16.90
150	-8.05	152.8799	1.31	2.49***
160	-20.60	103.8187	-0.24	-0.65
170	6.51	79.1715	-7.12	-8.85
175	22.47	111.7834	-1.79	0.73

***, **,* significant at 1%, 5% & 10%

Table depicts AAR, t –statistics & CAAR for each day in the event window. An AAR, CAAR & t-statistics value has been calculated using event study. MS-excel have been used for calculations. Figure 1 & 2 shows the values of CAAR & AAR corresponding to each day of the event window.

Table 1 depicts 175 days pre announcement of cross listing, starting from day $t_{(-175)}$ to day $t_{(-1)}$, there is a positive average abnormal returns. The returns are positive for approximately 120 days while they are negative for only 50 days. From the 120 positive AAR values, 104 values are statistically significant at 1%, 12 are significant at 5% & 6 are significant at 10%. The negative returns are not significant on any of the 50 days. During the post announcement window from day $t_{(1)}$ to day $t_{(175)}$, the pattern of positive AARs changes to negative pattern of returns. It has been observed that the AARs values are negative for nearly 115 days. From the 60 positive AAR values of post announcement, 50values are significant at 1%, 9 values is significant at 5% & 2 values are significant at 10%.

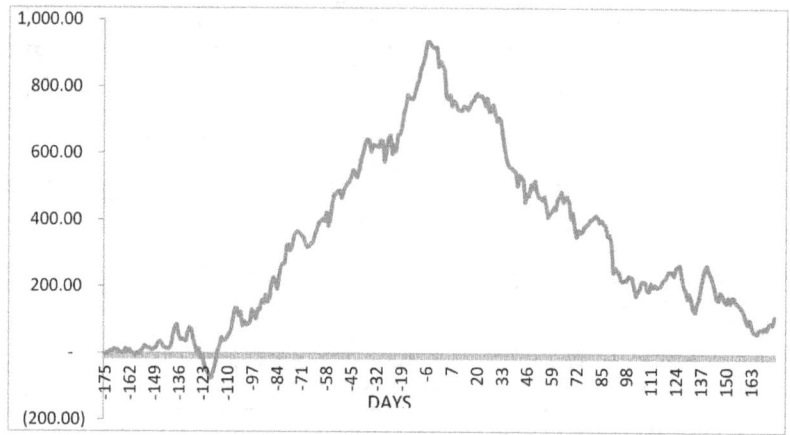

Figure 4.1.2 Cumulative Average Abnormal Returns during the event window

The returns are cumulated over the event window to assess the net magnitude of the overall returns. Table represents cumulative average abnormal returns (CAAR) for each day during the 350 day event window & their corresponding t-statistics values. The results indicate that till day $t_{(-116)}$, CAAR does not illustrate any obvious pattern, but from day $t_{(-115)}$ onwards, CAAR starts becoming positive. The CAAR value of day $t_{(-115)}$ starts from 7.425108%, reaches a peak of 935.1106 percent on $t_{(-5)}$ after that even though the CAAR is positive, but at an decreasing rate. At $t_{(-1)}$ CAAR value is 918.714, at $t_{(0)}$ the value decreased to 859.601. This decline CAAR is due to the fact that AAR values are mostly positive till day $t_{(1)}$, by & large negative during the post announcement window. The CAAR values around event window $t_{(0)}$ is 859.601 which is statistically insignificant.

From the 175 CAAR values of pre-listing period 115 values are statistically significant at 1%, 15 are significant at 5% & 7 are significant at 10%. This indicates that there is price run up of underlying shares in the pre listing period. The results show a decreasing stock price reaction on & around the listing announcement date. In the post listing period, out of 175 CAAR value which are decreasing rate, 58 values are statistically significant at 1%, 11 values are significant at 5%, 4 values are significant at 10%.

4.1.2   DR Impact on Indian stock returns listed on London stock exchanges:

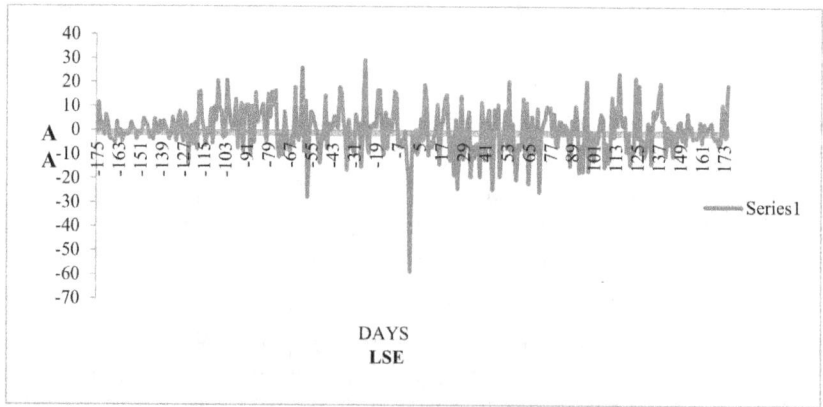

Figure 4.1.3 Average Abnormal Returns during the event window of stocks listed at LSE

Table 4.1.2 average abnormal returns (AARs), Cumulative average abnormal return (CAARs) and test statistics on and around the cross listings at LSE

LSE				
DAYS	AAR	CAAR	AAR t –sta	CAAR t-sta
-175	-0.63915	-0.63915	-0.599869836	-0.599869836
-170	6.42358	18.60677	-1.106418175	-1.592193536
-160	-2.12184	-0.40693	-0.77754673	0.450332786
-150	-0.11131	-7.20752	0.75586658	-0.918791426
-140	3.588259	0.453214	-0.089250045	-0.361887175
-130	4.230738	5.384429	3.144822792***	-1.393561412
-120	3.107607	4.085462	-2.05654086***	-4.10343508***
-110	-5.21282	26.9032	8.71809145***	2.327987394***
-100	3.450684	106.5017	4.191471378***	1.922546506*
-90	10.54655	153.9019	1.207958259	-0.216856981
-80	-4.58026	188.2875	3.71940466***	0.545555568
-70	7.771062	231.4433	-0.071035817	1.510858615
-60	26.06603	246.3745	-2.25234993***	-2.05599183***
-50	-13.3341	219.2399	-2.59745530***	-0.361887175
-40	0.852145	236.189	7.369800699***	-1.935614116*
-30	6.593081	246.5193	2.460284216***	-4.34350891***
-20	3.159795	265.5801	3.97641748***	2.79873944***
-10	3.238526	300.0429	1.466079748	0.677665389
-9	16.25083	316.2938	0.71911549	1.10858614
-8	14.9697	331.2634	4.7178345***	-2.9918364***
-7	-6.30284	324.9606	6.40322868***	-0.341243966
-6	-3.76169	321.1989	2.594709759***	1.181289016
-5	-6.75729	314.4416	-1.86976269**	-2.12480428***
-4	-3.37085	311.0708	0.964352445	-1.44568741
-3	-0.39939	310.6714	-2.17954672***	-1.452193536
-2	-12.69	297.9814	-9.58612006***	0.780332786
-1	-19.5976	278.3838	-15.3929837***	0.55555534
0	-58.808	219.5759	5.073103693***	1.3456778
1	-1.28214	218.2937	-7.55477355***	-2.05599183***
2	-8.74453	209.5492	-3.74643887***	-0.697377559

LSE				
DAYS	AAR	CAAR	AAR t –sta	CAAR t-sta
3	0.312817	209.862	-2.1830106***	-1.401157067
4	-9.88518	199.9768	-2.48073946***	0.589687505
5	-4.77013	195.2067	1.849530646***	-0.562394129
6	4.996965	200.2037	-2.38847243***	-1.909472525*
7	-4.03012	196.1736	6.74168141***	-2.35464985***
8	18.92823	215.1018	-0.261900684	-0.918791426
9	12.43543	227.5372	3.60059921***	-0.261887175
10	-10.2924	217.2448	-2.65423425***	-1.569356141
20	14.95393	232.9601	-1.512860611	-4.34034350***
30	-7.03197	167.0888	3.82621386***	2.22279873***
40	0.954385	121.4841	6.416732949***	0.026665389
50	-4.64023	87.7885	1.08583324	1.340858615
60	-7.80448	56.96441	-3.02928333***	-2.45599183***
70	9.236378	40.84147	-9.83692041***	-0.541243966
80	-4.99501	49.69004	9.18621764***	1.88128901*
90	-0.84951	39.11879	1.69714136*	-2.12480428***
100	-1.71527	19.29114	-6.0769713***	-1.444102953
110	-9.29126	-27.4991	1.609439888	-1.921935358*
120	-0.78816	24.6053	-0.469739312	0.033278633
130	-8.00338	-0.71453	-0.258265731	-1.909472525*
140	4.072968	52.22803	2.39194015***	-2.3546498***
150	-3.72989	24.91001	0.314152043	-0.918791426
160	3.603248	21.44505	-0.813976574	-0.361887175
170	-6.0576	10.82624	-0.562655108	-1.393561412
175	19.08753	36.21478	1.127962367	-4.10343508***

***, **,* significant at 1%, 5% & 10%

Table depicts average abnormal returns, cumulative average abnormal returns and their t-statistics of stocks listed on London Stock Exchange. Table depicts 175 days pre announcement of cross listing, starting from day $t_{(-175)}$ to day $t_{(-1)}$, there is a positive average abnormal returns.

The AAR and CAAR's are calculated period from 175 days prior to listings to 175 days after the listings for each of the 40 DRs. There is evidence of increase in the returns in the pre listing period. The increasing pattern starts declining in the post listing period. The returns are positive for approximately 100 days while they are negative for 75 days in the pre listing period. From the 100 positive AAR values,

55 values are statistically significant at 1%, 22 are significant at 5% & 13 are significant at 10%. This explains that there is price run up of underlying shares in the pre listing period. The negative returns are not significant on any of the 45 days. Daily AAR becomes significantly negative on and around the listing date. 7 days prior to listings and 7 days after the listings average abnormal returns turns out to be negative. The results show negative stock price reaction on the listing announcement date with an AAR of -58.808% and statistically significant at 1% level with a t-statistics of 5.073. During the post announcement window from day $t_{(1)}$ to day $t_{(175)}$, the pattern of positive AARs changes to negative pattern of returns. It has been observed that the AARs values are negative for nearly 105 days. From the 70 positive AAR values of post announcement, 55 values are significant at 1%, 10 values are significant at 5% & 5values are significant at 10%.

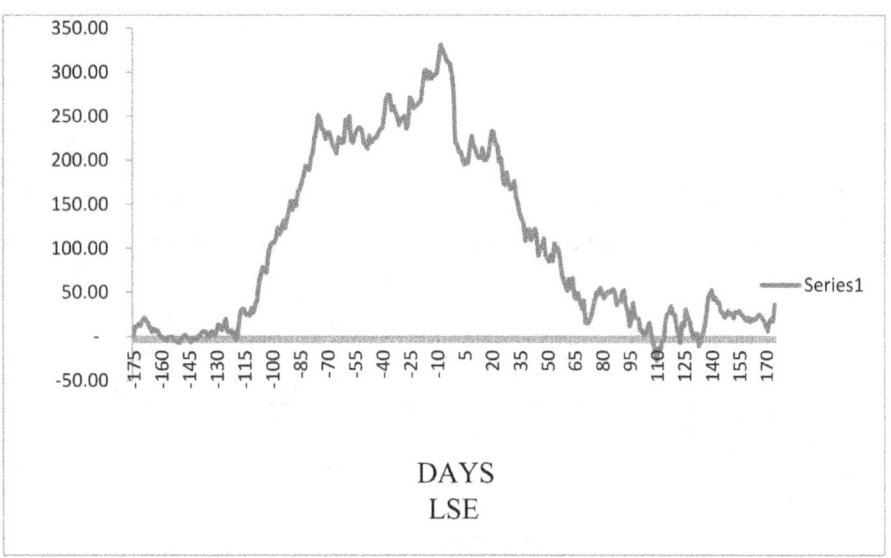

Figure 4.1.4 Cumulative Average Abnormal Returns during the event window of LSE

The returns are cumulated over the event window to assess the net magnitude of the overall returns. Table represents cumulative average abnormal returns (CAAR) for each day during the 350 day event window & their corresponding t-statistics values. The results indicate that till day $t_{(-141)}$, CAAR does not illustrate any obvious pattern, but from day $t_{(-140)}$ onwards, CAAR starts becoming positive. The CAAR value of day $t_{(-140)}$ starts from 0.45%, reaches a peak of 331.26 percent on $t_{(-8)}$ after that even though the CAAR is positive, but at an decreasing rate. At $t_{(-1)}$ CAAR value is 278.38, at $t_{(0)}$ the value decreased to 219.58. This decline CAAR is due to the fact that AAR values are mostly positive till day $t_{(1)}$, by & large negative during the post announcement window. The CAAR values around event window $t_{(0)}$ is 219.579 which is statistically insignificant. From the 175 CAAR values of pre-listing period 102 values are statistically significant at 1%, 21 are significant at 5% & 13 are significant at 10%. This indicates that there is price run up of underlying shares in the pre listing period. The results show a decreasing stock price reaction on & around the listing announcement date. In the post listing period, out of 175 CAAR value which are decreasing rate, 55 are statistically significant at 1%, 10 values are significant at 5%, 2 values are significant at 10%.

4.1.3   DR Impact on Indian stock returns listed on NYSE:

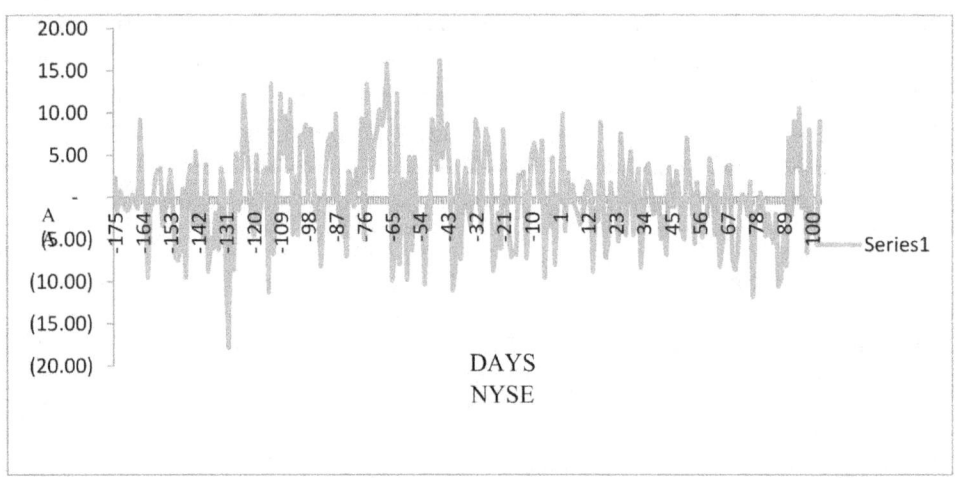

Figure 4.1.5: Average Abnormal Returns during the event window of stocks listed at NYSE.

Table 4.1.3 average abnormal returns (AARs), Cumulative average abnormal return (CAARs) and test statistics on and around the cross listings at NYSE.

NYSE				
DAYS	AAR	CAAR	AAR t -sta	CAAR t-sta
-150	(1.73)	0.58	(1.20)	0.41
-140	(1.32)	(4.84)	(0.92)	1.922546506**
-130	(3.36)	(2.06)	(0.83)	-.216856981
-120	2.23	(28.91)	1.06	0.052642239***
-110	(6.03)	(48.20)	(2.03)	1.510858615
-100	(1.54)	(82.46)	(0.05)	-2.05599183
-90	3.17	(62.11)	0.25	-0.34124396
-80	3.00	(34.74)	0.01	1.181289016
-70	3.08	3.35	(0.13)	-2.12480428**
-60	(1.64)	15.42	1.65	-1.44568741
-50	(5.03)	16.92	(2.12)	4.296426129**
-40	10.55	110.63	2.77	-3.37294332**
-30	4.72	95.68	1.29	-0.22220693
-20	16.16	107.68	3.64	-1.04889950*
-10	3.48	110.62	0.55	-2.74448474***
-9	(1.38)	109.24	0.84	-1.51950948
-8	(3.39)	105.85	0.09	1.920595219**
-7	1.84	107.69	0.07	-0.22238099

NYSE				
DAYS	AAR	CAAR	AAR t -sta	CAAR t-sta
-6	9.16	116.85	1.99	0.077677665***
-5	7.41	124.27	2.30	1.210858615*
-4	(3.72)	120.55	(0.71)	-2.04583648***
-3	2.47	123.02	0.92	-0.44124396
-2	8.10	131.13	1.08	1.281289016*
-1	6.78	137.91	0.60	-2.02480428**
0	3.09	141.00	1.13	-1.44568741*
1	(8.75)	132.24	(1.33)	4.296426129***
2	(5.98)	126.26	(1.74)	-3.37294332***
3	(1.89)	124.37	1.16	-0.222206937
4	(6.08)	118.29	(1.90)	-1.048899507
5	8.03	126.32	1.70	-2.744484747**
6	0.03	126.35	(0.82)	-1.519509487*
7	(3.35)	123.00	(0.81)	1.922546506**
8	(7.12)	115.87	(2.26)	-0.216856981
9	(6.40)	109.47	(1.87)	0.252343894
10	(6.84)	102.63	(1.86)	1.510858615**
20	6.70	125.26	1.98	-2.055991836**
30	2.84	116.23	0.66	-0.341243966
40	(8.80)	103.19	(3.30)	1.181289016
50	(5.22)	87.83	(1.38)	-2.124804287***
60	(2.91)	88.32	(1.04)	-1.434568741
70	3.56	81.75	2.23	4.459642613***
80	(5.50)	77.36	(1.74)	-3.572943324***
90	(8.31)	63.34	(1.89)	-0.322206937
100	(0.30)	42.14	(0.49)	-1.448899507*
110	(4.37)	14.52	(1.23)	-0.744484747*
120	3.68	(7.97)	0.66	-1.319509487**
130	-	2.49	-	1.722546506*
140	-	2.49	-	-0.126856981
150	-	2.49	-	0.037767767

***, **,* significant at 1%, 5% & 10%

Table depicts average abnormal returns, cumulative average abnormal returns and their t-statistics values of stocks listed on New York Stock Exchange. Table depicts 150 days pre announcement of cross listing, starting from day $t_{(-150)}$ to day $t_{(-1)}$, there is a positive average abnormal returns.

The AAR and CAAR's are calculated for 150 days prior to listings & 150 days after the listings for each of the 40 DRs. There is evidence of increase in the returns in the pre listing period. The increasing pattern starts declining in the post listing period. The returns are positive for approximately 80 days while they are negative for 70 days in the pre listing period. From the 100 positive AAR values, 50 values are statistically significant at 1%, 12 values are significant at 5% & 13 values are significant at 10%. This explains that there is price run up of underlying shares in the pre listing period. Daily AAR becomes significantly negative on and around the listing date.7 days after the listings average abnormal returns turns out to be negative. The results show a stock price reaction on the listing announcement date with an AAR of 3.09% and are not statistically significant. During the post announcement window from day $t_{(1)}$ to day $t_{(150)}$, the pattern of positive AARs changes to negative pattern of returns. It has been observed that the AARs values are negative for nearly 105 days. From the 70 positive AAR values of post announcement, 40 values are significant at 1%, 10 values are significant at 5% & 5 values are significant at 10%.

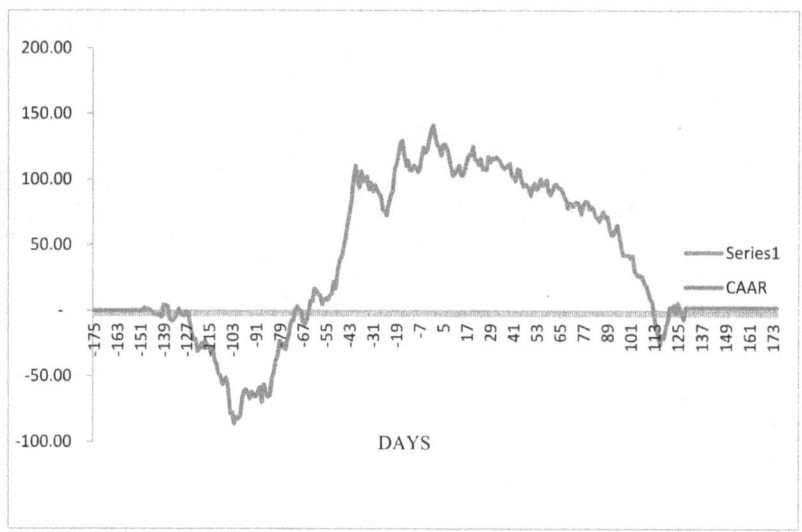

Figure:- 4.1.6 Cumulative Average Abnormal Returns during the event window of NYSE

The returns are cumulated over the event window to assess the net magnitude of the overall returns. Table represents cumulative average abnormal returns (CAAR) for each day during the 300 day event window & their corresponding t-statistics values. The results indicate that till day $t_{(-64)}$, CAAR does not illustrate any obvious pattern, but from day $t_{(-63)}$ onwards, CAAR starts becoming positive. The CAAR value of day $t_{(-63)}$ starts from 7.05%, reaches a peak of 141 percent on $t_{(0)}$ after that even though the CAAR is positive, but at an decreasing rate. At $t_{(-1)}$ CAAR value is 137.38, at $t_{(+1)}$ the value decreased to 132.24. This decline CAAR is due to the fact that AAR values are mostly positive till day $t_{(1)}$, by & large negative during the post announcement window. The CAAR values around event window $t_{(0)}$ is 141% which is statistically insignificant. From the 150 CAAR values of pre-listing period 82 values are statistically significant at 1%, 18 values are significant at 5% & 10 values are significant at 10%. This indicates that there is price run up of underlying shares in the pre listing period. The results show a decreasing stock price reaction on & around the listing announcement date. In the post listing period, out of 150 CAAR value which are decreasing rate, 52 are statistically significant at 1%, 10 values are significant at 5%, 12 values are significant at 10%.

4.1.4   DR Impact on Indian stock returns listed on LUXSE :

Figure 4.1.7 Average Abnormal Returns during the event window of stocks listed at LUXSE

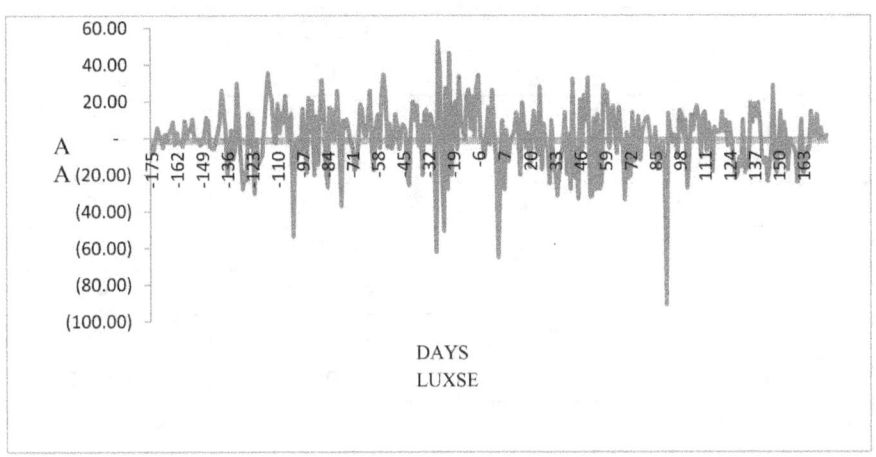

Figure: Average Abnormal Returns during the event window of stocks listed at LUXSE

Table 4.1.4 average abnormal returns (AARs), Cumulative average abnormal returns (CAARs) and test statistics on and around the cross listings at LUXSE.

LUXSE				
DAYS	AAR	CAAR	AAR t -sta	CAAR t-sta
-175	(2.88)	(2.88)	-0.6973776	-0.6973776
-170	(0.80)	(6.53)	-2.3546499	-6.3353636***
-160	(2.00)	(1.25)	-2.0559918	-9.5967273***
-150	(3.99)	16.11	-1.5195095	-16.938792***
-140	8.22	28.96	2.12604247	-0.3618872
-130	10.86	72.71	-0.6276607	-1.3935614***
-120	(14.31)	(35.80)	2.61971082	-4.1034351***
-110	18.61	67.71	1.50896952	2.32798739**
-100	(12.27)	60.42	-2.9922475	1.92254651**
-90	11.98	82.87	9.0597228	-0.216857
-80	2.98	116.20	-0.6074654	0.02666777
-70	(17.61)	111.77	6.01141403	1.51085861
-60	(17.41)	141.68	7.29075833	-2.0559918**
-50	(2.98)	229.09	-10.382554	-0.341244

DAYS	AAR	CAAR	AAR t -sta	CAAR t-sta
LUXSE				
-40	19.92	237.40	16.8125024	1.18128902**
-30	8.98	296.09	6.85176446	-2.1248043***
-20	(20.21)	282.47	-2.3641185	-1.4456874*
-10	4.95	409.84	6.72285926	4.29642613***
-9	22.45	432.28	2.42227211	-3.3729433***
-8	0.96	433.24	1.40199273	-0.2222069
-7	27.97	461.21	1.82264598	-1.0488995
-6	34.32	495.53	-6.2152196	-2.7444847***
-5	0.88	496.40	-1.8267238	-1.5195095*
-4	(1.24)	495.16	-7.6728213	0.363962
-3	(10.27)	484.89	-8.684746	-1.5921935*
-2	0.90	485.78	9.46623932	0.68033279
-1	16.64	502.42	5.86298309	-1.4392194
0	(3.40)	499.03	4.29391055	0.34033279
1	26.16	525.19	-2.2685848	-2.0559918***
2	3.57	528.76	0.51881439	-0.6973776
3	(10.68)	518.08	-3.1217898	-1.4011571*
4	(65.41)	452.67	-8.0657819	0.58968751
5	(12.15)	440.52	-8.7730317	-0.5623941
6	9.23	449.75	-0.3828384	-1.9094725*
7	(28.04)	421.71	-12.142586	-2.3546499**
8	4.17	425.88	5.07284481	-0.9187914
9	(12.94)	412.95	-2.58427	-0.3618872
10	(2.53)	410.42	5.25842012	-1.3935614*
20	(15.82)	421.79	-3.0024444	-0.3618872
30	(24.64)	413.57	5.09155374	-1.3935614
40	2.02	318.69	5.57821462	-4.1034351***
50	32.75	342.70	13.3081449	2.32798739***
60	24.73	295.63	-0.443089	1.92254651**
70	2.83	299.37	7.43279476	-0.216857
80	10.67	276.65	12.1970293	0.02776777
90	(18.97)	226.79	-1.7789763	1.51085861*
100	1.76	170.54	-9.9710744	-2.0559918***
110	11.96	201.16	8.9867393	-0.341244
120	14.28	228.79	7.61642295	1.18128902*

LUXSE				
DAYS	AAR	CAAR	AAR t -sta	CAAR t-sta
130	(15.57)	164.80	0.21202852	-2.1248043***
140	7.62	211.00	-12.391095	-1.4456874
150	(4.32)	125.48	3.80917345	4.29642613***
160	(24.21)	79.89	0.96030538	-3.3729433***
170	12.56	65.86	-7.2362096	-0.2222069
175	1.35	71.05	-2.5997402	-1.0488995

***, **,* significant at 1%, 5% & 10%

Table depicts average abnormal returns, cumulative average abnormal returns and their t-statistics of stocks listed on Luxembourg Stock Exchange. Table depicts 175 days pre announcement of cross listing, starting from day $t_{(-175)}$ to day $t_{(-1)}$, there is a positive average abnormal returns.

The AAR and CAAR's are calculated period from 175 days prior to listings to 175 days after the listings for each of the 40 DRs. There is evidence of increase in the returns in the pre listing period. The increasing pattern starts declining in the post listing period. The returns are positive for approximately 104 days while they are negative for 71 days in the pre listing period. From the 104 positive AAR values, 65 values are statistically significant at 1%, 20 are significant at 5% & 15 are significant at 10%. This explains that there is price run up of underlying shares in the pre listing period. The negative returns are significant for 28 days. Daily AAR becomes significantly negative around the listing date. The results show negative stock price reaction on the listing announcement date with an AAR of -3.40% and statistically significant at 1% level with a t-statistics of 4.29391055. During the post announcement window from day $t_{(1)}$ to day $t_{(175)}$, the pattern of positive AARs changes to negative pattern of returns. It has been observed that the AARs values are negative for nearly 95 days. From the 80 positive AAR values of post announcement, 65values are significant at 1%, 15 values is significant at 5% & 5values are significant at10%.

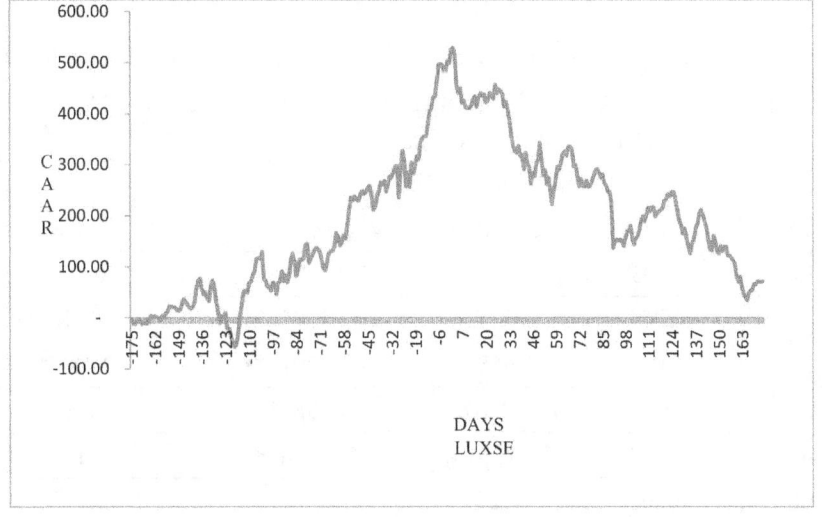

Figure: 4.1.8 Cumulative Average Abnormal Returns during the event window of LUXSE

The returns are cumulated over the event window to assess the net magnitude of the overall returns. Table represents cumulative average abnormal returns (CAAR) for each day during the 350 day event window & their corresponding t-statistics values. The results indicate that till day $t_{(-165)}$, CAAR does not illustrate any obvious pattern, but from day $t_{(-164)}$ onwards, CAAR starts becoming positive. The CAAR value of day $t_{(-164)}$ starts from 4.13736, reaches a peak of 502.4246 percent on $t_{(-1)}$ after that even though the CAAR is positive, but at an decreasing rate. At $t_{(-1)}$ CAAR value is 502.4246, at $t_{(0)}$ the value decreased to 499.029. This decline CAAR is due to the fact that AAR values are mostly positive till day $t_{(1)}$, by & large negative during the post announcement window. The CAAR values around event window $t_{(0)}$ is 499.029 which is statistically insignificant. From the 175 CAAR values of pre-listing period 120 values are statistically significant at 1%, 22 are significant at 5% & 15 are significant at 10%. This indicates that there is price run up of underlying shares in the pre listing period. The results show a decreasing stock price reaction on & around the listing announcement date. In the post listing period, out of 175 CAAR value which are decreasing rate, 55 are statistically significant at 1%, 25 values are significant at 5%, 3 values are significant at 10%.

4.1.5 DR Impact on Indian stock returns listed through GDR on LSE & LUXSE:

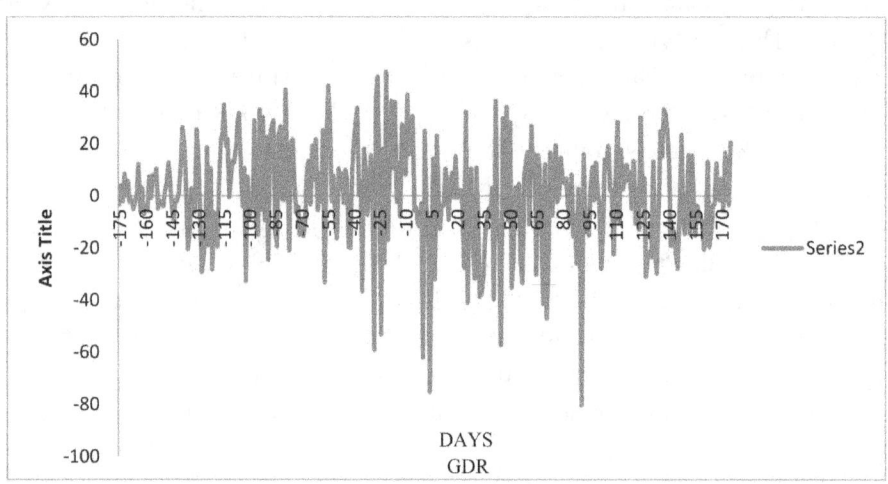

Figure: 4.1.9 Average Abnormal Returns during the event window of stocks listed through GDR.

Table 4.1.5 average abnormal returns (AARs), Cumulative average abnormal returns (CAARs) and test statistics on and around the cross listings listed through GDR.

GDR				
DAYS	AAR	CAAR	AAR t –sta	CAAR t-sta
-175	-3.52034	-3.52034	-2.573***	0.027768
-170	5.622647	12.08151	-2.61205***	1.510859
-160	-4.11874	-1.658	-4.41791***	-2.05599***
-150	-4.09702	8.900467	-2.05365***	-0.34124
-140	11.80615	29.4174	2.719714***	1.181289
-130	15.09085	78.09249	2.591283***	-2.1248***

GDR				
DAYS	AAR	CAAR	AAR t –sta	CAAR t-sta
-120	-11.1996	-31.7101	0.676782	-1.44569
-110	13.39468	94.60872	-2.28302***	4.296426***
-100	-8.8158	166.9238	-1.08476	-3.37294***
-90	22.52972	236.7712	12.76535***	-0.22221
-80	-1.6037	304.4877	-3.05995***	-1.0489
-70	-9.83483	343.2179	2.337618***	-2.74448***
-60	8.658858	388.0572	10.99139***	-1.51951
-50	-16.3167	448.3315	-10.9564***	0.363962
-40	20.76718	473.5862	16.81102***	-1.59219
-30	15.5688	542.6102	8.369455***	0.880333
-20	-17.051	548.0486	-4.37501***	-1.59219
-10	8.192474	709.881	6.925938***	0.880333
-9	38.69683	748.5778	6.83531***	-2.35465***
-8	15.92628	764.5041	7.892466***	-0.91879
-7	21.66407	786.1682	7.221527***	-0.36189
-6	30.55656	816.7248	3.64167***	-1.39356
-5	-5.88057	810.8442	-0.07564	-4.10344***
-4	-4.61235	806.2318	-8.9581***	2.327987***
-3	-10.6729	795.559	-10.7901***	1.922547***
-2	-11.7929	783.766	5.956569***	-0.21686
-1	-2.95766	780.8084	0.912088	0.027768
0	-62.2035	718.6049	-10.116***	1.510859
1	24.87946	743.4844	0.47907	-0.36189
2	-5.17036	738.314	-2.62403***	-1.39356
3	-10.3684	727.9456	-4.83808***	-4.10344***
4	-75.299	652.6466	-6.86146***	2.327987***
5	-16.9212	635.7254	-10.341***	0.027768
6	14.22801	649.9534	-0.38837	1.510859
7	-32.0677	617.8857	-14.791***	-2.05599***
8	23.0992	640.9849	11.98783***	-0.34124
9	-0.5013	640.4836	1.109314	1.181289
10	-12.8206	627.663	4.011083***	-2.1248***
20	-0.86134	654.7495	-1.78881**	-1.44569

		GDR		
DAYS	AAR	CAAR	AAR t –sta	CAAR t-sta
30	-31.6689	580.6549	-0.40477	4.296426***
40	2.976752	440.1789	7.01638***	-3.37294***
50	28.1115	430.4917	13.13335***	-0.22221
60	16.92277	352.5978	-3.82407***	-1.0489
70	12.06438	340.2146	7.802453***	-2.74448***
80	5.676915	326.3363	10.06192***	-1.51951
90	-19.8232	265.9103	-9.11456***	0.363962
100	0.04626	189.8347	-12.4342***	-1.59219
110	2.669954	173.6617	7.394032***	0.880333
120	13.49402	253.3937	6.599647***	-1.59219
130	-23.5737	164.0876	0.123347	0.880333
140	11.68926	263.2237	-8.29671***	-2.35465***
150	-8.04774	150.3946	1.308528	-0.91879
160	-20.6026	101.3334	-0.2423	-0.36189
170	6.506933	76.68621	-7.12394***	-1.39356
175	20.43655	107.2683	-1.79301**	-4.10344***

Table depicts average abnormal returns, cumulative average abnormal returns and their t-statistics of stocks listed on Luxembourg Stock Exchange. Table depicts 175 days pre announcement of cross listing, starting from day $t_{(-175)}$ to day $t_{(-1)}$, there is a positive average abnormal returns.

The AAR and CAAR's are calculated period from 175 days prior to listings to 175 days after the listings for each of the 40 DRs. There is evidence of increase in the returns in the pre listing period. The increasing pattern starts declining in the post listing period. The returns are positive for approximately 107 days while they are negative for 78 days in the pre listing period. From the 107 positive AAR values, 82 values are statistically significant at 1%, 22 are significant at 5% & 19 are significant at 10%. This explains that there is price run up of underlying shares in the pre listing period. Daily AAR becomes significantly negative on and around the listing date. 7 days prior to listings and 7 days after the listings average abnormal returns turns out to be negative. The results show negative stock price reaction on the listing announcement date with an AAR of -62.2035% and statistically significant at 1% level with a t-statistics of -10.116. During the post announcement window from day $t_{(1)}$ to day $t_{(175)}$, the pattern of positive AARs changes to negative pattern of returns. It has been observed that the AARs values are negative for nearly 95 days. From the 83 positive AAR values of post announcement, 65values are significant at 1%, 15 values is significant at 5% & 5values are significant at 10%.

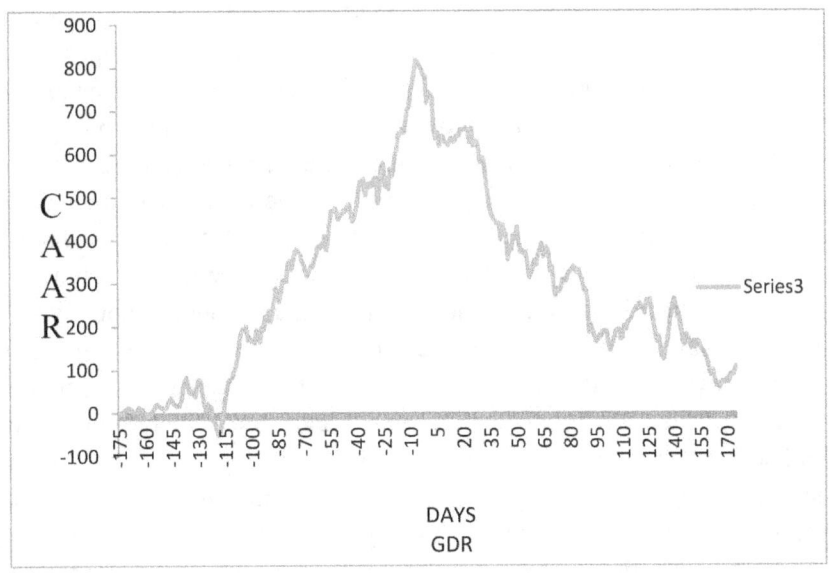

Figure:- 4.1.9 Cumulative Average Abnormal Returns during the event window listed through GDR.

The returns are cumulated over the event window to assess the net magnitude of the overall returns. Table represents cumulative average abnormal returns (CAAR) for each day during the 350 day event window & their corresponding t-statistics values. The results indicate that till day $t_{(-116)}$, CAAR does not illustrate any obvious pattern, but from day $t_{(-115)}$ onwards, CAAR starts becoming positive. The CAAR value of day $t_{(-115)}$ starts from 34.82551, reaches a peak of 816.7285 percent on $t_{(-6)}$ after that even though the CAAR is positive, but at an decreasing rate. At $t_{(-1)}$ CAAR value is 780.8084, at $t_{(0)}$ the value decreased to 718.6049. This decline CAAR is due to the fact that AAR values are mostly positive till day $t_{(1)}$, by & large negative during the post announcement window. The CAAR values around event window $t_{(0)}$ is 718.6049 which is statistically insignificant. From the 175 CAAR values of pre-listing period 125 values are statistically significant at 1%, 21 are significant at 5% & 14 are significant at 10%. This indicates that there is price run up of underlying shares in the pre listing period. The results show a decreasing stock price reaction on & around the listing announcement date. In the post listing period, out of 175 CAAR value which are decreasing rate, 54 are statistically significant at 1%, 21 values are significant at 5%, 7 values are significant at 10%.

4.1.6   CONCLUSION:

This section finds the impact of cross listings on the Indian stock returns. The study evaluates the cross listing impact on the Indian stocks listed on London stock exchange, Luxembourg stock exchange, New york stock exchange separately. More research has been done before on this issue. Traditional event study methodology was used, six months before & six months after cross listings announcement, 40 companies' data was taken & cumulative average abnormal returns & normal returns were drawn.

Study has considered 175 days as an event window for all the companies. 175 days pre announcement of cross listing, starting from day $t_{(-175)}$ to day $t_{(-1)}$, there is a positive average abnormal returns. The returns are positive for approximately 120 days while they are negative for only 50 days. From the 120 positive AAR values, 104 values are statistically significant at 1%, 12 values are significant at 5% & 6 values are significant at 10%. The negative returns are not significant on any of the 50 days. During the post announcement window from day $t_{(1)}$ to day $t_{(175)}$, the pattern of positive AARs changes to negative pattern of returns. It has been observed that the AARs values are negative for nearly 115 days. From the 60 positive AAR values of post announcement, 50 values are significant at 1%, 9 values are significant at 5% & 2 values are significant at 10%. Looking at the speed of the share price adjustment to the new information emanating from the cross listings announcement, study observed that there is no lagging response to the cross listings announcement. The observed results indicate that the investors perceive the announcement stock listings to be beneficial for them. Although the change of positive reaction prior to and on the announcement day to negative reaction, and after the announcement day indicates that the investors overreacted initially to these announcement, but a correction takes place quickly & positive returns turns to negative. The rationale for such results seems to be that the information about the event listing announcement reaches to the investors companies prior to the decision date as it will be mandatory for the listings companies to inform the exchanges and public regarding where it is listed locally, where it want to get listed itself on internationally stock exchanges through ADRs or GDRs. It has been observed that the companies usually inform the public around one month prior date of announcement. In such a situation, the moment the listings information about meeting & agenda is given publically, this becomes public information & investors starts reacting to it. In the pre listing period positive reaction clearly indicates that investors perceive stock cross listings to be beneficial for them. This further leads to an increase in the demand for the issuing companies' shares leading to the positive abnormal returns. AAR on the day of listing is also substantial indicating that the moment the decision of cross listing announced, its stocks jumps high, providing positive AAR to the investors. Later, a correction takes place & the AARs become negative. This result suggests that the Indian stock market responds quickly & efficiently to the corporate news contained in cross listing announcement.

The returns are cumulated over the event window to assess the net magnitude of the overall performance of the stocks. In the CAAR graph it has been observed that the increasing trend of returns starts declining after cross listing.

Similar studies have been observed for sample of GDR listed Indian firms, ADR listed firms, NYSE listed firms, LSE listed firms, and LUXSE listed firms. Separate analysis has been done for different stock exchanges. For all the samples, there is a clear evidence of increase in prices in the pre listing period & decrease in prices in the post- listing period.

From the present study it can be concluded that stock returns are affected by the cross listing announcements. It has been observed positive average abnormal returns prior to cross listings announcement, AAR is insignificantly negative after the cross listings. Indian firms deciding to list on a foreign exchange to increase their returns must take into account various factors such as market conditions, industry trends & listing & disclosure requirements, tax issues etc. Hence, it can be concluded that cross listings through ADRs and GDRs does not get any significant financial benefit for the stock investors.

4.2   Impact of Cross Listing on the Indian Stock Liquidity

Introduction:

Cross-listing advocates argue that cross-listing is advantageous for both the listed company and its Investors; a Depositary Receipt (DR) program is one such method to cross-list. It is suggested that by cross-listing, the firm can diversify and broaden their investor base, potentially enhancing liquidity.

Additionally, exposure to the global marketplace can strengthen the profile of the company, leading to heightened visibility, analyst following and media coverage. Benefits can also accrue to DR investors. Liquidity in secondary markets determines the success of public offerings, reduces the cost and risk for underwriters and market makers. It also reduces the cost for investors via ensuring lower volatility and transaction cost. Thus, from a macro perspective, liquid capital markets are essential for the efficient allocation of capital, which results in lower cost of capital for issuers. At the micro level, a liquid market ensures access to a diverse range of investors with various trading strategies (IOSCO).

Trading in the investor's home market reduces the cost of investing in an internationally diversified Portfolio; costly currency conversions and high transaction costs are averted.

Liquidity plays an important role in financial markets. The improvement and consistency of market liquidity is important for market participants and serves as a way to enhance financial market credibility. Without liquidity information, markets cannot provide exact price signals to shareholders and corporations, which plays a crucial role for efficient risk sharing and investment decision making.

Liquidity has multiple dimensions; it does not have a unique definition. Liquidity is the ability of trading assets quickly without manipulating prices. Liquidity is the easy way at which securities can be bought and sold in the market without significantly affecting stock price. Liquidity is an important attribute of common stocks because of its potential effect on the value of shares. Liquidity is an essential feature for the success of any exchange. As the liquidity of a stock (or the market) increases, the greater the access available to investors; this increased visibility can be exhibited through a tightening/reduction in the bid-ask spread or an increase in turnover (or a combination of both).

To examine the impact of cross listings on the liquidity, three commonly measures from the literature reviewed (Mehta, Jain & Yadav 2014, Olga 2011) have been employed. These measures use trading volume and stock price data to depict liquidity, higher the value of measure higher is the liquidity. Traditional measures of market liquidity include trade volume (or the number of trades), market turnover, bid-ask spreads and trading velocity. Additionally, liquidity also depends on many macroeconomic and market fundamentals. These include a country's fiscal policy, exchange rate regime as well the overall regulatory environment. Market sentiment and investor confidence are also key to improving liquidity conditions. On a more micro level, the type of instruments traded, the nature of participants involved as well as the structure of the market will have a significant impact on market liquidity. Market liquidity, an important factor that affects market efficiency, is primarily determined by the effectiveness and efficiency of the market's price discovery function. For instance, the uncertainty as to the execution price is low for liquid markets. This does not necessarily imply that the execution price is identical to the mid-price of the bid-ask spread; but rather that the deviation between the two should be predictable and minimal. In practice, this is likely to be associated with low and stable bid-ask spreads. Liquid markets should therefore facilitate entry and exit in a manner that is least disruptive i.e. at minimal loss to nominal values, low transaction costs, and within a short time frame. The more liquid a market, the wider the set of potential counter offers for any outstanding transaction, and hence the higher the probability of a favorable match. Thus, investors are generally attracted to markets with higher levels of liquidity. Therefore, liquidity is crucial to both the growth and development of markets. Market liquidity is also crucial to financial system stability as a liquid market is able to better absorb systemic shocks. For instance, a liquid market is able to cushion the price volatility brought about by sudden shifts in investor risk appetite. This in turn helps to limit the potential adverse knock-on effects on the rest of the financial system as well as the broad economy. Given its importance, it is therefore understandable why regulators place such a strong emphasis on improving overall market liquidity. Indeed, many regulatory, developmental and reform efforts within emerging markets are seen as having the key objective of establishing deep and liquid markets. The presence of liquid markets would in turn ensure a higher degree of investor confidence and market efficiency, and hence render the market more resilient.

Finance theories and empirical findings suggest that the liquidity of securities lower the cost of capital, which in turn has a favorable impact on share prices (Amihud and Mendelson, 1986). The present study examines how pre-listing liquidity of Indian shares affects the behavior of the market around event date.

Three liquidity measures are estimated for each stock over the period of 175 days with an event window of -175 to -25. The full sample is divided at the median into low and high liquidity sub-samples. Two tail t-tests are used to examine how the stock return for the low liquidity group differs significantly from the return of the high liquidity group.

In order to test the impact of cross listings on home market trading volume I first searched the overall trading volume behavior around the listing date. The liquidity of cross listed stocks is compared against the liquidity of 40 domestic stocks from the same countries. Several studies have been done to find an impact of cross listings on liquidity. This study contributes to the debate by providing evidence on the evolution of stock liquidity around cross listing and cross trading and their long run sustainability. The change in stock liquidity is evaluated in a time series frame work against those of the cross listed stocks over the pre-cross listing period of time.

The primary empirical finding is that cross-listing and cross-trading on a foreign market improve the liquidity of a stock. In the case of liquidity, this is also true in comparison to the pre-cross-listing/trading period of time. After controlling for the effects of factors that are known to affect stock liquidity and for the change in company characteristics after cross-listing/ cross-trading in the multivariate analysis, it is found that a presence on a foreign exchange, either through cross-listing or cross-trading, is associated with a significantly reduced bid-ask spread, increased trading volumes, Home market stock turnover does not improve after cross-listing. The documented effects of cross-listing and cross-trading are found to be sustained over a long period of time following the cross- listing/ cross-trading event.

Cross-listings on deeper and more liquid equity markets could lead to an increase in the liquidity of the stock and a decrease in the cost of capital. Foerster and Karolyi (1998) state that cross listings of Canadian firms in the US are associated with an increase in trading volume and a decline in effective bid-ask spreads. Smith and Sofianos (1997) document a substantial increase in the combined value of trading for a sample of foreign listings on New York Securities Exchange (NYSE). Silva and Chávez (2008) find that Latin American firms with an American Depository Receipts (ADR) do not always exhibit a liquidity advantage in the local market. Halling et al. (2008) document that for cross-listings on US exchanges, the fraction of trading that occurs on the destination market is greater for firms from countries that are geographically close to the US and for firms from less developed countries.

Mittoo (1992) and Bancel and Mittoo (2001) report, on the basis a survey done with Canadian and European firms, that managers perceive that international cross listing increase the total trading volume of the share of a firm. In fact several studies have looked upon the effects of cross listing on trading volume. Karolyi (1998) concludes that there is evidence that the total volume of trading increases following an international cross listing. In many cases the evidence shows that trading volume in the home market also increases. While Levine and Schmukler (2003) find a reduction in the trading volume of cross listed shares in the home market, Halling,et al. (2008) report that the increase in trading volume that occurs in the international market immediately after the international cross listing is followed by a decline later on.karolyi (2004) reports a significant positive relationship between the number of cross listings and a subsequent increase in the aggregate liquidity of the originating home market. This result seems to be driven by an increase in the liquidity of cross listed shares with no spillover effects for the other (non-cross listed) stocks. Thus the ratio of the turnover of non-cross listed and total home turnover necessarily decreases. Fernandes & Ferreira (2005) analyses the impact of the first ADR on the liquidity of non-cross listed home stocks and finds a positive effect. The study concludes that DR listings enhance the liquidity of the underlying shares following international cross listings. Kumar (2004) observed the overall volumes of the market had decreased in the post listing period. Mellon (2007) study concludes that DR program established by firms add significant value and improve home market liquidity to the benefit of both issuer and investors. Stoyan, novozhilova, kartashov, lemasson and Noronha (1996) concludes that there was no significant change in liquidity post cross listings. Arturo, salvatore & George (2006) states that liquidity of both stocks listed or unlisted in domestic market increases significantly. Gheaus(2010) states that cross listed stock firms experience a statistically significant increase in their home market liquidity following cross listings.

This study contributes to the literature by examining the impact of cross listings on the stock liquidity. More specifically, the main research question is: Does cross listings improve the stock liquidity? Cross listed stocks are expected to have a higher liquidity and lower return volatility compared to domestic stocks. Several measures are considered to capture various dimensions of stock liquidity, including trading volume, trading turnover. The impact of cross listings is evaluated in a multivariate framework after controlling the other factors such as company size, accounting practices, analyst and trading activity which potentially affect the stock liquidity. To find the impact of cross listings on the Indian stock liquidity, the following hypothesis is framed.

Hypothesis 2 H_0: There is no significant impact on liquidity of the underlying domestic Indian stocks due to cross listings.

EMPIRICAL RESULTS:-

4.2.1 DR Impact on Indian Stock liquidity by mean trading turnover

Average Stock Trading Turnover Pre and Post DR Listing

TURN OVER				
COMPANY	BEFORE LISTING	AFTER LISTING	DIFFERENCE	calculated t-value
APTECH	282147570	214956851.3	67190718.71	2.075572998***
AXIS BANK	395156440	303479390	91677050	1.575720702
BAJAJ HOLDING	460760316.6	129910146	330850170.6	9.545437804***
CIPLA	1967737520	734618859.9	1233118660	4.242868269***
DISH TV	248272134	152064558.3	96207575.73	4.637370897***
ELECTRO STEEL CASTING LTD	2596526621	732856632	1863669989	2.899677963***
FEDERAL BANK	772983963	471784979	301198984	3.707781849***
FINANCIAL TECNOLOGIES	3781.253265	2403.662	1377.591265	4.258901623***

TURN OVER				
COMPANY	BEFORE LISTING	AFTER LISTING	DIFFERENCE	calculated t-value
GAIL LTD	76.87946552	39.7857	37.09376552	2.969866078***
GEETANJALI JEWELLERS	124974203	181859704.8	-56885501.83	-2.379963962***
HDFC	504.9255725	379.4019	125.5236725	1.566012241
HINDUJHA FOUNDARIES	1732564.051	580950.6697	1151613.381	3.193408222***
HINDUSTAN CONSTRUCTIONS	82730711	79736025.35	2994685.653	0.261458762
ICICI BANK	26709623.47	24395938	2313685.47	0.584208285
INFOSYS LTD	13370549411	11793412379	1577137032	1.37145284
JINDAL COTEX	44427312	49024305.55	-4596993.547	-0.215665058
JINDAL STAINLESS STEEL	1080269.886	272171	808098.8857	4.442818475***
KARURTURI GLOBAL	184557835	115756787.7	68801047.25	1.949641116*
KOTAK MAHINDRA	74842533	80347953.7	-5505420.701	-0.495293773
LIC FINANCING	17672146	39729932.87	-22057786.87	-5.13871181***
LLYOD ELECTRICALS LTD	18224049.64	17368873	855176.6396	0.329374596
NEHA INTERNATIONAL	46903577.79	8401632	38501945.79	3.040555434***
NISSAN COPPER	1569769	10434718.18	-8864949.182	-3.328449194***
NOIDA TOLL BRIDGE	24770360	40846141.9	-16075781.9	-2.405398911**
REI AGRO LTD	185739511.7	384614005.8	-198874494	-3.510334154***
RELIANCE COM	1633233552	1987574333	-354340780.9	-2.06034177**
STERLITE LTD	65835062	105723769.2	-39888707.25	-3.358124708***
SUBEX	23232506	22150890.5	1081615.5	0.212781743
SUZLON ENERGY	3394394240	287072947	3107321293	1.715391496*
TATA GLOBAL BEVERAGES	1320825732	975321301.7	345504430.3	3.678642298***
TATA MOTORS	2210803287	1195773721	1015029566	14.44378417***
VIDEOCON	4218479.772	9422712.116	-5204232.343	-2.114839341***
WIPRO	937294980.4	1508062565	-570767584.7	-5.43426138***
ZYLOG	42238099.72	3687440.097	38550659.62	6.234257509***
ANANTH RAJ	22561697.06	8505309	14056388.06	2.70224174***
APOLLO	54899462	47887559.65	7011902.346	0.768854708
INDUSIND BANK	68134032	71269650.53	-3135618.526	0.270967409
RELIANCE CAPITAL	1386333762	830427962.8	555905798.7	9.16207302***
UNITED SPIRITS	455642823.1	292746854.1	162895969	-3.9752259***
ROLTA INDIA	331981842.3	158104806	173877036.3	6.660515716***

TURN OVER				
COMPANY	BEFORE LISTING	AFTER LISTING	DIFFERENCE	calculated t-value
SEL MANUFACTURING CO LTD	682997.619	2990095.238	-2307097.619	-5.026006363***

***, **,* significant at 1%, 5% & 10%

Table No. 4.2.1 Average Stock Trading Turnover Pre and Post DR Listing

Table reports the empirical results of the impact of cross listings on the liquidity of local stocks by using mean trading turnover. It is evident from the table the impact of cross listings on various liquidity measures varies. Out of 40 companies, 30 companies have decreased stock trading turnover in the post listing period. Using daily trading turnover data for a period of 175 days before and after the event window from home market, the study shares that cross listed stocks experience a decline in the level of trading turnover following listings. Last column in the table shows the results of paired t-test in the stock trading turnover for each firm around the time it lists its DR program on the international market. Stock trading turnover with a significance level 1%, 5% and 10% have been used for the study against a null hypothesis of a zero difference in the stock trading turnover. T-test signifies that 26 companies trading turnover is significant at 1%, 2 companies are significant at 5% & 2 companies are significant at 10% level of significance. Out of 30 companies whose stock trading turnover is decreased in the post listing period, 19 are significant which signifies that DR listings have a significant impact on stock trading turnover. Out of 10 companies whose stock trading turnover is increasing in the post listing period are significant at 1% and 5%.

4.2.2   DR Impact on Indian Stock liquidity by average means trading turnover

Table 4.2.2 Average Stock Trading Turnover Pre & Post DR Listing (All Markets)

STOCK MARKET	PRE-LISTING	POST-LISTING	% CHANGE	T-CAL VALUE
ALL MARKET	745744827.4	559307787.3	-25.00011	1.977878212**

***, **,* significant at 1%, 5% & 10%

Table above explains about the overall the market. Stock trading turnover have decreased in the post listing period with a decrease in percentage change of -25.00011%. It is statistically significant at 5%.

4.2.3   DR Impact on Indian Stock liquidity by means trading turnover (stock exchange wise)

Table 4.2.3 Average Stock Trading Turnover Pre & Post DR Listing

STOCK MARKET	PRE-LISTING	POST-LISTING	% CHANGE	T-CAL VALUE
ADRS				
NYSE	2816811925	2536444435	-9.95336	0.82504374
GDRS	390704753.5	220370076.3	-43.5968	1.768022945*
LSE	194267061	140664199	-27.5924	1.027933731
LUXSE	469279830.5	252252427.2	-46.2469	1.632062128

***, **,* significant at 1%, 5% & 10%

Table above explains that there is a decrease in the stock trading turnover in the post listing period which says that DRs are having a significant impact on stock trading turnover. GDRs are significant at 10% level of significance.

4.2.4   DR Impact on Indian Stock liquidity by mean trading volume
Average Trading Volume of DR Listing

COMPANY	VOLUME			
	BEFORE LISTING	AFTER LISTING	DIFFERENCE	calculated t-value
APTECH	952602.1	685410.9	267191.2	-5.59139988***
AXIS BANK	1813777	1301820.833	511956.1667	1.950025714*
BAJAJ HOLDING	189747.0149	253311.194	-63564.1791	-1.71783566*
CIPLA	932530.661	1964872.559	-1032341.89	-6.6678452***
Dr. Reddy's Laboratories	438566.4286	758927.1429	-320360.714	-5.5913998***
DISH TV	6361463	3073142.629	3288320.371	7.23653454***
FEDERAL BANK	4246261	2512474	1733787	4.01893189***
GEETANJALI JEWELLERS	529081	503611.4943	25469.50575	0.37221837
HINDUJHA FOUNDARIES	9875	4485.795455	5389.204545	2.3772616**
HINDUSTAN CONSTRUCTIONS	1111644	1245364.444	-133720.444	-0.98772426
ICICI BANK	242614.616	116432.6	126182.016	5.55815297***
INFOSYS LTD	5847197.842	5632595.683	214602.1583	0.538609095
JINDAL COTEX	454032.8	396942.9688	57089.83125	0.32126563
JINDAL STAINLESS STEEL	123.2092857	122.5671	0.642185714	0.247874405
KARURTURI GLOBAL	7808323	5032838.732	2775484.268	2.303794739**
KOTAK MAHINDRA	310998.9	287235.6356	23763.26441	0.536635748
LIC FINANCING	111009	202251.2121	-91242.2121	-4.1480165***
LLYOD ELECTRICALS	138679.2793	112082	26597.27928	1.37000851
NEHA INTERNATIONAL	228307.0588	63298.24	165008.8188	3.18151666***
NISSAN COPPER	44761.36	280427.2727	-235665.913	-3.7243503***
NOIDA TOLL BRIDGE	728631	869491.4729	-140860.472	-1.0585595
REI AGRO LTD	1643527.419	5042916	-3399388.58	-4.5978860***
RELIANCE COMMUNICATIONS	5785961	5013432.692	772528.3077	1.739768965*
STERLITE LTD	624621	842088.2617	-217467.261	-2.34582814**
SUBEX	39353.33	45003.33333	-5650.00333	-0.68876567
SEL MANUFACTURING CO LTD	682997.619	2990095.238	-2307097.61	-5.0260063***
SUZLON ENERGY	42161060.45	33748607	8412453.448	2.76808000***

VOLUME				
COMPANY	BEFORE LISTING	AFTER LISTING	DIFFERENCE	calculated t-value
TATA GLOBAL BEVERAGES	4119768	2562114.394	1557653.606	5.56767983***
TATA MOTORS	5446654.876	2602557	2844097.876	16.3974456***
VIDEOCON	10503.45	22101.72414	-11598.2741	-1.96062135**
WIPRO	381583.4074	650089.7	-268506.292	-8.9195392***
ZYLOG	327750.6951	193855	133895.6951	1.684763029*
ANANTH RAJ	53809.96694	45564	8245.966942	0.562002726
APOLLO	168631	110757.876	57873.12403	2.435247026**
INDUSIND BANK	1375195	1363733.475	11461.525	-0.05776945
RELIANCE CAPITAL	2881537.512	1439831.713	1441705.798	12.0212673***
UNITED SPIRITS	870592	385161.3109	485430.6891	6.99292040***
ROLTA INDIA	3580928.808	1626590	1954338.808	6.91684756***

***, **,* significant at 1%, 5% & 10%

Table reports the empirical results of the impact of cross listings on the liquidity of local stocks by using mean trading volume. It is evident from the table the impact of cross listings on various liquidity measures varies. Out of 40 companies, 27 companies have decreased stock trading volume in the post listing period. Using daily trading volume data for a period of 175 days before and after the event window from home market, the study shares that cross listed stocks experience a decline in the level of trading volume following listings. Last column in the table shows the results of paired t-test in the stock trading volume for each firm around the time it lists its DR program on the international market. Stock trading volume with a significance level 1%, 5% and 10% have been used for the study against a null hypothesis of a zero difference in the stock trading volume. T-test signifies that 27 companies trading volume are significant at 1%, 5% & 10%. Out of 27 companies, 10 companies trading volume are significant at 1%, 3 companies are significant at 5% & 4 companies are significant at 10% level of significance. Out of 27 companies whose stock trading turnover is decreased in the post listing period, 17 companies are significant which signifies that DR listings have a significant impact on stock trading volume. Out of 10 companies whose stock trading turnover is increasing in the post listing period, 8 companies are significant at 1%, 1 company is significant at 5% and 10%.

4.2.5   DR Impact on Indian Stock liquidity by mean trading volume (stock exchange wise)

Average Stock Trading Volume Pre & DR Listing

STOCK MARKET	PRE-LISTING	POST LISTING	% CHANGE	T-CAL VALUE
ADRS				
NYSE	2163539.695	1767115.065	-18.323	0.796576805
GDRS	2846052.231	2299740.052	-19.1954	1.669749437
LSE	1387026.106	1370684.937	-1.17814	0.028504663
LUXSE	3312940.591	2597037.689	-21.6093	1.831514569

***, **,* significant at 1%, 5% & 10%

Table above explains that there is a decrease in the stock trading volume in the post listing period which says that DRs are having a significant impact on stock trading volume. GDRs are significant at 10% level of significance.

4.2.6   DR Impact on Indian Stock liquidity by mean trading volume (All markets)

Average Stock Trading Volume Pre & Post DR Listing

STOCK MARKET	PRE-LISTING	POST-LISTING	% CHANGE	T-CAL VALUE
ALL MARKET	2701439.49	2210043.11	-18.1901682	1.68849541

***, **,* significant at 1%, 5% & 10%

Table above explains about the overall the market. Stock trading turnover have decreased in the post listing period with a decrease in percentage change of -18.1901682 %. It is statistically significant at 5%.

4.2.7   DR Impact on Indian Stock liquidity by Amivest Ratio

Average Stock Trading Amivest ratio Pre and Post DR Listing

Company	Amivest ratio			
	pre-li	post-li	Difference	t-value
Aptech	271573.8	131626	139947.883	0.722678
Apollo Hospitals	110954.6	35378.77	75575.8103	0.779517
Axis Bank	248886.5	964302.5	-715415.91	-0.7352
Bajaj holdings	-1226627	-48966.2	-1177660.3	-1.53011
Crompton greaves	5063.191	397.4427	4665.74807	2.071946*
Dish TV India	39897.68	392832.9	-352935.23	-0.31674
DR reddys lab	-814299	-106586	-707712.85	-1.0559
Electro steel casting	2677732	-1117167	3794899.74	2.278674*
Federal Bank	2642361	423590.3	2218770.5	0.94282
financial technologies	1559.173	2580.586	-1021.4128	-0.34787
Gail ltd	-5.3E+07	-8152259	-44350885	-0.7922
Geetanjali jewelers	-31806	184123.2	-215929.12	-1.14283
HDFC	183223.8	-75281.3	258505.099	1.274259
Hinduja foundries	78.8709	-2619.16	2698.03267	0.668289
Hindustan construction	734735.6	177603.3	557132.353	0.680151
ICICI bank	16623.97	-42744.6	59368.5736	0.715156
Indus India bank	101924.5	20194.72	81729.741	0.421599
Infosys	-1.7E+07	-3003565	-13562338	-1.26269
Jindal	60.49612	-2.10217	62.598284	1.21939
Jindal cotex	-60880.8	-32054.9	-28825.917	-0.12384

Company	Amivest ratio		Difference	t-value
	pre-li	post-li		
karurti global	67065.84	-1840172	1907238.04	1.551369
Kotak Mahindra	0.520862	0.154477	0.36638508	0.799881
LIC financing	12448.25	18259.01	-5810.7592	-0.0594
Lloyd electrical	3811.037	-16655.5	20466.5143	0.537763
neha international	347.2845	-18514.4	18861.6589	0.616259
Nissan copper	0.358217	-0.52992	0.88813926	1.026875
Noida toll bridge	-186936	37130.45	-224066.32	-1.69354**
rei agro	-1553305	-247106	-1306199.3	-1.0022
reliance capital	-904158	-663579	-240579.06	-0.22795
reliance communications	662374.5	2236153	-1573778.3	-0.54508
Rolta India	-171818	1640962	-1812780.5	2.387763***
Sel manufacturing	274178.2	-638742	912920.132	2.050759*
Sterlite	-8579.97	275722.6	-284302.57	-1.07304**
Subex	-79966.5	19448.89	-99415.416	-1.31404
Suzlonenergy	-1357452	-6070987	4713535.14	0.537323
Tata global beverages	3318572	5324911	-2006339	-0.67863
Tata motors	-2913081	-2146598	-766483.57	-0.17031
united spirit	-415934	480175.7	-896109.9	-1.5525
Videocon	823.8458	1781.192	-957.34594	-0.07385
Wipro	-50916.9	-44615.7	-6301.2155	-0.0684

***, **,* significant at 1%, 5% & 10%

Table reports the empirical results of the impact of cross listings on the liquidity of local stocks by using Amivest Ratio. It is evident from the table the impact of cross listings on various liquidity measures varies. Out of 40 companies, 18 companies have decreased stock Amivest ratio in the post listing period, 22 companies have increased Amivest ratio in the post listing period. Using daily trading Amivest ratio for a period of 175 days before and after the event window from home market, the study shares that cross listed stocks experience a decline in the level of trading volume following listings. Last column in the table shows the results of paired t-test in the stock Amivest ratio for each firm around the time it lists its DR program on the international market. Stock trading Amivest ratio with a significance level 1%, 5% and 10% have been used for the study against a null hypothesis of a zero difference in the Amivest ratio. T-test signifies that 6 companies Amivest ratio is significant at 1%, 5% & 10%. Out of 6 companies, 1 company Amivest ratio is significant at 1%, 2 companies are significant at 5% & 3 companies are significant at 10% level of significance. Out of 3 companies whose stock trading turnover is decreased in the post listing period, 3 companies are significant which signifies that DR listings have a significant impact on stock trading liquidity. Out of 3 companies whose stock trading turnover is increasing in the post listing period, 1 company is significant at 1%, 2 company are significant at 5%.

4.2.8   DR Impact on Indian Stock liquidity by Amivest Ratio (all markets)

Average Stock Trading Amivest Ratio Pre & Post DR Listing

STOCK MARKET	PRE-LISTING	POST LISTING	DIFFERENCE	% CHANGE	T-CAL VALUE
ADRS					
NYSE	-3389359	-844731	-2544628	-75.077	-1.15245
GDRS	-1376040	-160957	-1215083	-88.3029	-0.91624
LSE	-5310587	-615715	-4694872	-88.4059	-1.06227
LUXSE	263354.4	28525.44	234828.9	-89.1684	0.834265

***, **,* significant at 1%, 5% & 10%

Table above explains that there is increase in the stock Amivest ratio in the post listing period which says that DRs are having a significant impact on Amivest ratio. No DR is significant.

4.2.9   DR Impact on Indian Stock liquidity by Amivest ratio (Stock exchange wise)

Average Stock Amivest Ratio Pre & Post DR Listing

STOCK MARKET	PRE-LISTING	POST-LISTING	DIFFERENCE	% CHANGE	T-CAL VALUE
ALL MARKET	-1686762.759	-297526.0447	-1389237	-82.3611	-1.1872882

***, **,* significant at 1%, 5% & 10%

Table above explains about the overall the market. Stock Amivest ratios have increased in the post listing period with a decrease in percentage change of -1.187288268 %. Not significant.

4.2.10   Conclusion:-

This part of the section covers the impact of cross listings on the Indian stocks liquidity. Study tests the impact of DRs by examining the changes in stock liquidity. Sample of the study includes Indian companies listed through ADRs & GDRs on NYSE, LSE, and LUXSE. It is evident from the tables the impact of stock cross listings announcements on various liquidity measures varies. To find the impact three liquidity measures have been used, trading volume, turnover & Amivest ratio. Liquidity as a concept of trading quantity reduces significantly after the cross listings announcements. The average trading volume after the cross listings announcements has reduced significantly by - 18.1901682% compared to pre- listing period & is statistically significant at 5%. Stock trading turnover reduced significantly after these cross listings announcements. The average trading turnover has reduced by -25.00011% compared to pre-listing period which is significant at 5%. The stock mean Amivest ratio has increased after cross listings announcements with 82.3611%. The magnitude and direction of change for the first two measures are almost similar for 175 days period of time i.e. impact of cross listings decreased the liquidity, while in the case of Amivest ratio the results are mixed. The mean Amivest ratio for 175 days period increased by -82.3611%. A more liquid market should have a larger Amivest ratio, which says that DR market is more liquid market. The probable reason for this seems to be that the investor perceives the announcements of stock cross listings as providing signals about the firm's bright future prospects. Probably, the investors who own the shares at the time of cross listing announcement prefer to hold the shares expecting an increase in their wealth in future leading to decline in the liquidity. The information environment plays an important role in affecting the liquidity. The enhanced information environment affects the liquidity positively.

Similar results have been recorded for sample of GDR listed Indian firms, ADR listed firms, NYSE listed firms, LSE listed firms, and LUXSE listed firms. Separate analysis has been done for different stock exchanges. For all the samples, there is a clear evidence of decrease in liquidity in the post listing period. Hence, it can be concluded that stock liquidity are affected by the cross listings announcements.

4.3   Impact Of Cross Listing on the Indian Stock Price

Introduction

International capital flows are playing a very important role, but there are hampered by different barriers such as transaction costs, information costs & legal requirements. One of the aspects of globalization is the listing of firm's equity securities on international stock exchange. The answer for this problem is cross listings through depository receipts.

Numerous earlier researches have been carried out in this area of cross listings through depository receipts both in India and overseas. Kato, Linn, and Schallheim (1991) investigate the underlying share and ADR prices of 8 Australian, 7 English, and 8 Japanese firms. Their findings show no significant differences between the prices, and thus no arbitrage opportunities seem to exist. Rosenthal and Young (1990) examine two Anglo-Dutch groups (Unilever and Royal/Dutch Shell) which trade on the London Stock Exchange, on the Amsterdam Stock Exchange, and as ADRs on the NYSE. Although they report persistent deviations from the theoretical pricing relationships, the direction and the magnitude of the mispricing is not sufficiently large enough to formulate profitable intra- or inter market trading rules. Kim, Mathur, and Szakmary (1995) examine 21 Japanese, 21 British, 5 Dutch, 5 Swedish, and 4 Australian companies which trade as ADRs in the US. To investigate informational efficiency and the dynamics of information transmission of ADRs and underlying shares, they perform multivariate cointegration tests and a vector autoregressive analysis (VAR). Their results show that ADRs respond to unexpected movements in the underlying shares, the S & P 500 index, the domestic index, informationally and the exchange rate, implying that ADR markets are efficient. Moreover, their findings show that currency shocks have become a more important factor for pricing ADRs in recent years.

To explore the transmission of pricing information for identical assets trading in different markets, Garbade and Silber (1979) develop a model that examines short-run relationships for dually- traded securities on the NYSE, the Midwest Exchange (MSE), and the Pacific Stock Exchange (PSE). Their results indicate that regional market prices always adjust to NYSE prices. Hence, the NYSE is the dominant market while the regional stock exchanges are satellites of NYSE. The "Garbade Silber approach" is also used by Pagano and Roell (1991 to investigate whether the London market for Italian equities and the Milan Stock Exchange are integrated. Their examination of the direction of information flows between both markets shows that a mutual feedback relationship over time between prices exists but in most cases Milan stock exchange seems to lead London stock exchange. Chakraborti (2003) reports there are several dimensions likely to influence the dynamics of ADR prices and volume. Research also mentions that, due to ADRs dollar- price entitlements to foreign shares, movements in prices and returns are naturally expected to be affected by those in the underlying shares and the exchange rates. Saxena (2005) analyzed the relationship in the ADR prices with the underlying equity prices, and concludes that ADR prices do not move in lock- step with the underlying equity prices. Kato, Linn, and Schallheim (2008) claims that there are no significant differences between the prices of these two identical types of claims, no arbitrage opportunity existing between the international capital markets encompassed in the study. Patel (2015) investigated the dynamic linkages between American depository receipts and their respective underlying stock prices of Indian stock market. He applied five proxies to find the linkages- augmented Dickey-Fuller unit root test, Johansen cointegration test, Granger causality test, vector error correction model & impulse response function and variance decomposition. Gupta, Yuan & Roca (2016) investigated dynamics of information flows between the ADRs & its respective underlying stock prices in both the short run & long run period by using Vector auto regression & error correction model. The main objective is to study the causality pattern between Depository receipts prices and Indian stock prices. In order to fulfill the objective the following hypothesis is framed.

HYPOTHESIS:-

H_0: The cross listings of Indian firms on the international stock exchanges has no abnormal effect on the prices in the home market.

Granger Causality test is used to find out whether the prices of Indian DRs are affecting the prices of underlying stocks listed in local stock markets or vice versa. All the prices of underlying securities and respective indices were checked with the help of dickey fuller test for stationery. Thornton & Battern (1984) studied about lag- length selection criteria for granger causality test & suggested that Akaike's FPE criteria performs well compared to other models for lag selection. We can take any lag length criteria, but we must be very careful while selecting the appropriate criteria. Lag values are chosen by the Akaike information criterion (AIC) and Schwarz criterion (SC) for the study. Study choose lowest lag which ensures the lack of autocorrelation of residuals. In all cases var models with at most four lags fit the best. Then study estimated var (vector auto regression models) for $k+1$ lags (the additional lag comes from the degree of integration of series). Under the null hypothesis of the Granger non causality the test statistic is asymptotically $\chi 2\ k$ distributed. 40 Indian companies listed on international stock exchanges for a period of 2011-16 has been considered for the study. In the table below presents the 40 companies, AIC criterion and SC criterion values along with lag values for noise process.

4.3.1   AIC criterion, SC criterion & lag values for noise process.

VAR lag order selection criterion

Companies	Log L	AIC	SC	Lag Values
Ambuja cements	-9845.2123	15.43551	15.23451	4
Anant raj ltd	-218.7967	2.660637	2.982390	4
Apollo hospitals	-8432.7621	14.56342	14.97231	4
Arvind ltd	-280.9466	4.096481	4.385212	4
Axis ltd	-2428.606	22.45671	22.04567	4
Bajaj Holdings	-2993.865	19.54309	19.61593	3
Ballapur ltd	-437.8248	3.550771	3.852895	3
Balrampur chinni	-1209.130	10.69412	10.84453	4
BSEL infra	-1133.938	14.70887	14.82668	3

Companies	Log L	AIC	SC	Lag Values
CESC ltd	-1713.443	15.77470	15.86785	4
Cipla ltd	-1123.705	19.67854	18.76747	3
Crompton Greaves	-1518.470	22.75329	22.88304	3
Dr reddy lab	-7923.7823	16.78321	15.9768	2
Elder pharma ltd	-2128.835	18.80912	18.89964	2
Financial technologies	-3424.504	21.34512	21.98342	4
Ranbaxy ltd	-3454.2981	20.78561	20.67345	4
Gammon ltd	-1452.694	13.08246	13.17413	4
Granules Ltd	-1412.764	12.72434	12.81601	3
Great eastern co	-2527.063	23.02785	23.12040	4
Gujarat Narmada valley	-2034.749	16.00587	16.08920	4
HDFC ltd	-5465.6712	12.45653	12.65782	4
Hex aware technologies	-4210.033	32.30677	32.38871	3
Hindustan construction	-1175.907	12.22354	12.59150	4
ICICI Bank	-7642.7634	11.08761	11.07604	4
India cements	-901.5217	11.86480	12.21823	4
INFOSYS LTD	-7374.769	20.81343	20.90345	4
Jindal cotex	-6534.5621	23.65451	23.54671	4
Kotak Mahindra	-5342.765	32.30653	32.45012	4
Larsen & turbo	-4200.618	20.89637	20.99560	4
LIC housing finance ltd	-2610.799	23.58043	24.21811	4
Lloyd electric & engineering ltd	-1534.381	11.84908	11.93125	2
Mahindra & Mahindra	-3442.543	21.02770	21.09709	4
Oriental hotels	-1928.906	14.82686	14.90881	4
Reliance infrastructure	-7624.865	38.00431	38.14349	4
SBI	-3542.846	26.12386	26.25643	3
Sterlite	-7698.7541	17.87123	17.5667	4
Steel authority of India	-3840.055	23.14748	23.30758	4
Tata Motors	-8757.6754	12.56421	12.6754	4
Videocon industries ltd	-1735.547	13.39652	13.47869	3
Wipro	-5632.5320	10.98231	11.8945	4

Table above represents VAR selection criterion by using BIC and SC. Mostly 4 lag were selected for all the companies to have approximate white noise.

4.3.2 Causality Pattern Between Security Prices and Their GDR Prices.

Company	Granger's F	p-value	Causality Conclusion
AMBUJA CEMENTS	3.42213	0.0661	No conclusion
ANANT RAJ LTD	3.57696	0.0791	No conclusion
APOLLO	64.4267	0.2233	No conclusion
ARVIND LTD	1.04568	0.3745	No conclusion
AXIS BANK	0.50885	0.6762	No conclusion
BAJAJ HOLDING LTD	91.9988	0.5234	No conclusion
BALLAPUR LTD	2.51074	0.3072	No conclusion
BALRAMPUR CHINNI MILLS	1.38286	0.2530	No conclusion
BSEL INFRAST	2.00578	0.1587	No conclusion
CESC LTD	1.60929	0.2060	No conclusion
CIPLA LTD	72.7427	$1.E-25$	Security prices –GDR prices
CROMPTON GREAVES	1.45882	0.2293	No conclusion
ELDER PHARMA	7.76721	0.0580	No conclusion
FINANCIAL TEC	1.15991	0.2831	No conclusion
GAMMON LTD	7.04604	0.0851	No conclusion
GRANULES LTD	0.35112	0.5541	No conclusion
GREAT EASTERN CO	47.9641	5.E-11	Security prices –GDR prices
GUJARAT NARMADA	1.14516	0.2856	No conclusion
HINDUSTAN CONST	30.5252	1.E-22	Security prices –GDR prices
INDIA CEMENTS	4.77166	0.1222	No conclusion
JINDAL LTD	2.92606	0.3470	No conclusion
KOTAK MAHINDRA	2.13878	0.1449	No conclusion
LARSEN & TURBO	74.7752	3.E-28	Security prices –GDR prices
LIC HOUSING FINAN	4.8050	0.2344	No conclusion
LLOYD ELECTRONICS	0.50834	0.4765	No conclusion
MAHINDRA & LTD	141.854	0.2344	No conclusion
ORIENTAL HOTELS	1.17670	0.2790	No conclusion
RANBAXY LAB	45.8923	4.E-12	Security prices –GDR prices
RELIANCE INFRA	4.82419	0.2680	No conclusion
SAIL	1.33993	0.2613	No conclusion
SBI	0.53039	0.5890	No conclusion
VIDEOCON IND LTD	0.53897	0.4635	No conclusion
Hexa ware tech	56.2356	3.E-13	Security prices –GDR prices

Table above represents the causality pattern between security price and GDR price. There are 33 GDR programs listed on European stock exchanges. Out of 33 GDR, 6 company security prices are having an impact on the GDR price. Remaining 27 company stock prices don't have any impact on the GDR prices. The study's results are local security price don't have any impact on GDR price.

4.3.3   Causality Pattern Between GDR Price and Their Security Price.

Company	Granger's F	p-value	Causality Conclusion
AXIS BANK	102.627	3.E-59	GDR prices – Security prices
CIPLA LTD	1.21182	0.0445	GDR prices – Security prices
FINANCIAL TEC	52.1461	2.E-11	GDR prices – Security prices
KOTAK MAHINDRA	145.587	1.E-26	GDR prices – Security prices
JINDAL LTD	3.35366	0.0198	GDR prices – Security prices
APOLLO	55.4798	1.E-12	GDR prices – Security prices
AMBUJA CEMENTS	163.049	2.E-26	GDR prices – Security prices
ANANT RAJ LTD	3.12781	0.0163	No Conclusion
ARVIND LTD	5.54454	0.0013	No Conclusion
BAJAJ HOLDING LTD	0.03880	0.0018	GDR prices – Security prices
BALLAPUR LTD	143.069	6.E-71	GDR prices – Security prices
BALRAMPUR CHINNI MILLS	70.9141	1.E-24	GDR prices – Security prices
BSEL INFRAST	138.700	4.E-23	GDR prices – Security prices
CESC LTD	283.473	4.E-41	GDR prices – Security prices
CROMPTON GREAVES	26.3520	1.E-06	GDR prices – Security prices
ELDER PHARMA	398.928	1.E-51	GDR prices – Security prices
GAMMON LTD	286.045	1.E-41	GDR prices – Security prices
GRANULES LTD	520.362	7.E-60	GDR prices – Security prices
GREAT EASTERN CO	38.7018	3.E-09	GDR prices – Security prices
GUJARAT NARMADA	230.854	2.E-37	GDR prices – Security prices
HINDUSTAN CONST	5.96927	4.E-05	GDR prices – Security prices
INDIA CEMENTS	13.7346	2.E-09	GDR prices – Security prices
LARSEN & TURBO	2.47809	0.0852	No Conclusion
LIC HOUSING FINAN	9.18563	2.E-12	GDR prices – Security prices
LLOYD ELECTRONICS	925.102	4.E-87	GDR prices – Security prices
MAHINDRA & LTD	8.65003	0.0035	GDR prices – Security prices
ORIENTAL HOTELS	8990.07	2E-202	GDR prices – Security prices
RELIANCE INFRA	12.9320	4.E-08	GDR prices – Security prices
SBI	110.489	1.E-35	GDR prices – Security prices

Company	Granger's F	p-value	Causality Conclusion
SAIL	57.6192	7.E-30	GDR prices – Security prices
VIDEOCON IND LTD	495.495	7.E-62	GDR prices – Security prices
RANBAXY LAB	2.45663	0.0023	No Conclusion
Hexa ware tech	3.45553	0.1245	No Conclusion

Table above represents the causality pattern between GDR price and local Indian stock prices. There are 33 GDR programs listed on European stock exchanges. Out of 33 GDR, 5 companies Indian security prices are having an impact on the GDR security price. Remaining 28 companies GDR prices have an impact on the Indian local stock prices. The study's results are GDR security price have an impact on local stock price.

4.3.4   Causality pattern between security price and their ADR price

Company	Granger's F	p-value	Causality Conclusion
ICICI (ADR)	1.89125	0.0792	No conclusion
WIPRO (ADR)	2.99560	0.0504	No conclusion
HDFC	0.32473	0.5689	No conclusion
DR REDDY LAB	5.89960	0.0153	No conclusion
STERLITE	3.51106	0.0302	Security prices –ADR prices
INFOSYS LTD (ADR)	3.83321	0.0097	Security prices –ADR prices
TATA MOTORS	0.62867	0.4280	No conclusion

Table above represents causality pattern between security prices & ADRs. Out of 7 companies listed on US stock exchange, 2 company's security prices are having an impact on ADR prices. Remaining 5 stock prices don't have any impact on ADR prices. The results are local stock prices don't have any impact on ADR prices.

4.3.5   Causality pattern between ADR prices and their security prices

Company	Granger's F	p-value	Causality Conclusion
ICICI (ADR)	41.8091	2.E-46	ADR prices – Security prices
WIPRO	5.78829	0.0031	ADR prices – Security prices
HDFC	0.00616	0.0374	ADR prices – Security prices
DR REDDY LAB	0.00683	0.0341	ADR prices – Security prices
STERLITE	2.18217	0.1133	No conclusion
INFOSYS LTD	40.1418	6.E-24	ADR prices – Security prices
TATA MOTORS	0.00069	0.9791	No conclusion

Table above represents causality pattern between security prices & ADRs. Out of 7 companies listed on US stock exchange, 5 company's ADR prices are having an impact on security prices. Remaining 2 ADR prices don't have any impact on security prices. The results are local stock prices don't have any impact on ADR prices. The study shows that DR prices are having an impact on local stock prices but less vice versa.

4.3.6   CONCLUSION:-

Study used Granger Causality Test by using E-views software to find impact. The study tests the causality pattern between Indian stock prices & DR prices & vice versa. Is there any impact of DRs on Indian local stock prices or Indian prices on DR prices?

Due to cross border trading, the DRs and the local underlying shares will have a same pay off, as they reflect the same information, price of the local stock & the DR lies close to each other. For this reason, most of the times DR Price & local stock price will be perfectly correlated resulting in least profitability arbitrage.

Earlier studies found that DR issuer gets lower cost of capital, improved liquidity & less risk. When there is a lower cost of capital, more liquidity it is reflected in the DR stock prices. They also found that there is a positive price reaction to the DR offering announcement; it may vary in the long term.

Study used a sample of 40 Indian companies listed through ADRs & GDRs on different stock exchanges (NYSE, LSE & LUXSE). Out of 40 listed Indian companies, 33 companies are listed through GDRs on London & Luxembourg stock exchanges. Remaining 7 are listed on New York stock exchange through ADRs. Out of 33 GDR listed programs, 27 Indian local stock prices don't have an impact on GDR prices. Secondly, causality pattern between GDR prices & Indian local stock prices. Out of 33 GDR listed programs, 28 GDRs stock prices have an impact on Indian local stock prices.

Same causality pattern was done between ADR prices & Indian stock prices & vice versa. 7 ADR programs listed on NYSE. Five ADRs prices were having an impact on the Indian local stock price. Study concludes that cross listings through DRs are having an impact on the Indian local stock price.

4.4   Impact of Cross Listing on the Indian Stock volatility

Companies, corporates investors, speculators & regulatory agencies are very much interested in information of international stock listings which has an impact on capital cost incurring & the risk returns of the stocks which are underlying. A major motivation for examining the volatilities of the stocks emerged from market segmentation. Foreign listing provides opportunity by which companies & corporate investors can side steps some of the barriers on capital flow that contribute to the international capital market segmentation. These helps to reduce the degree of market segmentation which is associated with systematic changes in capital costs & stock volatility has a significant effect on stock valuation. Volatility is the fluctuations in the stock prices.

One of the objectives of the study is impact of cross listings on the volatility of the underlying domestic stocks. Share price volatility can be measured in the terms of standard deviation (σ) of its daily stock prices around its event window. Earlier studies McConnell, Dybevik, Haushalter & Lie (1996), Barclay (1990), Makhijha & Nachtmann (1990), Howe (1993), Jayaram (1993) analysed volatilities of foreign dual listed stocks. They used variances of international stocks to find the changes in volatilities during trading & non trading days.

Studies by Dodd, Olga (2011), Leuz & Verrecchia (2000) used three proxies to measure variances to quantify stock risks. They tested stock return volatility as a proxy for information asymmetry[11]. They find that high level of Information asymmetry between companies & shares holders are associated with high variability in stock returns (Barry & Brown (1985), Wang (1993), Dodd, Olga (2011), Leuz & Verrecchia (2000)). Second measure used is firm to market volatility ratio [12]. The study includes companies that were listed on a foreign stock exchange & continued trading in the home market. Study used the third measure (High- Low ratio) to find the volatility impact. High- low ratio focuses on intraday volatility of stock prices. The impact of cross listing on stock volatility has been captured using event study methodology.

Study includes DR program listed by 138 Indian companies. The data about listing dates was collected from Yahoo finance India, Google finance & Economic times. Daily stock prices have been calculated by computing standard deviation. In order to measure the variances or the changes in volatility, the study splits the sample into pre & post listings periods & the mean volatilities of two pre & post listings sub periods have been compared. Stock is said to be volatile when it tend to rapidly change to extreme fluctuations in its stock prices (Kumar, 2001). Therefore, it is said that stocks with larger standard deviation are more volatile than the stocks with smaller standard deviation. The intraday volatility pattern becomes flatter post cross listings. In order to find the effect of cross listings on the Indian stock volatility, the following hypothesis is framed.

Hypothesis 4 H_0: Depository receipts listings do not significantly affect the volatility of underlying stocks.

RESULTS

4.4.1   DR Impact on Indian Stock Volatility Listed On all stock exchanges

TABLE: 4.4.1 Comparison of variances of sample companies before and after the DR listings.

COMPANIES	var after	var before	variance ratio
ANANT RAJ	22.888508	50.5686577	0.452622413
APOLLO HOSPITAL	8.742014	6.10597883	1.431713773*
APTECH	14.34166	8.68053744	1.652162681*
AXIS	3.6727174	8.19799853	0.448001709
BAJAJ HOL	44.017885	30.3078493	1.452359241*
CIPLA LTD	83.110411	10.1715312	8.170884914*
COX & KING	55.839432	58.7076105	0.951144698
CROMPTON GREAV	8.6073	3.69545971	2.329155404*
DISH TV	5.401811	10.3161421	0.523627048
ELECTRO STEEL	2.7120691	6.40113314	0.423685786
FEDERAL BANK	7.2254695	7.47643212	0.966432839
FINANCIAL TECH	8.351234	6.51565747	0.281717773
GAIL LTD	12.386153	10.2226173	0.211642044

---

11 Information asymmetric is the monthly standard deviation of stocks daily returns including dividend income.

12 Volatility ratio is Ratio of monthly standard deviation of stocks daily total turnover to monthly standard deviation of daily total returns of home market index.

COMPANIES	var after	var before	variance ratio
GEETANJALI	11.386943	10.2449415	0.111469776
HDFC	5.5078537	5.79934341	0.949737457
HINDUJA FOUND	15.483174	17.1138377	0.904716668
HINDUSTAN CON	8.3472206	6.68483152	1.248680775*
ICICI BANK	11.159024	24.5663838	0.454239582
INDUSIND BANK	15.560266	14.4468245	1.077071689*
JINDAL COTEX	13.527261	4.0877884	3.309188215*
KARURTURI GLOBAL	15.348205	14.7450488	1.04090567*
KOTAK MAHINDRA	12.873269	8.06231155	1.596721818*
LIC FINANCING	5.144027	4.27557587	0.2031191
LLYOD ELECTRIC	7.3028847	10.9384027	0.667637209
NEHA INTERNATIONAL	11.533212	21.4959198	0.536530304
NISSAN COPPER	82.045859	11.0640628	7.415527176*
NOIDA TOLL BRIDGE	15.519684	8.8144087	1.760717584*
REIGRO	17.807752	6.95684673	2.559744712*
RELIANCE CAPITAL	2.9094888	10.1854362	0.285651861
RELIANCE COMM	3.0309349	10.1189909	0.299529364
ROLTA INDIA	9.689576	5.83260274	1.66127824*
SEL MANUFA CO	10.526918	8.90364247	1.182315868*
SUBEX	2.7249901	16.3407077	0.166760836
SUZLON ENERGY	11.400831	19.0715017	0.597794108
TATAGLOBAL BEVERAGES	3.5189909	4.33686343	0.811413812
TATA MOTORS	1.5932822	2.51918608	0.632459111
UNITED SPIRITS	8.2721349	10.3894453	0.796205637
VODEOCON INDUST	4.4646283	6.65914148	0.670451034
WIPRO LTD	12.371452	14.8347719	0.83394961
ZYLOG LTD	15.916997	19.821864	0.803002009

Table above shows variance of pre & post listing period, variance ratio of stocks listed on London stock exchange. It shows that twenty five variance ratios out of forty variance ratios are less than one, indicating decrease in variances of the underlying domestic shares during the post listing period. Remaining 15 stocks variance ratios are greater than one indicating increase in variances of the underlying domestic shares and are statistically significant. The statistical significance is judged using the F-ratio test that compares two variances before and after the listing date and tell if they are significantly different (df=150-1). The twenty five firms in the sample have variance ratios less than one but statistically insignificant implying the decrease in the return variance after the listing date. Overall, we can conclude that the variances of the all underlying domestic stocks of foreign listed Indian firms have reduced aftermath to listings of their DR program on the international stock exchange.

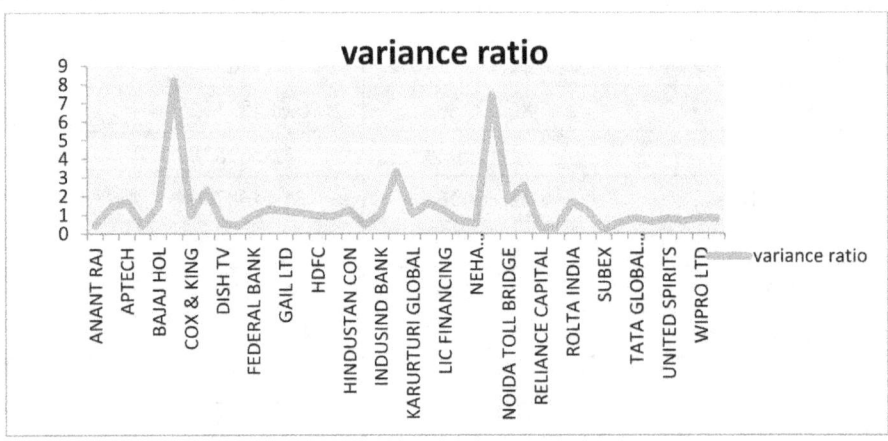

Figure: -4.4.1 Variance ratio of different stocks listed on all stock exchanges

4.4.2   DR Impact on Indian Stock Volatility Listed On London Stock Exchange.

TABLE: Comparison of variances of sample companies before and after the DR listings on LSE.

COMPANIES	var after	var before	variance ratio
AXIS	3.67272	8.198	0.448
CROMPTON GREAV	8.6073	3.69546	2.329155404*
FEDERAL BANK	7.22547	7.47643	0.96643
FINANCIAL TECH	8.35123	6.51566	0.28172
GAIL LTD	12.3862	10.2226	0.21164
GEETANJALI	11.3869	10.2449	0.11147
HDFC	5.50785	5.79934	0.94974
LLYOD ELECTRIC	7.30288	10.9384	0.66764
NOIDA TOLL BRIDGE	15.5197	8.81441	1.760717584*
REIGRO	17.8078	6.95685	2.559744712*
ROLTA INDIA	9.68958	5.8326	1.66127824*
SUBEX	2.72499	16.3407	0.16676

Table above shows variance of pre & post listing period, variance ratio of stocks listed on London stock exchange. It shows that 8 company's variance ratios out of 12 company's variance ratios are less than one, indicating decrease in variances of the underlying domestic shares during the post listing period. Remaining 4 stocks variance ratios are greater than one indicating increase in variances of the underlying domestic shares and are statistically significant. The statistical significance is judged using the F-ratio test that compares two variances before and after the listing date and tell if they are significantly different (df=150- 1). The 8 firms in the sample have variance ratios less than one but statistically insignificant implying the decrease in the return variance after the listing date. Overall, we can conclude that the variances of the all underlying domestic stocks of India have reduced aftermath to listings of their DR program on the London stock exchange.

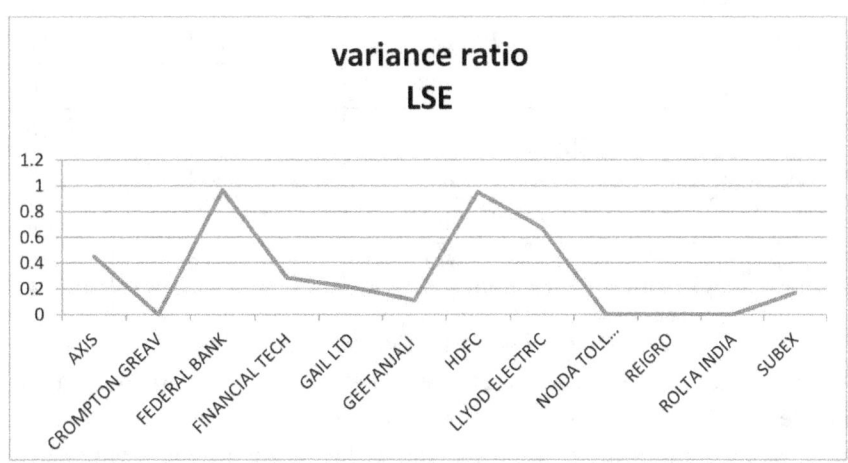

Figure: - Figure above shows the variance ratio of stocks listed on LSE.

4.4.3   DR Impact on Indian stock Volatility listed on LUXSE

TABLE: Comparison of variances of sample companies before and after the DR listings on Luxembourg stock exchange.

COMPANIES	var after	var before	variance ratio
ANANT RAJ	22.8885	50.5687	0.45262
APOLLO HOSPITAL	8.74201	6.10598	1.431713773*
APTECH	14.3417	8.68054	1.652162681*
CIPLA LTD	83.1104	10.1715	8.170884914*
COX & KING	55.8394	58.7076	0.95114
DISH TV	5.40181	10.3161	0.52363
ELECTRO STEEL	2.71207	6.40113	0.42369
HINDUJA FOUND	15.4832	17.1138	0.90472
HINDUSTAN CON	8.34722	6.68483	1.248680775*
INDUSIND BANK	15.5603	14.4468	1.077071689*
JINDAL COTEX	13.5273	4.08779	3.309188215*
KARURTURI GLOBAL	15.3482	14.745	1.04090567*
KOTAK MAHINDRA	12.8733	8.06231	1.596721818*
LIC FINANCING	5.14403	4.27558	0.20312
NEHA INTERNATIONAL	11.5332	21.4959	0.53653

COMPANIES	var after	var before	variance ratio
NISSAN COPPER	82.0459	11.0641	7.415527176*
RELIANCE CAPITAL	2.90949	10.1854	0.28565
RELIANCE COMM	3.03093	10.119	0.29953
SEL MANUFA CO	10.5269	8.90364	1.182315868*
SUZLON ENERGY	11.4008	19.0715	0.59779
TATAGLOBAL BEVERAGES	3.51899	4.33686	0.81141
UNITED SPIRITS	8.27213	10.3894	0.79621
VIDEOCON INDUST	4.46463	6.65914	0.67045
ZYLOG LTD	15.917	19.8219	0.803

Table above shows variance of pre & post listing period, variance ratio of stocks listed on Luxembourg stock exchange. It shows that 15 company's variance ratios out of 25 company's variance ratios are less than one, indicating decrease in variances of the underlying domestic shares during the post listing period. Remaining 10 stocks variance ratios are greater than one indicating increase in variances of the underlying domestic shares and are statistically significant. The statistical significance is judged using the F-ratio test that compares two variances before and after the listing date and tell if they are significantly different (df=150-1). The 15 firms in the sample have variance ratios less than one but statistically insignificant implying the decrease in the return variance after the listing date. Overall, we can conclude that the variances of the all underlying domestic stocks of listed Indian firms have reduced aftermath to listings of their DR program on the Luxembourg stock exchange.

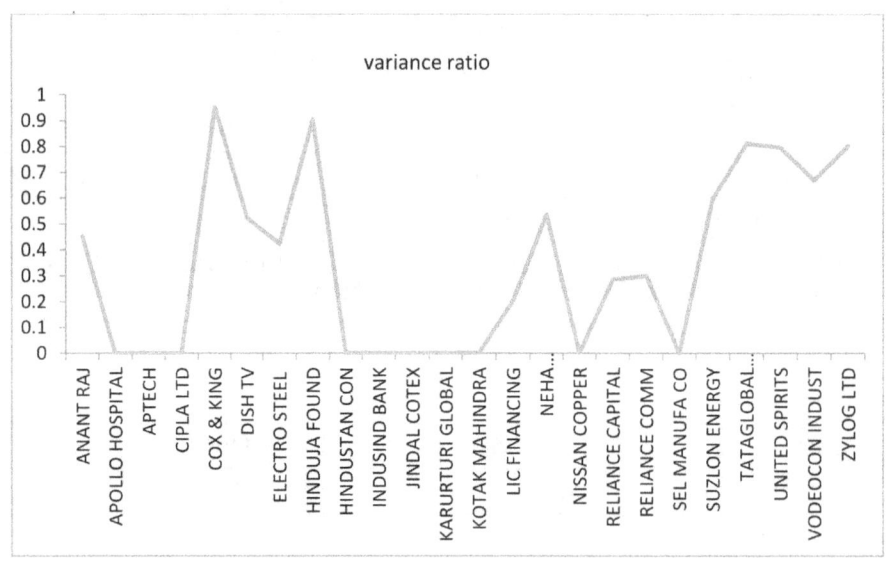

Figure: - 4.4.3 Figure above shows the variance ratio of stocks listed on LUXSE.

4.4.4   DR Impact on Indian stock Volatility listed on NYSE

TABLE: Comparison of variances of sample companies before and after the DR listings on New York stock exchange (ADR)

COMPANIES	var after	var before	variance ratio
ICICI BANK	11.159	24.5664	0.45424
TATA MOTORS	1.59328	2.51919	0.63246
WIPRO LTD	12.3715	14.8348	0.83395

Table above shows pre- listing & post listing period, variance ratio of Indian stocks listed on NYSE through ADRs. Study includes three Indian stocks listed; all three companies variance ratio is less than one indicating that there is a decrease in volatility of Indian stock. The firms in the sample have variance ratios less than one but statistically insignificant implying the decrease in the return variance after the listing date. Overall, we can conclude that the variances of the all underlying domestic stocks of India have reduced aftermath to listings of their DR program on the New York stock exchange.

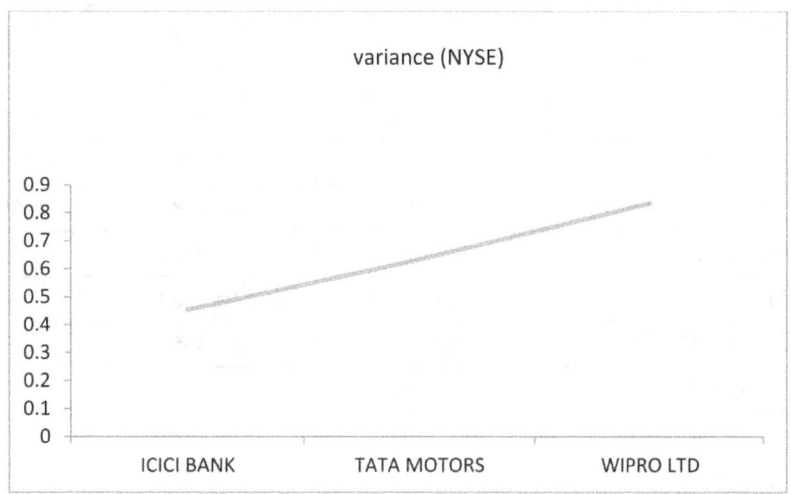

Figure: -4.4.4 Figure above shows the variance ratio of stocks listed on NYSE.

4.4.5 DR Impact on Indian Stock Volatility Listed Through GDR

TABLE: Comparison of variances of sample companies before and after the GDR listings.

COMPANIES	var after	var before	variance ratio
ANANT RAJ	22.8885	50.5687	0.452622413
APOLLO HOSPITAL	8.74201	6.10598	1.431713773*
APTECH	14.3417	8.68054	1.652162681*
AXIS	3.67272	8.198	0.448001709

COMPANIES	var after	var before	variance ratio
BAJAJ HOL	44.0179	30.3078	1.452359241*
CIPLA LTD	83.1104	10.1715	8.170884914*
COX & KING	55.8394	58.7076	0.951144698
CROMPTON GREAV	8.6073	3.69546	2.329155404*
DISH TV	5.40181	10.3161	0.523627048
ELECTRO STEEL	2.71207	6.40113	0.423685786
FEDERAL BANK	7.22547	7.47643	0.966432839
FINANCIAL TECH	8.35123	6.51566	0.281717773
GAIL LTD	12.3862	10.2226	0.211642044
GEETANJALI	11.3869	10.2449	0.111469776
HDFC	5.50785	5.79934	0.949737457
HINDUJA FOUND	15.4832	17.1138	0.904716668
HINDUSTAN CON	8.34722	6.68483	1.248680775*
INDUSIND BANK	15.5603	14.4468	1.077071689*
JINDAL COTEX	13.5273	4.08779	3.309188215*
KARURTURI GLOBAL	15.3482	14.745	1.04090567*
KOTAK MAHINDRA	12.8733	8.06231	1.596721818*
LIC FINANCING	5.14403	4.27558	0.2031191
LLYOD ELECTRIC	7.30288	10.9384	0.667637209
NEHA INTERNATIONAL	11.5332	21.4959	0.536530304
NISSAN COPPER	82.0459	11.0641	7.415527176*
NOIDA TOLL BRIDGE	15.5197	8.81441	1.760717584*
REIGRO	17.8078	6.95685	2.559744712*
RELIANCE CAPITAL	2.90949	10.1854	0.285651861
RELIANCE COMM	3.03093	10.119	0.299529364
ROLTA INDIA	9.68958	5.8326	1.66127824*
SEL MANUFA CO	10.5269	8.90364	1.182315868*
SUBEX	2.72499	16.3407	0.166760836
SUZLON ENERGY	11.4008	19.0715	0.597794108
TATAGLOBAL BEVERAGES	3.51899	4.33686	0.811413812
UNITED SPIRITS	8.27213	10.3894	0.796205637
VODEOCON INDUST	4.46463	6.65914	0.670451034
ZYLOG LTD	15.917	19.8219	0.803002009

Table above shows variance of pre & post listing period, variance ratio of stocks listed on Luxembourg stock exchange. It shows that 22 out of 37 company's variance ratios are less than one, indicating decrease in variances of the underlying domestic shares during the post listing period. Remaining 15 stocks variance ratios are greater than one indicating increase in variances of the underlying domestic shares and are statistically significant. The statistical significance is judged using the F-ratio test that compares two variances before and after the listing date and tell if they are significantly different (df=150-1). The 22 firms in the sample have variance ratios less than one but statistically insignificant implying the decrease in the return variance after the listing date. Overall, we can conclude that the variances of the all underlying domestic stocks of listed Indian firms have reduced aftermath to listings of their GDR program on the Luxembourg & London stock exchanges.

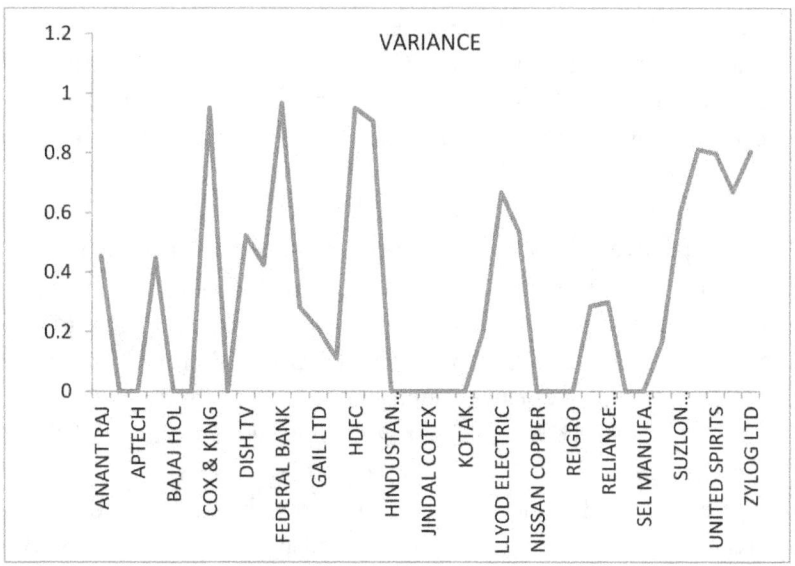

Figure: - 4.4.5 Figure above shows the variance ratio of stocks listed through GDR.

4.4.6   CONCLUSION:

This part of the chapter examined the impact of cross listings through DRs on Indian stock volatility. Event study was conducted to study the changes in variances of the underlying domestic stocks. Results of the study are shown in the table. Table reports the ratios of post to pre listings variances.

The data presented in the table shows, there is a wide variation in the effect of foreign listings on the underlying domestic stock variances. The variance ratio in our sample varies from a low 0.1667 variance to a high 8.1708 variance. Summarized results in table provide some interesting insights. Twenty five variance ratios out of forty variance ratios are less than one, indicating decrease in variances of the underlying domestic shares during the post listing period. Remaining 15 stocks variance ratios are greater than one indicating increase in variances of the underlying domestic shares and are statistically significant. The statistical significance is judged using the F-ratio test that compares two variances before and after the listing date and tell if they are significantly different (df=150-1). The twenty five firms in the sample have variance ratios less than one but statistically insignificant implying the decrease in the return variance after the listing date.

Similar results were drawn while analyzing performance of Indian stocks listed on international stock exchanges. Separate volatility test was done differently for stocks listed through DRs on NYSE, LSE & Luxembourg stock exchange. For Indian stock listed on LSE & Luxembourg & NYSE majority of the stocks listed, volatility was decreased.

At an aggregate level, DR listings seem to have decreased the volatility of the domestic underlying shares. Volatilities declined for most of the Indian companies in the sample that listed their DR programs on the European and US markets.

4.5   Comparison of depository receipts regulatory framework

Past few decades have witnessed great development in internationalization of companies through cross listings on international stock exchanges. Cross listings through depository receipts has become one of the avenues for integration of global market securities. Globally markets for DRs are 90 years old. DRs are traded on major international stock markets with large investment banks running this program. The depositary receipts were intended as both an investment vehicle as well as an investment option. Today, DRs are not only used for capital raising purpose but also used for number of benefits like strategic, reputational & risk mitigation.

Previously, companies from emerging economies listed either on the US or European stock exchanges through ADRs or GDRs, respectively. However, the phenomenal success of DRs in the US and in European countries combined with the evolving liberal conditions that are conducive for capital market development in Latin American and Asian countries prompted the securities market regulators to allow DR programs in these countries. Another factor that contributed to the popularity of DRs is that investors are looking beyond their national borders to take advantage of new opportunities for diversifying their portfolio. Even many multinational firms are interested in the local DR programs to take advantage of the growth prospects of Latin American and Asian countries.

Securities of a firm are deposited with a domestic custodian in the firm's domestic jurisdiction and a corresponding DR is issued abroad which can be purchased by foreign investors. A Depositary Receipt is a negotiable instrument denominated in US dollars or Euro, which is issued to the investors in one or more foreign countries. DRs are issued by the overseas depositary bank to the international investors against the delivery of local currency shares of the issuer company to the domestic custodian bank. A Depository Receipt contains features of equity shares and carries rights, which are similar to rights attached to equity shares. The Depository Receipt holder, thus, enjoys the right to appropriate disclosures by the foreign company issuing Depository Receipts; The right to corporate benefits/ dividends attached to the Depository Receipts; the right to vote under certain circumstances. "Depository" means a company formed and registered under the Companies Act, 1956 (1 of 1956) and which has been granted a certificate of registration under subsection (1A) of section 12 of the Securities and Exchange Board of India Act, 1992 (15 of 1992).(Gaurav, 2012). Depository Receipt'(DR) means a negotiable security issued outside India by a Depository bank. A Depository Receipt (DR) is a negotiable instrument in the form of securities that is issued by a foreign public listed company and is generally traded on a domestic stock exchange. For this, the issuing company has to fulfill the listing criteria for DRs in the other country. Before creating DRs, the shares of the foreign company—which the DRs Represent—are delivered and deposited with the custodian bank of the depository creating the DRs. Once the custodian bank receives the shares, the depository creates and issues the DRs to the investors in the country where the DRs are listed. These DRs are then listed and traded in the local stock exchanges of the other country.(Shipra, Pallavi, NSE, 2012).

Objective of the study:- The main objective is to study the DR regulatory frame work of the capital market regions representing some western and Asian economies. The study compares the DR regulatory frame works in these countries namely, Taiwan, Brazil, Russia, India & Hong Kong.

The study focuses on analyzing the performance of each of them. The study discusses requirements of the companies to get listed as DRs, respective capital market DR regulatory frame work, their performance records, number of companies listed as DRs, problems faced by the firms listed. The study also attempts to categories these capital markets into strictly regulated or sparsely regulated markets by examining their regulatory frame work.

Depository receipts framework in, Brazil, Taiwan, Russia, India & Hong Kong.

4.5.1   Depository receipts framework in Brazil

Brazilian depository receipts:-

Brazilian Depository receipts are the instruments for the foreign stocks to get presence in the dynamic capital markets of Latin America. Foreign stocks listings their Depository Receipts on the Brazilian stock exchanges are called Brazilian Depository Receipts (BDRs). It is a certificate representing securities issued by publicly listed companies based abroad and issued by a depository bank in Brazil.

A Brazilian depository receipt is a negotiable instrument that represents an ownership interest in the stocks of a non-Brazilian publicly traded company which must be backed by its own securities listed in its home country or other market.

In accordance with CVM instructions 332, updated by CVM 431,456,480 and 493[13], BDR is a certificate of deposit securities of a public company or similar company with headquarters abroad and issued by a depository bank in Brazil, whose assets are located in Brazil corresponding to 50% or more of these contained in the annual financial statements, consolidated or separate, which ever better represents the economic substance of business finds this classification.

BDRs were first introduced in 1990's to attract foreign stocks to get listed in the Brazilian stock exchange. The national monetary council (CMN) established the BDRs regulations and the Brazilian Securities and Exchange Commission (CVM) and the central bank of Brazil in 1996[14]. The BDRs regulations were reformulated with an objective of incorporating better international standards which make the regulatory framework attractive to international firms.

4.5.1.1   Requirements of the company to get listed as BDR:-

Foreign companies must register itself as a publicly held company as an issuer of BDRs. Then a depository will issue BDRs, under Level I, II or III programs depending on the disclosure requirements. BDRs Level I do not require any previous registration with CVM. Despite lower disclosure requirements such BDRs are limited to

- Qualified investors
- Employees of issuer
- Pension funds, and
- Portfolio managers and traders

---

13   http://www.legalink.ch/xms/files/CROSS_BORDER_QUESTIONNAIRES/IPO/IPO_SaoPaulo.pdf
14   http://www.bmfbovespa.com.br/pt_br/listagem/bdrs-brazilian-depositary-receipts/#

Company need to provide following information by its legal representative:

- Articles of association which regulate the company
- Correlating legislation which regulates the company
- Shareholders agreements
- Companies' financial information related to previous three tax years drawn up accordance with Brazilian accounting standards. The preparation period from decision to list until the filing date would be typically 120 days. Stock exchange cannot list a company or a tender without CVM registration[15].

4.5.1.2   BDR program:- There are two categories of BDR program sponsored and unsponsored level program.

Brazilian Depository Receipts

	Level I – not sponsored	Level I- sponsored	Level II – sponsored	Level III - sponsored
Company involvement	No	Yes	Yes	Yes
Registration at CVM	Program	Program	Program and business	Program and company
Public offering	No	No	No	Yes
Trading market	BN & FBOEVESIA	BN & FBOEVESIA	BN & FBOEVESIA	BN & FBOEVESIA
Authorised investors	Qualified	Qualified	All	All
Accounting standard of financial statements	Country of origin	Country of origin	BRAZIL	BRAZIL

Source: - Wikipedia/BMF BOVESPA [16] Table no. 4.5.1

- Sponsored Brazilian Depository Receipts are securities issued in Brazil, which an asset value overseas. The sponsored Brazil depositories receipts are issued by a depository bank or an institution contracted by the foreign enterprise issuing the securities and are classified as Level I, Level II and Level III. Sponsored BDRs, issued once, may be traded on the secondary market through the BM & FBOVESPA exchange in a manner similar to shares. An investor by acquiring the BDRs, indirectly acquires the shares of the company with the headquarters of another country, without opening an account with a foreign brokerage company.
- The unsponsored Brazilian depository receipts (Level I) are issued by a depository bank or a financial institution, without the involvement of foreign issuer stocks with only Level I programme. Depository

---

15 http://www.bmfbovespa.com.br/pt_br/produtos/listados-a-vista-e-derivativos/renda-variavel/empresas-listadas.htm
16 https://pt.wikipedia.org/wiki/Brazilian_Depositary_Receipt

institutions are responsible for ensuring that non- sponsored BDRs issued in Brazil are effectively backed up by securities issued overseas. Depository institutions make sure that there is mismatch between the balance of shares abroad and BDRs issued.

BDRs are governed by CVM (Securities and Exchange Commission of Brazil) Instruction 332, CVM Instruction 480, BM & FBOVESPA (Brazilian Mercantile and Futures Exchange) Regulation and Manual of Issuers, as well as other applicable legal and regulatory provisions. Sponsored Level II and Level III BDRs are traded on BM & FBOVESPA (Mega Bolsa, is an electronic trading platform, and an only securities, commodities and future exchange in Brazil). On Mega Bolsa exchange, 99.5% of the orders are sent to the system and takes less than a second time to be processed. Products like Equities, Exchange traded funds (ETFs) and Brazilian Depositary receipts are traded on it. In the sponsored BDR program, the company issuing the securities which is a sponsoring company is responsible for bearing the cost of the DR program. In the non-sponsored BDR program, there are one or more depository institutions working with the DR certificate and not required any formal agreement with the company issuing the securities. The depository institutions are responsible for disclosing to the local market the corporate financial information of the foreign companies issuing Non-Sponsored BDRs.

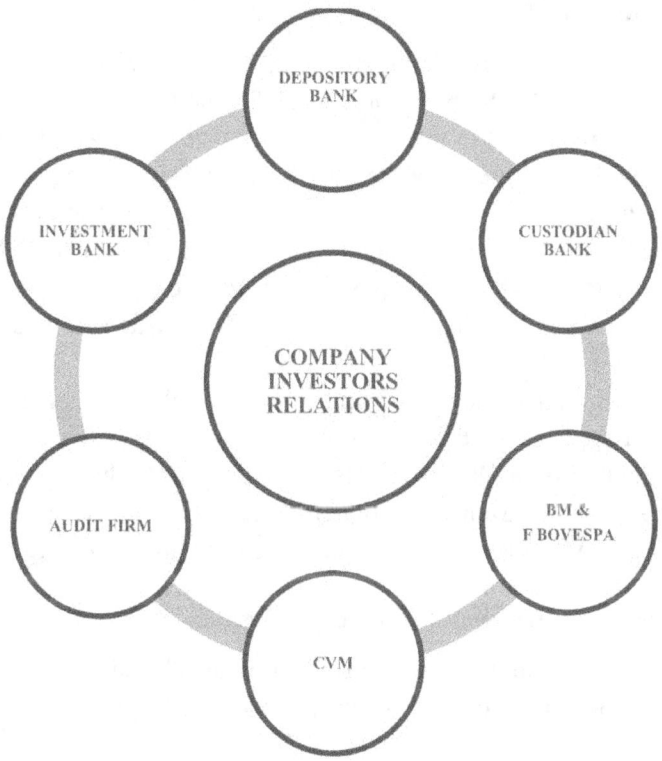

BDR Program: - Figure no. 4.5.1 Participants and roles

- Company group: - Company personnel need to share the necessary information required to prepare documents on a consistent basis and to be actively involved in all the aspects of registration process.

- Depository bank:- Depository bank issues brazil the corresponding certificates based on the securities in the custody abroad and is responsible for the filings with the CVM for the purpose of registering the BDR program.
- Custodian bank:- Custodian bank are responsible for custody of equities underlying the BDRs, which back the BDRs in the home or other country where these shares are traded.
- BM & F BOVESPA:- It is the only market for capital market transactions in Brazil. The role of BM & F BOVESPA[17] includes providing a secure trading environment, market monitoring while listing of BDR program. It is responsible for keeping market updated as to all relevant facts submitted by the BDR issuer.
- CVM:- It is a Brazilian capital market regulator. CVM is charged with ensuring a fair and level playing field for public companies in Brazil and their investors[17]. CVM has the authority to pursue against those who don't follow the rules and regulations applicable to a public company.
- Audit firm:- CVM registered auditors[17] and home offices play an decisive role throughout the registration process in providing opinions, review reports and advice on the transactions.
- Investment bank:- The investment bank will provide the underwriting services, define the features of the offering and conduct the Due Diligence in case of public offering of BDRs[17].

4.5.1.3   Brazilian depository receipts regulatory frame work:-

- CVM:-BDRs are governed by the regulatory bodies CVM (Securities and Exchange Commission of Brazil) Instruction no. 331and CVM instructions no.332[18], both dated April 4 2002, deals mainly with the registration of the company and the BDR program, respectively, with the CVM. On December 29, 2003, the provisions were set in the CVM instruction no.400, which regulates the public offering for the distribution of securities in primary and secondary markets of Brazil, and also is applicable for the issuance of Level III BDRs. CVM Instruction 480[17], through which CVM circulates instructions dealing with various capital market instruments, including disclosure requirements. CVM instructions no. 476 has permitted the fast tracking of issuance, CVM instructions nos. 554, 564 and 566 have further modified the regulations.
- BM & FBOVESPA: - (Brazilian Mercantile and Futures Exchange) is a Regulation and Manual of Issuers, as well as other applicable legal and regulatory provisions.
- Brazilian Monetary Council (CMN): - The rules and regulations which govern the negotiation of the BDRs are contained in Brazilian Monetary Council.
- Brazilian Central Bank (BACEN): - Rules and regulations are also contained in BACEN Circulars.

4.5.1.4   Performance record of Brazilian depository receipts:-

There are altogether 22 sponsored and unsponsored BDR programs listed on Brazilian stock exchange (BM & FBOVESPA). 10 are of sponsored and 12 are of unsponsored BDR programs.

---

17 How-to-launch-a-BDRs-program-Handbook.pdf

18 BDR PROGRAM, Operating Procedure Manual https://www.itau.com.br/_arquivosestaticos/SecuritiesServices/defaultTheme/ PDF/PROCEDIMENTO_BDR_EN.pdf,

COMPANY	LEVEL	CUSTODIAN SHARES	RATIO BDR*shares
Aventis S.A	Level I	SOCIETE GENERALE S.A	1:1
GP Investments	Level III	The bank of New York – LONDRES	1:1
DUFRY A.G	Level III	The bank of New York – LONDRES	1:1
Wilson Sons LTD	Level III	The bank of New York – LONDRES	1:1
BANCO PATAGONIA S.A	Level III	BANCO ITAU Argentina - BUENOS	1:20
COSAN LTD	Level III	The bank of New York – New York	1:1
AGRENCO LTD	Level III	The bank of New York – LONDRES	1:1
BANCO SANTANDER S.A	Level III	SANTANDER INVESTMENTS SECURITIES – SPAIN	1:1
TGLTS.A	Level III	BANCO ITAU Argentina – BUENOS AIRES	1:5
LATAM AIRLINES	Level III	BANCO ITAU CHILE- SANTIAGO	1:1

Source: BDR Program, Operating Procedural Manual[18]

Table 4.5.2 Sponsored BDRs

Table above shows a 10 sponsored level I & III BDR programs. Banco Patagonia with a ratio of 1:20. While the TGLTS.A with a BDR ratio of 1:5 (one BDR equals to 5 foreign shares). The other 8 companies have a ratio of 1:1; most of them have a bank of New York-Londres as custodian.

4.5.3   Unsponsored BDR

COMPANY	LEVEL	CUSTODIAN SHARES	RATIO BDR*shares
AMAZON.COM	Level I	The Bank of New York Mellon	2:1
CATERPILLAR	Level I	The Bank of New York Mellon	1:1
CHEVRON CORP	Level I	The Bank of New York Mellon	2:1
COLGATE- PALMOLIVE	Level I	The Bank of New York Mellon	1:1
MASTERCARD INC	Level I	The Bank of New York Mellon	1:1
NIKE INC	Level I	The Bank of New York Mellon	1:1
ORACLE	Level I	The Bank of New York Mellon	1:1
SCHLUMBERGER N.V.	Level I	The Bank of New York Mellon	1:1
THE COCA COLA CO.	Level I	The Bank of New York Mellon	1:1
TIFFANY & CO.	Level I	The Bank of New York Mellon	1:1
UNITED TECHNOLOGIES	Level I	The Bank of New York Mellon	1:1
US BANCORP	Level I	The Bank of New York Mellon	1:1

Source: BDR Program, Operating Procedural Manual[18]

Table above shows a 12 unsponsored level I BDR programs. Amazon.com & Chevron CORP has a BDR ratio of 2:1(2 BDR program equals to 1foreign share). The other 10 companies have a ratio of 1:1; most of them have a bank of New York-Mellon as custodian.

US are the largest investor in Brazilian equities with 43% of total Brazilian equity investment holdings, and a 46% held in depository receipts. By sector, the largest Brazilian depository receipts market capitalization was found in the utility sector with 22%, consumer discretionary with 17%, basic materials with 15%, financials13% and 11% industrials, with all other sectors comprising 22% balance.

BDRs are popular much among international foreign stocks that have strong ties with Brazil. Spanish telecommunications Telefonica which is a telephone service provider for Sao Paulo Brazilian stock exchange set up its BDR program to facilitate local trading.

Few companies with operations initiation in Brazil have incorporated in foreign jurisdictions for tax purposes and issued BDRs back into Brazil. One of them is Banco Patagonia[19], an Argentina bank, combined an initial public offering in Argentina with an issue of BDRs in Brazil.

Brazilian banking giant Bradesco has become the fourth financial institutions to be selected to issue Unsponsored Level I BDRs on BM & BOVESPA. BDR were allowed to be traded only by financial institutions, investment funds, asset managers and stock consultants authorized by CVM. On march 24, the CVM issued instructions 493, which allows private pension plans, individuals and companies with financial investments of over $ 1 million to trade Level I BDRs, sponsored or not.

Spanish financial company Banco Santander[20] SA has raised $8.1 billion with an initial public offering of shares in Brazilian subsidiaries. Santander's Brazilian shares slipped 2.1 % in their trading debut on Brazilian Bovespa exchange in Sao Paulo. Santandar is Brazil's third largest private sector bank after ITAU-UNIBANCO and BRADESCO[21].

Brazil was one of the last countries hit by the economic meltdown and was able to recover because government has put in huge tax breaks in 2010. Early of twenty first century witnessed great economic policies of Brazilian government. Brazilian economy got additional boosts by upgrade infrastructure, played a host to soccer's world cup 2014 and was a host to summer Olympics 2016, the positive effects of which were evident in the growth of Brazilian capital market.

4.5.2   Depository receipts framework in Taiwan

Taiwan depository receipts: - International company's listings its depository receipts on the Taiwan stock exchange are called Taiwan Depository Receipts. Taiwan has emerged as one of the most favorites destinations for foreign issuers in the Asian region. The liberalization of the Taiwan stock market and the regulations governing changes in the listing of foreign enterprises allow the securities of non-Taiwan stocks to be listed on Taiwan stock exchanges have increased the demand of Taiwan Depository Receipts. There are also numbers of other factors that are making capital markets appealing are its developed extensive clusters, positive P/E ratios of the stocks listed on it, and improved liquidity levels.

---

19 https://www.itau.com.br/_arquivosestaticos/SecuritiesServices/defaultTheme/PDF/PROCEDIMENTO_BDREN.pdf

20 http://www.cbsnews.com/news/banco-santanders-brazilian-ipo-raises-81b/

21 http://www.thetradenews.com/Regions/Americas/Bradesco-selected-to-issue-unsponsored-Brazilian-depository-receipts/

4.5.2.1   TDR regulatory system:-

Taiwan stock market regulators and the securities exchange commission (SEC) announced the regulations in 1992 governing the issuance of Taiwan Depository Receipts. The Taiwan depository receipts are listed on the Taiwan stock exchange and are denominated in New Taiwan dollars (TWD)[22].

The main regulations need to be followed to get listed in the Taiwan stock exchange[23].

- Company size should be at least 20 million shares or a market value of at least New Taiwan dollars (TWD) 300 million which is around USD 10 million[23].
- The company must have shareholder equity value equivalent to TWD 600 million (USD 20 million).
- The company must have a pre-tax profit of at least 6% of shareholder's equity in the most recent years and 2.5% of shareholder value in last two consecutive years, with a profitable stage better year by year.
- The company should have a pre-tax profitability should be TWD 250 million (USD 8.5 million) each in the last two consecutive fiscal years.
- There should not be less than 1000 TDR holders at the proposed listing period in Taiwan, and shareholders should have at least 20% of the shares or 10 million shares.
- The shares of the foreign stocks need to be registered and they should get listed on an international stock exchanges or securities market approved by competent authority for issuing Taiwan Depository Receipts.
- The underlying shares of the TDR should be either already issued shares or new shares; there is no upper limit on the quantity issued. A TDR holder must request the depository institution to redeem the TDR into shares. On request by a TDR holder, the depository could either redeem the TDR into shares or could sell the TDR in the market where it is listed.
- The depository system may reissue TDRs with the original redemption amount or issue new TDRs if the capital rises.

4.5.2.2   Regulatory Frame Work of TDRs:-

There are seven regulations governing the Taiwan Depository receipts[24].

- ➢ Taiwan stock exchange corporation rules governing review of securities listings
- ➢ Taiwan stock exchange corporation procedures for verification and disclosure of material information of listed companies. This regulation requires the foreign listed stocks to disclose their material information as it is needed by the laws of the home country or the country of listings.
- ➢ Taiwan stock exchange corporation operational procedure for review of Taiwan depository receipt listings. The listing of securities issued by foreign listed stocks shall be conducted accordance to these operational procedures.

22 http://www.pwc.tw/en/publications/assets/tdr.pdf, Taiwan depository receipts, price water house coopers Taiwan.
23 http://twse-regulation.twse.com.tw/ENG/EN/tree/tree.aspx#law01, tree structure of rules & regulations, Taiwan.
http://www.pwc.tw/en/ipo-in-tw/feature/tdr.html
24 http://www.twse.com.tw/en/listed/alien_business/download/qa.pdf

> Taiwan Stock Exchange Corporation rules governing contracts for the listing of Taiwan depository receipts. These rules govern the contracts between the foreign stock issuer and the depository system for the exchange listings of previously issued TDRs.

> Additional provisions to the Taiwan stock market exchange corporation rules for review of securities listings.

4.5.2.3   Performance record of Taiwan depository receipts:-

The first Taiwan depository receipts was issued in 1999, although there were introduced in 1992. TDRs became popular among international investors only after 2006.

Table no. 4.5.4 Performances of TDRs year wise

Year	No of TDRs	Trading amount	Trading volume
2006	5	29,053,630,350	53,57,988,176
2007	5	91,926,426,436	11,052,523,236
2008	5	28,610,911,241	42,661,112,510
2009	14	128,488,924,006	9,526,960,568
2010	26	261,905,819,089	17,608,811,281
2011	34	142,183,965,243	11,082,100,915
2012	34	35,183,963,263	4600438,226
2013	31	27,745,641,385	385,0454,672
2014	27	22,573,559,644	3357,382,732
2015	26	22,217,403,292	4274,376,488

Source: - Taiwan stock exchange fact sheet 2015[25]

In the above table, it is visible that in the early years of Taiwan depository receipts listings of stocks were very less in number because the regulations at that time permitted only few foreign stocks that were listed in major foreign stock exchanges (such as NYSE, AMSE,NASDAQ,LSE etc) to be listed under TDR program. Additionally, stock regulations requirements were to have a very strong capital and profitability records. The Taiwan government has taken serious steps in order to improve the regulatory conditions for the stock listings of TDRs, Which includes steps as elimination of restrictions on the settlement of funds from Taiwan to mainland china in 2008. The financial supervisory commission is the government agency responsible for regulating securities market in Taiwan decreased the threshold for the first listing of foreign stocks on Taiwan's stock exchanges and OTC market. One more reason for success of Taiwan depository receipts was the agreement signing of Cross- Straits Economic Cooperation Frame Work (ECFA) with China in 2010. After these changes many companies from Asia- Pacific regions (China, Singapore, and Hong Kong) issued several TDRs[26].

---

25   http://www.twse.com.tw/en/statistics/statistics_list.php?tm=07 & stm=005 & gt, Taiwan stock exchange fact sheet 2015.

26   Shipra, Pallavi, (2012). Depository Receipts: Comparison of Regulatory Frame Work in Taiwan, Brazil, Hong Kong & India, National Stock Exchange, India.

In 2006, one more factor that has contributed immensely to the success of TDRs was that TSE (Taiwan Stock Exchange) permitted various investors to borrow cash and to use the same securities as collateral which resulted in 20 new listings of TDRs during 2008 to 2010. The listings of TDRs are a speedy and easy process with fewer investment structures or tax planning issues.

4.5.3   Depository receipts framework in Russia

RUSSIAN DEPOSITORY RECEIPTS:-

Depository receipts trading on the Russian stock exchange are known as Russian depository receipts. An RDR is a Russian registered security with no nominal value that (a) certifies a right of ownership of an RDR holder to a certain number of underlying shares and (b) provides for a right of the RDR holder to demand from the depository provision of certain services related to the rights attached to the underlying securities or delivery of the corresponding number of the underlying securities in exchange for an RDR.

The much awaited legal frame work of Russian depository receipts came in to force in Jan 2007. In 2012, the Russian state Duma adopted amendments to certain primary legislation including the federal law "on joint companies" & "on the securities market law". The amendments further developed and simplified the regulatory frame work of Russian financial markets. Amendments came in to force on 2 January 2013[27]. As a result of the Amendments, Russian issuers and foreign depository banks are not required to disclose the ultimate beneficial owners of the depository receipts on a quarterly basis.

They are different ways foreign stocks can access the Russian market, one of the way is through issuing Russian depository receipts. Under the securities law, a RDR means a registered security without a nominal value, which certifies both the right to a specified amount of shares or bonds and the provisions of services in connection with realization of rights by a RDR holder. In order to issue RDRs, the company must deposit its shares with a depository bank which will issue RDRs. Depository banks which are licensed, incorporated in Russia operating as a depository business for at least three years with an equity capital amounting to at least 200 million RUB are allowed to issue RDRs. RDRs are circulated immediately after the registration of the issue.

Definition:-A Russian depository receipt is a registered uncertified security that:

- Does not have a par value
- Confers ownership rights to a certain number of shares or bonds of a foreign issuer (underlying securities)
- Carries the RDR holder's right to receive from the RDRs issuer the relevant number of underlying securities in exchange for the depository receipts and to provide with services in relation to the exercise of rights attached to the underlying securities by the RDR holder.[28]

4.5.3.1   Regulatory frame work of Russian depository receipts[29]:-

- Russian Federal service of financial market (FSFM)
- Russian ministry of finance
- Central bank of the Russian federation (CBR)

---

27   https://www.lw.com/thoughtLeadership/amendments-to-russian-financial-regulatory-regime

28   http://moex.com/a1128, Moscow Stock Exchange.

29   http://uk.practicallaw.com/3-518-7086

- Federal antimonopoly service of the Russian federation (FAS)
- Moscow exchange group (MOEX)

Amendments relating to deposit agreement were to be registered with the FSFM. On Sep 1, 2013, the FSFM was declared invalid by president Decree no. 64. On July 25, 2013, the functions of regulation, control and supervision of financial markets were transferred to the Central bank of Russian federation[30]. The central bank of Russian federation is the main regulator in Russian markets. CBR regulates the securities issues, prospectus and supervises the compliances by issuer with the requirements of the federal legislation on securities, issues listing rules and regulations of Russian depository receipts. It regulates, control and supervises the financial markets & institutions. Russian ministry of finance is responsible for strategic issues related to the development of financial markets. The Russian finance ministry determines the procedures for issuing federal government securities. Russian finance ministry (Minfin) also prepares the regulations on minimum capital requirements for market participants and their asset structure, with the participation of bank of Russia. The role of federal antimonopoly service is to secure competition, restrict monopolistic activities in strategic enterprises. FAS supervise foreign investor's activities in strategic enterprises. Moscow stock exchange is among the first top 30 leading stock exchanges. MOEX has a broad variety of markets including securities, derivatives, foreign exchange, money and precious metal markets. RDRs are listed on MOEX exchange. Amendments relating to deposit agreement will have to be registered with the FSFM.

4.5.2   Russian depository receipt participants:-

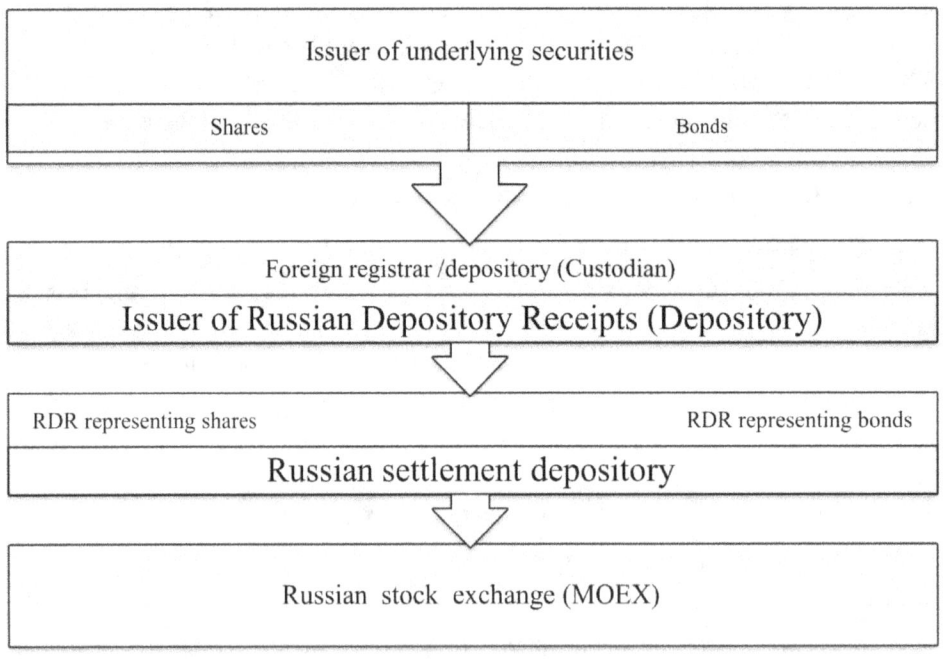

Source:-Russian Depositary Receipts issuance scheme (Moscow exchange)

---

30   RTS MARKET, issue Jan/Feb 2011.

- Issuer of underlying securities (company):- Issuer Company is responsible in preparation of issue proposal, financial objectives, obtaining the approvals from board of directors, shareholders, having investor relation plan. Issuer of underlying securities must take up obligations to RDR security holder that are provided in the agreement signed with the depository. The agreement constitutes an integral part of the issuance decision.
- Depository bank: - Sberbank of Russia is the largest credit institution in Russia. It acts as an issuer and depository of RDRs. Sberbank[31] depository is the authorised bank by the issuer company to issue RDRs against the equity shares of the issuer company deposited with the custodian. Sberbank is responsible for appointing the custodian, preparation and issue of RDR certificate, communicating with lawyers, accountants and investment bankers to ensure RDR program is implemented. Depository was set up in accordance with the Russian law and fulfil the requirements established in regulatory acts of the Bank of Russia regarding the equity capital maximum size and should have at least three years of depository activity.
- Custodian Bank:- Clear stream banking S.A was appointed as a custodian of securities underlying the RDRs in Russia. Depository may replace custodian with another custodian from the list of custodians approved by the Russian Federal service for the financial markets (FSFM) at any time. Custodian is responsible for holding the underlying shares, contacting with depository on corporate decisions and related issues, dividends payments to the investors through depository. Custodian maintains records of ownership rights to the securities represented by RDRs & is included in the list approved by bank of Russia.
- MOEX stock exchange:-MOEX was created after the merger of two major Russian stock exchanges MICEX (Moscow interbank currency exchange) & Russian trading system (RTS) in 2011. It has a broad variety of markets including securities, derivatives, foreign exchange, money and precious metal markets. RDRs are listed both MOEX stock exchange and Russian trading system. These stock exchanges are incorporated under the Russian law that allow RDRs to trade with or without undergoing the listing procedure.

4.5.3.2 Requirements of the company to get listed as RDRs :-

- Disclosure by depository:- The depository is required to disclose to public, its quarterly reports and notices of material events related to its business, as well as other information related to federal law on the securities market No. 39-FZ dated 22 April 1996 & the federal law on the joint stock companies no. 208-FZ dated 26 December 1995.
- Disclosure by company & shares:- As such depository is responsible to disclose on going periodic requirements with respect to company and shares under the Russian securities law. The company needs to furnish the depository the annual reports, financial statements prepared in accordance with IFRS, as well as public announcements of price- sensitive information related to company and shares.
- Disclosure on Interfax Russian newswire: - Notices related material events, financial statements of the company will be made available on the Interfax Russian newswire by the depository.

4.5.3.3 Performance record of Russian depository receipts:-

RDRs are new instruments in Russia. The Russian securities saw its first RDR from united company RUSAL PLC (Jersey) in December 2010. RUSAL PLC is a parent company of a group, being the world's largest

---

31 "Terms & conditions", UC RUSAL Plc', Russian depository receipts.

producer of aluminium located in Jersey. Sberbank was the first company to issue RDRs, on the ordinary shares of United Company RUSAL Plc. RDRs is listed on MICEX (Moscow interbank currency exchange and Russian trading system which after merger of two exchanges in 2011, now is called as MOEX). This was done to increase the company's market visibility and brand enhancement in Russia. The maximum size of the RDR program is 2000,000,000[32] RDRs which represents 100% of the total authorized share capital of the company. Each RDR represents a right of its holder to receive 10 common shares. RDR do not have any nominal value. There is no time limit on the issue of RDRs with in the RDR program. There is Fungibility, company's shareholders will be able to receive RDRs against the deposit of shares and vice versa, RDR holder will be able to receive shares. RDRs represent ownership rights to the companies' ordinary shares with nominal value of US $ 0.01each. On December 24, 2010 RTS (Russian trading system) launched its first Russian depository receipt of Sberbank representing rights on ordinary shares of united company RUSAL Plc (with a registration no. 5-01- 01481-B as of 07.12.2010)[33]. On the first trading day the following parameters were followed: starting price is RUB460.0 per 1RDR which is to be converted into US dollars at the exchange rate of the Central bank of the Russian federation as of 24.12.2010; price limits were +/- 35%[33].

Problems faced by RUSAL PLC while trading through RDRs:-

- Due to derivative nature of the RDRs, the depository company's business, financial condition and results of operations had a significant impact on the market price of shares.
- As such RDRs are securities traded and listed in Russia. As Russia is an emerging market, it is subject to greater risks than more developed markets. Political, economic and social conditions in Russia have an adverse effect on the price and liquidity of RDRs.
- As the RDRs were new instruments for Russia, there was a limited float of RDRs resulting increased price volatility. In order to maintain listings on Russian stock exchanges, depositories were required to comply with the listing requirements.
- Lack of clarity of taxation. Russian tax consequences are based on the limited available clarification issued by the Russian ministry of finance which do not have a force of law.

4.5.4   Depository receipts framework in India

Indian depository receipts:-

Indian company's trades on foreign markets through various instruments are American depository receipts, global depository receipts & foreign currency convertible bonds on overseas stock exchanges like NYSE, Luxembourg stock exchange, London stock exchange & European stock exchanges. As the Indian securities markets have become deeper with BSE Sensex and NSE nifty giving higher returns as compared to other indices of the world. Foreign companies have started showing interest in the Indian securities market. India is becoming popular among foreign investors as a preferred investment destination for investment; the Indian government has introduced and modified various financial instruments through which investment can be made by different investors. Indian government has introduced the concept of Indian depository

---

32 "Terms & conditions", UC RUSAL Plc', Russian depository receipts.

33 RTS MARKETS, ISSUE JAN/ FEB 2011

receipts (IDRs) to facilitate listings by foreign firms on Indian stock markets. An international company can now access Indian stock market by raising funds through issuance of IDRs. The government of India notified the companies issue of Indian depository receipts rules, 2004 (companies IDRs rules), amended till date, pursuant to section 642 read with section 605 A of the companies act, 1956 of India[34]. First IDR was launched by Standard Chartered bank PLC on 13th May, 2010.

Section 2(48) of the companies act, 2013 defines an IDR as 'any instrument in the form of a depository receipt created by a domestic depository in India and authorized by a company incorporated outside India making an issue of such depository receipts'

4.5.4.1 Regulatory legal framework of Indian Depository receipts:-

IDRs issue is governed by the companies act, 1956, SEBI regulation 2009 & RBI circular. The Indian government has liberalized India's corporate and securities laws to allow foreign stocks to raise capital in the early twenty century. The Indian government companies' act, 1956 notified the corporate company's issues, rules, amendments, provisions related to IDRs were presented in the form of section 642 read with section 605 A in 2004. Companies residing outside India are allowed to issue IDRs through a domestic depository pursuant to a circular No. SEBI/ CFD/ DIL/ DIP/20/ 2006/3/4 dated April 3, 2006 and the provisions of issue of capital and disclosure requirements (ICDR) regulation 2009, which replaced the SEBI guidelines, 2000. The ICDR regulation 2009 circular allows individuals residing in & outside India to purchase, possess, transfer & redeem IDRs. SEBI, Ministry of corporate affairs & RBI are the regulatory bodies for IDRs governance.

The Indian legal framework for IDRs consists of[35]:

- Section 2(48), 234, 390 & 469 of the companies Act, 2013;
- Rule 13 of the companies for (registration of foreign companies) Rules, 2014;
- Chapter X of the SEBI (Issue of capital and disclosure requirements) regulations, 2009;
- SEBI circulars dated August 28, 2012 & March 01, 2013.
- Schedule 7 of the FEMA 20;
- Part I, Section 4, Para 2 of the master circular on Foreign Investment in India;
- Income tax Act, 1961.
- Section 605 A of the companies act, 1956
- Companies (issue of Indian Depository receipts) Rules 2004

4.5.4.2 Requirements of the company to get listed as IDRs

Companies rules Act, 2014 & SEBI (issue of capital & disclosure requirements) regulation 2009 has lay down the eligibility criteria for foreign companies to issue IDRs are as follows:

- Companies pre-issue paid up capital & free reserves of at least $50 million, minimum average market capitalisation of at least $ 100 million during the last three years in its home country[36];

---

34 https://en.wikipedia.org/wiki/Indian_Depository_Receipt

35 Report of committee to review the frame work of access to domestic & overseas Capital markets, Indian Depository Receipts, Ministry of finance, 2014

36 Rule 13 (2) (a), ministry of corporate affairs, Companies, rules, 2014,.

- Company should have a track record of distributable profits for at least three of the immediately preceding five years[37];
- Company has been continuously trading in its home countries stock exchange for at least three immediately preceding years[38];
- Company is not been prohibited by any regulatory body from issuing securities;
- It has a record of compliance with the stock market regulations in its parent company;
- Companies issue size should not be less than ₹50 crore and a minimum application amount shall be ₹20000; &
- At least 50% of IDRs issued should be allotted to qualified institutional investors on proportionate basis.

4.5.4.3   Performance of IDRs:-

Standard Chartered bank was the first company to launch IDRs in India on 13th May, 2010[39]. Standard Chartered PLC is a holding company which operates 1700 branches in 70 countries using various subsidiaries. Income of the standard chartered bank is majorly from Asia, Africa & West Asia. Shares of the standard Plc bank are already listed on London & Honk Kong stock exchanges. As Indian government has allowed two-way Fungibility in IDRs, standard chartered IDR has become more attractive for various investors. Investors trade by taking advantage of price disparity in price between two locations (exchanges) through Fungibility.

There was an issue of 240 million Indian depository receipts (IDRs). First issue was open for subscription from May 25, 2010 to May 28, 2010[40]. IDRs issue price band was fixed between ₹ 100 & ₹ 115[40]. Foreign bank raises ₹ 2400 crore at the lower end and ₹ 2760 crore at the higher end of the price band. On May 25, 2010, the standard chartered bank PLC offered price at ₹ 104 & raised ₹ 2490 crore ($ 530 million) by selling 240 million IDRs. Out of the 240 million of the IDRs sold, 36 million IDRs were placed with six anchor investors at a rate of ₹ 104 & remaining 204 million shares were normally offered, bids of 449 million shares were placed. Subscribers of the first IDRs included reliance mutual fund for 1.05 crore IDRs, ICICI Prudential AMC for 96 lakh, HDFC AMC 60 lakhs, Franklin Templeton AMC for 48 lakh, Birla Sun Life mutual fund for 35.5 lakh, Sundaram BNP Paribas for 14 lakhs. On the same date, 30% of IDRs were allotted to retail investors, 50 % of the IDRs were reserved for qualified institutional buyers (QUIBs) & high net worth individuals with 18%.

On June 11, 2010, IDRs was opened at BSE & NSE at a listing price of ₹ 105.05 and on the same day raised up to ₹ 106.40, raised a profit between ₹ 2521crores to ₹ 2553 crore. Standard chartered bank PLC gained a net profit of ₹ 26,278[41] crore for the year ended December, 2011. The bank has met the regulations stipulated by Basel III with a strong capital position. Total numbers of bids received at NSE

---

37 Rule 13(2) (c), IBID

38 Report of committee to review the frame work of access to domestic & overseas Capital markets, Indian Depository Receipts, Ministry of finance, 2014

39 Shipra, Pallavi, (2012). Depository Receipts: Comparison of Regulatory Frame Work in Taiwan, Brazil, Hong Kong & India, National Stock Exchange, India.

40 http://www.thehindubusinessline.com/todays-paper/tp-markets/article992575.ece

41 http://www.thehindubusinessline.com/portfolio/standard-chartered-idr-buy/article3266297.ece

were 312,025,000 & at BSE was 137,680,000 IDRs with a cut-off price of 15,033,200[42]. In November 2015, standard chartered bank PLC has raised ₹ 14 crore by selling rights issue entitlements of IDR holders.

Problems faced by companies while issuing IDRs:-

➤ In 2015, British standard chartered bank said it will not undertake the rights issue of IDRs due to procedural hindrance and IDR holders will be given a cash-out option[43].

➤ Asia- focused standard chartered bank PLC reported a loss of $ 139 million for the third September quarter as against a net profit of $ 1.5 billion in the previous year. Bank blamed the poor asset quality as one of the major factors for a loss.

➤ In august, 2016 the standard chartered bank expressed disappointment with its Indian operations, said the impact of Indian reforms has been slower and corporates are still struggling.

➤ Currency risk was there due to the strengthening of the US$ verses Indian rupee.

➤ Price fluctuations were directly linked to the share price of standard chartered bank of London stock exchange, if at all any fluctuations in the European economy would be there, it will affect the valuation of banks & in turn affects the IDR price movements.

➤ IDRs are having a lack of clarity on the issue of taxation. IDRs are not having securities transaction tax. IDRs are neither subjected to securities transaction tax nor to dividend distribution tax[44]. Income tax act 1961 doesn't have clarity about IDR taxation. Law is not clear on tax treatment on conversion of IDRs into underlying securities. Section 47(X) was introduced by Income tax act 1961, deals with transfer by way of conversion of DRs is applicable to GDRs & ADRs but not to IDRs.

➤ IDRs are having a restricted Fungibility[45]. There is a tremendous confusion about the mode and the extent of Fungibility permitted. Even though government has accepted two ways Fungibility, the guidelines impose furthermore restrictions, such as reservation of 20% for retail investors, redemption on proportionate basis etc. This circular further prohibits fungibility during the first year after the issue and limits fungibility to 25% of the original issue in the subsequent financial years. Thus, there is partial two-way fungibility[46] with lot many restrictions with no clarity.

➤ Certain group of investors are not allowed to invest in IDRs. Insurance companies & pension funds are prohibited under insurance laws from investing in IDRs.

➤ Indian schemes related to IDRs should be a mirror image of ADR/GDR. Because, how we treat to overseas companies while facilitating issue IDRs, the same treatment we will be receiving while our companies invest in other stock exchanges.

➤ FEMA 20, schedule 7 describes the proceeds of issue of IDRs to be early repatriated outside India by the issuer company which prevents foreign firms from using the IDRs route to fund its Indian operations.

42 Shipra, Pallavi, (2012). Depository Receipts: Comparison of Regulatory Frame Work in Taiwan, Brazil, Hong Kong & India, National Stock Exchange, India.

43 http://profit.ndtv.com/news/market/article-stanchart-not-to-undertake-rights-issue-of-indian-depository-receipts-on-impediments-1244906

44 IDR_Fungibility_-_FAQs.pdf

45 Report of committee to review the frame work of access to domestic & overseas Capital markets, Indian Depository Receipts, Ministry of finance, 2014

46 Partial two way fungibility means the IDR issuer will make available up to 25% of the original issue of IDRs per annum for redemption in to underlying equity shares together with the ability to convert equity shares into IDRs.

➢ There is a restrictive eligibility criterion while issuing IDRs. This criterion allows those investors which meet the eligibility requirements to use IDR instrument. Apart from the above mentioned eligibility criteria, the present DR regime does not allow an issuer to issue IDRs in India unless the companies' shares are listed and traded for at least three years overseas. Companies are not allowed to issue IDRs unless it issues half of the issue size to qualified institutional buyers (QIBs).

➢ Approval process for the issue of IDRs is very complicated. The company is required to obtain a written approval from SEBI on an application form. SEBI has brought in limited merit based regulation which gives power to SEBI to reject draft offer documents in most cases. The requirements of the approval for an issue of IDRs takes India back to two decades to a merit based regulatory regime.

4.5.5   Depository receipts framework in Hong Kong

Hong Kong depository receipts:-

Hong Kong depository receipts are a negotiable instrument issued by a depository bank which evidences ownership of company shares organized outside Hong Kong. It is market situated in the high- growth Asia & serves as a vital financial hub for Hong Kong, China & the rest of Asia- pacific region[47]. Hong Kong is one of the leading financial centers in the world for trade & finance. Hong Kong has a good reputation of most popular destinations for capital rising among global financial markets. Hong Kong exchanges are often a prime choice for companies incorporated in the people's republic of China. Listings on the Hong Kong stock exchanges boost a company's brand in the Asia-Pacific region. Number of international stocks listed on Hong Kong has increased substantially from 2006-11. In 2011, Hong Kong topped as the world's top finance center keeping behind both U.K & U.S stock exchanges in the world's economic forum financial index. According to a study produced by international accounting firms, overseas companies raised only 4% of total funds raised in Hong Kong, in 2007 & by 2011 the share shot up to 52% which signifies most of the overseas firms are interested trading in Hong Kong stock exchanges. The first Hong Kong depository receipts were launched on 1st July, 2008[48]. The Chinese stocks listed on Hong Kong stock exchanges can be divided into direct and indirect listings. Direct listings shares are referred to as H-shares which mean companies incorporated in China & approved by the China security regulatory commission (CSRC)[49]. One of the example of indirect listings are Red chips, are stocks of companies incorporated at least 30% of its shares in aggregate held by main land China firms & remaining either in Hong Kong or in Tax Havens such as Cayman Islands or Bermuda.

4.5.5.1   Requirements of the company to get listed as HDRs

Foreign stocks willing to list on a Hong Kong stock exchange through HDRs have to comply with same listing regime as issuers listing in the form of normal shares. All the existing Hong Kong share holder protections in the listing rules shall apply to HDR issuer[50]. The listings requirements should comply with the Main Board listing rules (chapter 8)

---

47   BNY MELLON, Hong Kong depository receipts, 2009.

48   Financial services development council, positioning Hong Kong as an international IPO center, FSDC Paper no.9.

49   Shipra, Pallavi, (2012). Depository Receipts: Comparison of Regulatory Frame Work in Taiwan, Brazil, Hong Kong & India, National Stock Exchange, India.

50   http://www.hkex.com.hk/eng/rulesreg/listrules/mbrules/vol1_2.htm, chapter no 8, main board listing, HKEX.

- A trading record of not less than three financial years;
- The issuer must have a trading record of not less than HK$ 20,000,000, in most recent years & not less than HK$ 30,000,000, in respect of the two preceding years.
- The issuer management must have a continuity for at least three preceding financial years
- Issuer must have a market capitalisation of at least HK$2,000,000,000 at the time of listings.
- Revenue of at least HK$5,00,000,000 for the most audited financial year &
- Issuer must have a ownership continuity and control for at least the most recent audited financial year;
- Positive cash flow from operating activities of at least HK$ 100,000,000 in the three preceding financial years.
- Free flow requirement should not be less than 25% for primary listing.
- All disclosures & materials must be in English
- Immediate disclosure of major transactions or price sensitivity information
- Issuer allowed preparing the financial statements under Hong Kong financial reporting standards, IFRS & U.S GAAP[51].

4.5.5.2   Regulatory frame work of Hong Kong depository receipts

Hong Kong regulatory environment is well respected globally. Its legal system are based on English common law principles and accounting requirements which includes Hong Kong reporting standards, International financial reporting standards & U.S GAAP. Hong Kong stock exchange listing rules are user friendly with other international exchange standards. Main board listing rules Chapter 19B includes rules related to HDRs.

Regulatory bodies of HDRs include [52]

- Securities & Futures Commission
- Hong Kong Securities Clearing Company Limited (HKSCC)
- Stock Exchange of Hong Kong Limited
- Hong Kong Futures Exchange Limited
- Clearing houses
- Hong Kong Centralised Securities Depository (CCASS)
- Hang Seng Foreign Companies Composite Index (HSFCCI)[53]
- Section 13.46 (2), 13.47 & 13.48 of the listing rules explains financial reporting.
- The issuer should comply with the trading & settlement rules under13.58 to 13.62.

Exchange listing rules of Hong Kong depository receipts is included in chapter 19 & 19 B[54] on 1st July, 2008. HKSCC determines the manner in which issue of securities deposited, cleared and settled in CCASS. HKSCC will collect instructions from CCASS participants and take actions on their behalf. CCASS & HKSCC will support the depository by providing its nominee services in relation to the corporate actions

---

51 BNY MELLON, Hong Kong depository receipts, 2009.

52 http://www.hkex.com.hk/eng/rulesreg/regintro/introreg.htm, Introduction to regulatory frame work, HKEX.

53 http://www.hsi.com.hk/HSI-Net/static/revamp/contents/en/dl_centre/brochures/hsfcci_E.pdf

54 http://www.hkex.com.hk/eng/rulesreg/listrules/mbrules/documents/chapter_19b.pdf

or activities affecting HDRs. Hang Seng serves as a bench mark that reflects the overall performances of foreign stocks listed on Hong Kong Stock exchange.

Certain amendments are included under HDR frame work of listing rules of the stock exchange main board are as follows[55]:

- Describes the applicable rules for the HDR issuer
- Setting out the requirements for the depository and the obligations of the HDR issuer on any change of depository
- Setting out the required contents of the deposit agreement that defines the rights of the HDR holder.

4.5.5.3   Performance of Hong Kong Depository Receipts:

On 13th May, 2014 there were only five listed Hong Kong Depository Receipts on the Main board. List of five listed HDR are

- Vale Common-DRS (Brazil)
- Vale Pref -DRS (Brazil)
- Fast Retail- DRS (Japan)
- Coach- DRS-RS (USA)
- SBI holdings –DRs (Japan)

A SBI holding is a Japanese company listed as a HDR on Hong Kong Stock Exchange. Company raised US$ 207 million after issuing 20,000,000 HDRs at an issue price of USD 10.35 (HKD80.23 per unit)[56]. On June 25, 2014, SBI holding has decided to delist its HDRs from Hong Kong Stock Exchange to reduce costs & stream line operations arising from the maintenance of the HDR listing. Fast retail DRS and Coach –DRS RS are the two only companies presently trading through HDRs on Hong Kong stock exchanges[57]. Other three companies are delisted. Fast retailing company belongs to Japan, issued shares of 500,000,000 with a market capitalization of 12,000,000,000 HKD of JPY 1.65 per HDR. Coach –DRS-RS is a U.S.A company listed as an HDR with 293,603,937 shares issued, market capitalization of HKD 8,235,590,433 of HKD 0.261765 per HDR. Hong Kong is a great place to do business due to its progressive financial and tax land scape. There are no capital flow restrictions while trading in HDRs. It has a many tax advantages compare to other countries. Easy currency convertibility is observed while trading in HDRs. The HDRs securities are freely transferable. A Hong Kong depository receipt has a very friendly regulatory environment. Issuer can follow English common law principles, Hong Kong financial reporting standards or international financial reporting standards or U.S GAAP while trading through HDRs[58]. Due to these Hong Kong has earned lot of respect among traders.

---

55   https://www.hkex.com.hk/eng/newsconsul/hkexnews/2008/080509news.htm

56   https://investor.shareholder.com/jpmorganchase/releasedetail.cfm?releaseid=569089

57   https://www.hkex.com.hk/eng/market/sec_tradinfo/stockcode/eisdhdr.htm

58   BNY MELLON, Hong Kong depository receipts, 2009.

4.5.3   Comparative Analysis of Selected Foreign Jurisdictions

S.no	Parameters	India	Brazil	Taiwan	Hong Kong	Russia
1	Paid-up capital	Pre- issued paid up capital of at least $ 50 million	Foreign companies must register itself as a publicly held company and an issuer of BDRs, and issue shares held in custody in the issuer's home market	company must have shareholder equity value equivalent to TWD 600 million (USD 20 million)	Issuer must have a trading record of not less than HK$ 20,000,000, in most recent years & not less than HK$ 30,000,000, in respect of the two preceding years.	equity capital amounting to at least 200 million RUB are allowed to issue RDRs.
2	Market capitalization	Minimum average market capitalization of at least $ 100 million during the last three years in its home country	None	market value of at least New Taiwan dollars (TWD) 300 million which is around USD 10 million	Issuer must have a market capitalization of at least HK$2,000,000,000 at the time of listings.	None
3	Profitability	Company should have a track record of distributable profits for at least three of the immediately preceding five years	Companies' financial information related to previous three tax years profits should be disclosed	company should have a pre-tax profitability should be TWD 250 million (USD 8.5 million) each in the last two consecutive fiscal years	Revenue of at least HK$5,00,000,000 for the most audited financial year	Company should have a track record of profits for three years.
4	Financial reporting compliance	Indian GAAP, IFRS or U.S GAAP	Unsponsored level I : no need to comply with Brazilian requirement; level II & III Brazilian standards or IASB standards	Taiwan standards, IFRS or US GAAP	Hong Kong financial reporting standards, IFRS, US GAAP	IFRS, Russian standards, GAAP U.S
5	Issue size	Companies issue size should not be less than ₹50 crore and a minimum application amount shall be ₹20000	No specification	There should not be less than 1000 TDR holders at the proposed listing period in Taiwan, and shareholders should have at least 20% of the shares or 10 million shares	None	maximum size of the RDR program is 2000,000,000 RDRs which represents 100% of the total authorized share capital of the company

S.no	Parameters	India	Brazil	Taiwan	Hong Kong	Russia
6	Regulators bodies	SEBI, Ministry of corporate affairs & RBI	National monetary council (CMN), Brazilian securities & exchange commission (CVM), BM & FBOVESPA (Brazilian Mercantile and Futures Exchange), Brazilian central bank (BACEN)	Taiwan stock exchange rules governing contracts, Taiwan stock market regulators and the securities exchange commission (SEC)	Securities & Futures Commission, Hong Kong Securities Clearing Company Limited (HKSCC), Stock Exchange of Hong Kong Limited, Hong Kong Futures Exchange Limited, Hong Kong Centralized Securities Depository (CCASS), Hang Seng Foreign Companies Composite Index (HSFCCI)	Russian Federal service of financial market (FSFM), Russian ministry of finance, Central bank of the Russian federation (CBR), Federal antimonopoly service of the Russian federation (FAS), and Moscow exchange group (MOEX).
7	Instruments	IDRs	BDRs	TDRs	HDRs	RDRs
8	Level of instrument or structure	Sponsored only	Sponsored I, II or III, unsponsored I	Sponsored & unsponsored level I	Two tier DR structure	Sponsored only
9	Fungibility	Partial Two-way fungibility with 20 % reservation to retail investors	Two- way fungibility	TDR holder must request the depository institution to redeem the TDR into shares. On request by a TDR holder, the depository could either redeem the TDR into shares or could sell the TDR in the market where it is listed.	Two-way fungibility	Two-way fungibility, companies' shareholders shall be able to receive the deposit of shares & vice versa
10	Cost	₹ 20000 initial listing fees, annual fees starting from ₹ 100000 (increase with increase in listed capital)	Listing annuity = R$ 35000+ (stock capital -50,000,000*0.00473%) An auction cost to the depository bank upwards of R$1000000, a registration fees of R$ 51000.	Maximum listing fees is Taiwan $450000, minimum fees is Taiwan$ 50000.	Listing fees for DR issuer follows the same schedule as for the issuer of shares. 0.20% of the total issued capital.	Annual service fees will be up to R$ 0.9 per one RDR

S.no	Parameters	India	Brazil	Taiwan	Hong Kong	Russia
11	Time span to list		60 days after filing to CVM	11 to 45 business days after application	Time frame for DR issuer follows the same schedule as for the issuer of shares.	-
12	Tax norms	No clarity	Least tax requirement	least tax planning issues	Least tax requirements	High tax load
13	No. of listed companies	01 company listed in 2010	22 companies, 10 are sponsored DR program, 12 are unsponsored DR program	26 DR program listed	05, right now 02 shares	01 company listed in 2010
14	Operating history	At least three years of continuous trading at home country.	Companies' financial information related to previous three tax years drawn up accordance with Brazilian accounting standards	shares of the foreign stocks need to be registered and they should be getting listed on an international stock exchanges or securities market approved by competent authority for issuing Taiwan Depository Receipts	Management continuity of at least three preceding financial years	At least three years of continuous trading at home country.
15	Investor restrictions	Minimum application of ₹ 20000 for retail investors, & ₹ 100000 for QUIBs & non institutional buyers	Level I sponsored or unsponsored is available to only to sophisticated & FIIs investors, no restrictions on level II & III unsponsored programs.	Least restrictions	No restrictions	More restrictions
16	Currency denomination	Rupees	R dollar	Taiwan $	Hong Kong $	Rubles
17	Stringent or not stringent	Stringent	Not stringent	Moderately stringent	Not stringent	Stringent

4.6   Conclusion:-

The study examined the DR regulatory frame work of five countries- Taiwan, Brazil, Russia, India & Hong Kong. Study compared the DR regulatory frame work of five capital markets & states which capital markets is sparsely regulated & strictly regulated one. A DR issuer may list its shares on an international stock market for gaining visibility, to increase international customer base, to improve liquidity, to expand business.

Taiwanese government has taken various steps from time to time to improve the regulatory conditions of TDRs, steps like elimination of restrictions on the settlement of funds from Taiwan to main land china through getting into an agreement with cross –straits economic cooperation frame work in 2010. Financial supervisory commission is responsible for regulating stock market & has decreased the restrictions of first listings of foreign stocks on Taiwanese stock exchanges. Another reason for the success of TDRs was government has permitted various investors to borrow cash & use the same securities as collateral resulting in 20 new listings during 2008-10. One more benefit TDRs which is the reason of its popularity among foreign issuer is same tax laws for local & international shares (TDRs). TDRs listing process takes least time compare to an IPO listing is an added advantage compare to other capital markets. In the study, if we compare the TDR regulatory system with the others, in terms of profitability to issuer, TDR is considered as a strictly regulated one. Despite of these, the Taiwanese government attracts number of foreign investors every year.

Brazilian government has witnessed a great change in the economic policies resulted in the growth of Brazilian capital market base in the early 21st century. Several foreign stocks listed on Brazilian capital markets have raised huge profits. Brazil has less stringent norms compared to other capital markets with least stringent three- tier BDR program. BDR issuer has an option to select between sponsored & unsponsored level DR programs. Sponsored level I BDR program has a less stringent norms & disclosure requirements. For unsponsored level program, an issuer does not require any particular eligibility criteria for paid-up capital, market capitalization, time period of listing as a normal DR program requires. Brazilian DR programs with less stringent norms are considered as a sparsely regulated DR program.

U.S RUSAL PLC was the first & only company listed on Russian stock exchange. As Russia is an emerging market, with more stringent norms is subjected to greater risk than many other developed markets. There is a limited float of RDRs resulting in increased price volatility with complicated listing requirements. Like Indian tax law, Russian government doesn't have clarity about taxation of DRs. For these reason Russian capital market is strictly regulated market. Due to its stringent rules, regulations, weak regulatory environment & lot many disclosure requirements, Russian depository receipts are not very popular among foreign issuers. A failure to comply with the listing requirements may result in delisting of RDRs. For these, Russian capital markets are considered as strictly regulated one. Russian capital market should introduce less disclosure & listing requirements in order to attract more foreign issuers.

Hong Kong has earned a lot of respect among foreign issuers due to its friendly regulatory environment. Issuer can follow English common law principles, Hong Kong financial reporting standards or international financial reporting standards or U.S GAAP while trading through HDRs. HDRs securities are freely transferable. Hong Kong is a great place to do business due to its progressive financial and tax land scape. There are no capital flow restrictions while trading in HDRs. It has a many tax advantages compare to other countries. Easy currency convertibility is observed while trading in HDRs. Another advantage to issuer while trading through HDRs is similar listing requirements for local & foreign issuers resulting in more clarity. Issuers who listed through HDRs had an opinion that "the good thing about HDR as a product is that it allows more foreign issuers to be list in Hong Kong, whether raising funds or not, by eliminating some legal issues".[59] HDRs are popular among DRs to be transferable at a high speed. "Ability raise reminbi is also important", most of the companies are choosing Hong Kong dollars as the currency for HDRs, rather than US$. Number of foreign Jurisdictions like (Brazil, India, Japan, and Russia & South Korea) does not allow companies to maintain an offshore ordinary share registrar; HDRs do allow is an advantage among the DRs. Due to its issuer friendly regulatory environment, HDRs are considered as sparsely regulatory environment.

Standard Chartered PLC was the one & only company got listed on the Indian stock exchange through IDRs till date. Though SEBI has introduced two-way fungibility, the guidelines have more restrictions, such as reservation of 20% for retail investors. Indian government as introduced two-way fungibility should have more clarity with less restriction. In 2015, Indian stringent rules & eligibility criteria has been greatly criticized by foreign issuers. Out of these five countries, India has most stringent norms; as such it cannot be favorable. British standard chartered giant bank also stepped back due to its procedural hindrances. Indian government should take proper steps to improve relations with the foreign issuers. Like Hong Kong is having issuer friendly norms, issuer can use Hong Kong reporting standards, international financial reporting standards or U.S GAAP. India also should introduced likewise friendly norms with all international investors. Indian government should try to introduce similar norms related to listing & disclosure requirements for local & foreign issuers with more clarity.

India, Russia is considered as having the most stringent norms among all the capital markets in the study. Both the countries are emerging countries, does not have clarity on tax issues, listing & disclosure requirements, fungibility, eligibility of both the issuer & the investor. Taiwan also has stringent rules & regulations, but less compare to India & Russia. Taiwan comes with a strong DR market with lot many foreign issuers every year. Brazil & Hong Kong capital markets are sparsely regulated one. Brazil with least restrictions on sponsored & unsponsored programs are attracting more foreign issuers with least requirements & huge benefits. Hong Kong with issuer protecting regulatory environment & least restrictions gained much popularity among issuers. All these capital markets, even though they are performing better, they need to work harder to reach the level of ADRs & GDRs, by introducing issuer friendly regulatory environment without compromising on investor protection.

---

59   J.P Morgan, Hong Kong depository receipts, the innovation continues.

FINDINGS & CONCLUSIONS

The thesis examines the impact of cross listings on the valuation of Indian stocks. The impact of cross listings & cross border trading on the international stock exchanges & its impact on local stocks returns, liquidity, price & volatility. The study also compares the regulatory frame work of five capital markets.

Studies include five objectives or issues and are addressed in 4th chapter. First chapter includes introduction of Cross listings. Chapter 2 comprises of review of literature. Chapter3 include Research Methodology. Chapter 4 includes data analysis & interpretation. Chapter 4 comprises of 5 sections of 5 objectives. 1st section analyses the impact of cross listings on the Indian stock returns. 2nd section evaluates the impact of cross listings on the Indian stock liquidity. Section 3 examines the impact of cross listings on the Indian stock price. Section 4 examines the impact of cross listings on the Indian stock volatility. Section 5 includes the comparison of regulatory frame work of five capital markets. Over all, the findings shows that Indian stocks returns, liquidity, volatility & price are significantly affected by the international cross listings.

The findings of the study have several important implications for foreign issuers, companies, regulatory bodies, stock exchange authorities, investors & depository banks. The study also serves as a useful guide to the Indian investors who want to expand their business by crossing the borders.

Section 1 examines the impact of cross listings on the Indian stock returns. The study evaluates the cross listing impact on the Indian stocks listed on London stock exchange, Luxembourg stock exchange, New york stock exchange & London stock exchange separately. Separate analysis has been done for different stock exchanges. Study has considered 175 days as an event window for all the companies. It has been observed positive average abnormal returns prior to cross listings announcement, AAR is insignificantly negative after the cross listings. For all the samples, there is a clear evidence of increase in prices in the pre listing period & decrease in prices in the post- listing period. Similar results have been observed for sample of GDR listed Indian firms, ADR listed firms, NYSE listed firms, LSE listed firms, and LUXSE listed firms.

Study has considered 175 days as an event window for all the companies. The returns are positive for approximately 120 days while they are negative for only 50 days. From the 120 positive AAR values, 104 values are statistically significant at 1%, 12 are significant at 5% & 6 are significant at 10%. The negative returns are not significant on any of the 50 days. During the post announcement window from day $t_{(1)}$ to day $t_{(175)}$, the pattern of positive AARs changes to negative pattern of returns. It has been observed that the AARs values are negative for nearly 115 days. From the 60 positive AAR values of post announcement, 50values are significant at 1%, 9 values are significant at 5% & 2 values are significant at 10%. Looking at the speed of the share price adjustment to the new information emanating from the cross listings announcement, study observed that there is no lagging response to the cross listings announcement. The observed results indicate that the investors perceive the announcement of stock listings to be beneficial for them. Although the change of positive reaction prior to and on the announcement day to negative reaction, and after the announcement day indicates that the investors overreacted initially to these announcement, but a correction takes place quickly & positive returns turns to negative. The rationale for such results seems to be that the information about the event listing announcement reaches to the investors companies prior to the decision date as it will be mandatory for the listings companies to inform the exchanges and public regarding where it is listed locally, where it want to get listed itself internationally through ADRs or GDRs. It has been observed that the companies usually inform the public around one month prior date of announcement. In such a situation, the moment the listings information about meeting & agenda is given publically, this becomes public information & investors starts reacting to it. In the pre listing period positive reaction clearly indicates that investors perceive stock cross listings to be beneficial for them. This further leads to an increase in the demand for the issuing companies' shares leading to the positive abnormal returns. AAR on the day of listing is also substantial indicating that the moment the decision of cross listing announced, its stocks jumps high, providing positive AAR to the investors. Later, a correction takes place & the AARs become negative. This result suggests that the Indian stock market responds quickly & efficiently to the corporate news contained in cross listing announcement.

The returns are cumulated over the event window to assess the net magnitude of the overall performance of the stocks. In the CAAR graph it has been observed that the increasing trend of returns starts declining after cross listing. The listing of an Indian firm on international stock exchanges is a wealth enhancing point for DR issuers. Indian firms deciding to list on a foreign exchange to increase their returns must take into account various factors such as market conditions, industry trends, listing & disclosure requirements, tax issues etc. Hence, it can be concluded that cross listings through ADRs and GDRs does not get any significant financial benefit for the stock investors.

Section 2 covers the impact of cross listings on the Indian stocks liquidity. Study tests the impact of DRs by examining the changes in stock liquidity. Sample of the study includes Indian companies listed through ADRs & GDRs on NYSE, LSE, and LUXSE. It is evident from the tables the impact of stock cross listings announcements on various liquidity measures varies. To find the impact three liquidity measures have been used, trading volume, turnover & Amivest ratio. Liquidity as a concept of trading quantity reduces significantly after the cross listings announcements. The average trading volume after the cross listings announcements has reduced significantly by -18.1901682% compared to pre- listing period & is statistically significant at 5%. Stock trading turnover reduced significantly after these cross listings announcements. The average trading turnover has reduced by -25.00011% compared to pre-listing period which is significant at 5%. The stock mean Amivest ratio has increased after cross listings announcements with 82.3611%. The magnitude and direction of change for the first two measures are almost similar for 175 days period of time i.e. impact of cross listings decreased the liquidity, while in the case of Amivest ratio the results are mixed. The mean Amivest ratio for 175 days period increased by -82.3611%. A more liquid market should have a larger Amivest ratio, which says that DR market is more liquid market. The probable reason for this seems to be that the investor perceives the announcements of stock cross listings as providing signals about the firm's bright future prospects. Probably, the investors who own the shares at the time of cross listing announcement prefer to hold the shares expecting an increase in their wealth in future leading to decline in the liquidity. Hence, it can be concluded that stock liquidity are affected by the cross listings announcements.

Section 3 analyses the impact of cross listing through DRs on the Indian stock prices. Study used Granger Causality Test by using E-views software to find impact. The study tests the causality pattern between Indian stock prices & DR prices & vice versa. Is there any impact of DRs on Indian local stock prices or Indian prices on DR prices?

Due to cross border trading, the DRs and the local underlying shares will have a same pay off, as they reflect the same information, price of the local stock & the DR lies close to each other. For this reason, most of the times DR Price & local stock price will be perfectly correlated resulting in least profitability arbitrage.

When there is a lower cost of capital, more liquidity it is reflected in the DR stock prices. They also found that there is a positive price reaction to the DR offering announcement.

Study used a sample of 40 Indian companies listed through ADRs & GDRs on different stock exchanges (NYSE, LSE & LUXSE). Out of 40 listed Indian companies, 33 companies are listed through GDRs on London & Luxembourg stock exchanges. Remaining 7 are listed on New York stock exchange through ADRs. Out of 33 GDR listed programs, 27 Indian local stock prices don't have an impact on GDR prices. Secondly, causality pattern between GDR prices & Indian local stock prices. Out of 33 GDR listed programs, 28 GDRs stock prices have an impact on Indian local stock prices.

Same causality pattern was done between ADR prices & Indian stock prices & vice versa. 7 ADR programs listed on NYSE. Five ADRs prices were having an impact on the Indian local stock price. Study concludes that cross listings through DRs are having an impact on the Indian local stock price.

Section 4 examined the impact of cross listings through DRs on Indian stock volatility. Empirical tests are conducted to study the changes in variances of the underlying domestic stocks. The stud observed a wide variation in the effect of foreign listings on the underlying domestic stock variances. The variance ratio in the study sample varies from a low 0.1667 variance to a high 8.1708 variance. Summarized results in table provide some interesting insights. Twenty five variance ratios out of forty variance ratios are less than one, indicating decrease in variances of the underlying domestic shares during the post listing period. Remaining 15 stocks variance ratios are greater than one indicating increase in variances of the underlying domestic shares and are statistically significant. The statistical significance is judged using the F-ratio test that compares two variances before and after the listing date and tell if they are significantly different (df=150-1). The twenty five firms in the sample have variance ratios less than one but statistically insignificant implying the decrease in the return variance after the listing date. Similar results were drawn when analyzing of Indian stocks listed on international stock exchanges. At an aggregate level, DR listings seem to have decreased the volatility of the domestic underlying shares. Volatilities declined for most of the Indian companies in the sample that listed their DR programs on the European and US markets.

Section 5 examined the DR regulatory frame work of five countries- Taiwan, Brazil, Russia, India & Hong Kong. Study compared the DR regulatory frame work of five capital markets & concluded which capital markets is sparsely regulated & strictly regulated one. A DR issuer may list its shares on an international stock market for gaining visibility, to increase international customer base, to improve liquidity, to expand business.

India, Russia is considered as having the most stringent norms among all the capital markets in the study. Both the countries are emerging countries, does not have clarity on tax issues, listing & disclosure requirements, fungibility, eligibility of both the issuer & the investor. Taiwan also has stringent rules & regulations, but less compare to India & Russia. Taiwan comes with a strong DR market with lot many foreign issuers every year. Brazil & Hong Kong capital markets are sparsely regulated one. Brazil with least restrictions on sponsored & unsponsored programs are attracting more foreign issuers with least requirements & huge benefits. Hong Kong with issuer protecting regulatory environment & least restrictions gained much popularity among issuers. All these capital markets, even though they are performing better, they need to work harder to reach the level of ADRs & GDRs, by introducing issuer friendly regulatory environment without compromising on investor protection.

SUGGESTIONS:

Findings of the thesis are useful for various companies, policy makers, international investors, stock exchanges & the regulators of financial system. Findings represent national & international perspectives; as they are based on experiences of companies from Indian markets that are listed on international stock markets. Suggestions are as follows:

➢ The Indian financial system must offer a complete set of services available in international financial market in terms of depository receipts & must be offer a competitive environment internationally.

➢ One of the important factors for the failure of DR market is consumer protection. The Indian law (regulators) must be designed regulations by keeping investor protection in view.

➢ In our study, one of the point needed attention is Indian financial norms, rules & regulations are highly stringent. World reciprocates, how we treat other countries firms, the same manner Indian firms, issuers will be treated. Indian stringent rules & eligibility criteria has been greatly criticized by foreign issuers. Indian norms must be made clear with less stringent norms so that it can attract more international investors.

➢ Every stock market requires a regulator. Too many regulators to one particular stock market create confusion to the issuer. Each stock market must have one regulator, to have clarity about the rules & regulations need to be followed by the DR issuer.

➢ Concept of Bharat Depository receipts (BhDRs) is new for Indian law, policy makers, regulators, international issuers & Indian investors. Indian norms related to Bhdrs must be transparent & less stringent with improved tax structure, so that it can attract more foreign investors.

➢ Tax issues are not clear related to DRs under Income Tax act 1961. Proper Indian tax structure needs to be improved.

➢ It is evident from the studies; capital markets with more investor protection & better insider trading have an ability to attract more foreign issuers. Capital markets like Europe & U.S are having a very good DR market & preferred destinations of many international investors. Indian country need to work more on its regulatory environment (listing & disclosure requirements, tax issues & fungibility etc.) India should introduce less stringent norms with transparency & high investor protection.

➢ Firms from various countries should educate the domestic shareholders about the benefits of DR listings. Need to conduct workshops of what DR listing is all about.

➢ Regulatory bodies should come up with certain schemes to encourage DR investors & create awareness about DR benefits among the investors.

➢ Though SEBI has introduced two-way fungibility, the guidelines have more restrictions, such as reservation of 20% for retail investors. Indian government as introduced two-way fungibility should have more clarity with less restriction.

Scope for Further Research:

➢ Further research can be done by finding the impact of cross listings by non US & non-European markets.

➢ Liquidity impact was found by using three measures volume, turnover ratio & Amivest ratio. More research can be done by using bid-ask spread & zero trading methods.

➢ Study used long term (i.e. 175 days as an event window) impact of cross listing, further both long term & short term performances can be done.

➢ Industry wise performance can also be done on cross listings by taking a sample of companies from different industries.

➢ Bharat depository receipts have been introduced in India, new research can be done in this regard.

➢ Studies investigated the effect of cross listings through ADRs, GDRs on the Indian stocks returns, volatility, liquidity & price. It will be useful to compare the effect of cross listings across different DR programs offered around the world.